W9-AGQ-130

DOCTOR
OF THE
HEART

My Life in Medicine

DOCTOR OF THE HEART

My Life in Medicine

ISADORE ROSENFELD, M.D.

Mary Ann Liebert, Inc. publishers

Library of Congress Cataloging-in-Publication Data

Rosenfeld, Isadore.
  Doctor of the heart : my life in medicine / by Isadore Rosenfeld.
    p.   cm.
  Includes index.
  ISBN 978-1-934854-15-0
  1. Rosenfeld, Isadore.   2. Cardiologists—United States—Biography.   I. Title.
  RC666.72.R67A3 2010
  616.1'20092—dc22
  [B]

                                                                2009027024

Mary Ann Liebert, Inc.
140 Huguenot Street
New Rochelle, NY 10801

Printed in the United States of America.

I am dedicating this book to Dr. Phineas Rabinovitch, the general practitioner who inspired me to become a physician when I was only four years old. He remains my medical role model to this day. I have also written this in memory of my parents, who made it possible for me to fulfill my dream of becoming a doctor, and for my wife, Camilla, whose love, support, and high moral standards have continued to motivate and guide me throughout my career. My pride in and love for my four wonderful children—and theirs—have brought me the happiness one needs to withstand the stress and pressure of a doctor's life. I am grateful to my many teachers over the years who taught me how to help the sick. Above all, this book is for my patients—past, present, and future—whose health and well-being will always remain the focus of my life.

ISADORE ROSENFELD, M.D.

CONTENTS

ACKNOWLEDGMENTS

It took me almost as long to finish this one book as it did to write my other twelve. I started working on it more than ten years ago after I decided to provide my children and grandchildren with a family history dating back to their grandparents and great-grandparents and ending with an account of my own career. The first draft was about one quarter of the size of the one you're now reading, and my kids told me they enjoyed it. I believe they stashed it away somewhere with their old photo albums to be looked at years from now when they might want to reminisce. However, as time went by, I kept adding my ongoing experiences as a doctor to the original manuscript. I wanted to keep a record somewhere, for someone—anyone—of all the interesting men and women I was privileged to treat and, often, befriend. I came to realize how much I had learned in almost sixty years of practicing cardiology, how times have changed, how new treatments have evolved, and yet how human nature has remained the same. I wanted to illustrate and share the basic facts that no two patients are alike and that there is always room for hope.

And so as the number of pages in my manuscript multiplied, I sent them not only to my children but also to several friends, anxious to know whether they would find it interesting and useful. My son Herbert read drafts countless times and always had useful suggestions; my son-in-law, Richard Silbert, an attorney, reviewed it from a legal viewpoint. I want to thank Gwen and Lester Fisher for their patience as I subjected them to one draft after another and Raymond and Beverly Sackler, who religiously evaluated each update and revision with which I bombarded them. Joni Evans, my long-time editor and agent, reviewed the manuscript, too. She liked it, as did my old friend, Ambassador Richard Holbrooke. My colleague, Dr. Holly Andersen, must have read ten versions over the years and could never understand why I kept changing them. But perhaps most important of all, Camilla, my wife and most immovable critic, encouraged me to continue writing it.

Since the feedback was positive and the majority of those who read the manuscript seemed to identify with many of my stories, I decided to go full steam ahead. In so doing, I imposed on yet more friends and colleagues to read the drafts until I was ready, finally, to publish this memoir.

Once I had decided to "go public," I needed help to make my story readable and enjoyable. That's where Jules Bass entered the picture. Jules is a very special friend of many years. He and Arthur Rankin created the animations for *Rudolph the Red-Nosed Reindeer*, *Frosty the Snowman*, and many others that continue to bring joy to millions of men, women, and children throughout the world. I'm so sorry that he was unable to convert this volume into one of his wonderful animated cartoons. But he did enliven some of my more "factual" accounts. I also appreciate Rock Brynner's helpful suggestions.

Finally, I am grateful to Mary Ann Liebert, who took the bull by the horns, insisted that I stop procrastinating, and published this book. She is one of the most successful women in publishing, especially in the medical field; she regularly turns out some eighty-four specialty journals, several magazines, and many books. She and her other officers Vicki Cohn, Larry Bernstein, and Marianne Russell took a particular interest in my book and edited it to a fault. Their attention and input has been invaluable.

ISADORE ROSENFELD, M.D.

INTRODUCTION

In these pages I recount some of the more interesting experiences I've had in the almost sixty years (and counting) of my medical career. I hope you enjoy reading about them as much as I relished reminiscing. My goal was to provide you with some insight into what it was like to be a doctor during the most productive era of medicine, and what the inevitable discoveries portend for us down the line. Many of you will identify with some of my medical "stories," how my patients and I dealt with a variety of problems: vascular disease, malignancies, neurological problems, intestinal and psychiatric illnesses, and others. You will read about men and women from all walks of life who followed my medical advice—and those who didn't—and about physicians (including me) who sometimes chose alternative treatments in addition to or in place of conventional approaches when doing so raised eyebrows among the lay public and met with frank disapproval from the medical establishment.

A good portion of this book also describes relationships and situations that resulted from my having been catapulted into an international medical practice. This happened by accident, not by design—and I share with you the story behind it. Some of these international "high level" experiences are medical; others are not. They occasionally turned out to be pure fun—as, for example, when I seduced the leaders of the Soviet Kremlin to toast Golda Meir at a time when Russia and Israel were not on speaking terms, or when my cuff links found their way on to the ears (yes, the ears—it's not a typo) of the General-Secretary of the Soviet Union.

I have also included some personal details of my family background and what it was like to be a husband and father while devoting most of my time to caring for the sick. You will read how the attitudes and expectations of physicians and patients have changed over the years and about their impact on medical care today.

This book starts off with the story of why I decided to become a doctor at the age of four and ends with my thoughts about the future of our medical care system.

Sometimes I feel as if I never really went to medical school. Much of what I was taught almost sixty years ago has turned out to be wrong; and we never, in our wildest dreams, foresaw all the mind-boggling advances in the prevention, diagnosis, and treatment of disease—everything from new antibiotics to cancer cures to robotic surgery to gene and stem cell therapy. In my own specialty of cardiology, there have been more breakthroughs in my lifetime than there were in the three centuries after William Harvey first explained how blood circulates throughout the body. For example, when my father developed coronary artery disease and angina pectoris in his late forties, there was no way to assess the severity of his disease or to treat it: no cardiac catheterization to visualize the arteries, no echocardiography to assess the strength of the heart muscle, no nuclear stress tests to evaluate whether enough blood was reaching the heart muscle when it was stressed, and no multislice CT angiograms of the chest to view the coronary arteries noninvasively. All these were years away when I started practice. My dad's doctor diagnosed his angina by taking a careful history (still very important today), listening to his heart with a stethoscope (not very revealing), and recording an electrocardiogram (which is normal in about 80 percent of patients with angina). Nor were we aware of the risk factors that close up the coronary arteries. As far as treatment was concerned, all we doctors could do was advise our patients to "take it easy"; there was no coronary artery ballooning and stenting to unblock arteries that were narrowed or blocked, and no bypass surgery.

This primitive state of affairs was not limited to heart disease. There wasn't much we could do about cancer either. My brother died a few months after he developed leukemia because none of the life-saving drugs that can cure this malignancy today had yet been developed.

These advances became available gradually as I practiced medicine over the years. They blended almost imperceptibly into my day-to-day work. Keeping abreast of them is what made it possible for me as a cardiologist (and for my colleagues in every other specialty) not only to save and prolong life but also to dramatically improve its quality.

1

I WANT TO BE A DOCTOR

The House Call That Changed My Life

My childhood horizons were very limited. My older brother, John, and I grew up in a low-income family in Montreal in the late 1920s. There was no TV, we didn't even have a radio in our home until I was ten, and my parents couldn't afford to take us to the movies. So I knew nothing of the outside "world," what other kids were doing or what their lives were like. Since there were no pre-kindergarten classes for me to attend, I was alone at home with my mother when John, four years older than I, left for school. I played with my makeshift toys on the kitchen floor while mama cooked, cleaned, baked, stirred the soup, sipped her tea—and sang to me.

She was always philosophizing about life; her main message to me was that all good and obedient children grow up to be either doctors or lawyers. This had nothing to do with goals of wealth or material things; she simply wanted to make sure that if I was ever uprooted and forced to flee to another country (as happened to her and my father), I would have a marketable skill. She believed that medicine and law were the only professions that would provide protection for me and my family should the need arise.

Gremlins in My Throat

1930: I was four years old. One day, I caught a bad cold; my throat was sore, I was coughing, and I had some fever. My parents tried the usual remedies from the "old country"—weak tea with honey, hot lemon juice, and, of course, chicken soup. Nothing helped. I felt miserable; I hurt all over, and I cried inconsolably. Then, when my temperature reached almost 104 degrees, I had a seizure. My parents had never seen a convulsion before and were terrified. They'd obviously have to call a doctor even though they couldn't afford to. Times were very bad. This was 1930, one year after the start of the Great Depression in the United States. Canada's economy, then as now, was closely linked to America's. Unemployment was rampant. My dad was lucky to have a job but was earning only six dollars a week. A house call cost seventy-five cents, more than 10 percent of his salary (night visits were a dollar). Still, they had no choice, and called a local GP named Phineas Rabinovitch, who had a small clinic a few doors down the street. He answered the phone himself. My mother described my symptoms and told him how worried she was. The doctor reassured her and promised to come as soon as he could. She spent the next two hours getting the house "in order" for his visit.

I begged her not to call him. I remembered vividly the last time I'd been to a doctor—how he had hurt me with what seemed like a three-foot-long needle! I trembled when I heard the doorbell ring.

Dr. Rabinovitch came in carrying a little black bag. (When was the last time you saw a doctor with one of them?) He was thin, with a black mustache, and short, like my father. I was relieved when he left his bag at the door of my little bedroom before coming in to see me, but I worried that he would go back to get one of those needles before he was through with me.

Dr. Rabinovitch sat down on my bed; gave me a warm, loving, "I'm your friend" smile; squeezed my hand reassuringly; and then started telling me about his little dog! I couldn't understand it! Had my parents called a vet to treat me?

"I have this great little pup, Hughie," he said. "I wish I'd brought him; maybe I will the next time I come. I want you two to be friends. You'll love him. But guess what? He thinks he's a cat," Dr. R chuckled. "He doesn't bark, but sort of meows, and loves to drink milk. The other day I saw him chasing a poor mouse that had found its way into my office. Have you ever seen a dog do that?" he asked.

I forgot about the bag and the needle because I liked this man! He was so calm, so friendly, so funny, and so reassuring. I felt better just listening to him, although frankly, I can't remember the end of the story.

He finally asked me how I was feeling and I told him my throat was sore. "That's what I expected," he said. "It's those darn gremlins. I've had them myself. Look, Issie, do me a favor. Take this flashlight, look into my throat and tell me whether you see any gremlins there." He opened *his* mouth and said, *"Ahh"* as I looked into it with his flashlight. "Well", he asked, "any green gremlins?"

I told him I saw lots of red and pink things in his throat, but no green gremlins. He was obviously very relieved. "I guess I got rid of them before I came to see you, but I wanted to make sure they're gone."

That, in effect, was the beginning of my medical career. At four years of age, I had examined my first patient—and he was a doctor! *Now it was his turn.*

"Those gremlins can make your throat really sore. Believe me, I know," he said. "You may have the same ones I did. Let me take a look."

I returned his flashlight, eagerly opened my mouth, and said, *"Ahh"* while he looked in. I wasn't the least bit scared. After a moment or two, he gave an enthusiastic whoop!

"I see one! I've found him! Get out of there, you nasty gremlin," he shouted.

I was excited and thrilled!

"Is he gone? Is he gone?"

Dr. R turned to me, beaming. "No, not yet, but don't you worry. I'll get him out of your throat just like I threw his friend out of mine. You see, gremlins are scared of these little white pills," he said, taking a packet of aspirin out of his pocket. "I took two of these myself this morning and then brought the rest for you. Here, swallow one with a little water. I promise it will chase that nasty greenie out in a hurry and your throat will stop hurting. I'm also going to give you a couple of teaspoons of this delicious medicine to help get rid of your cough. You'll love it."

I believed him. Right after I swallowed the pill and took a sip of the syrup, I said, "Hey, I feel better already. I'm sure I don't need a shot."

He laughed. "No, Issie. I'm your friend. I would never give you a shot just to get rid of some gremlins."

My cold gradually improved in the next couple of days, and all I remembered about being sick was how much I enjoyed that house call. It was probably the most memorable experience of my four-year life. If truth be told, I couldn't wait to get sick again! It was then and there that I decided to become a doctor. I still remember that visit as if it had just happened: the smile, the handshake, my "patient's" throat, and even the gritty feel of the aspirin as I swallowed it. *It was pure magic!*

But there was more to that house call than aspirin and gremlins. Doctors didn't send bills in those days, and there was no such thing as health insurance. Patients were expected to pay for a doctor's services at the time they were rendered. As he was leaving, my parents asked Dr. R how much they owed him. He looked around our tiny apartment.

"When did you arrive in Canada?" he asked.

"Four years ago," my dad answered.

"And what kind of job do you have?"

Dad was embarrassed. Before the Communist Revolution in Russia, he'd been a successful businessman. But then, along with other "capitalists," he was forced to leave Russia. The best he could do in this new country whose language he couldn't speak and where he had no friends or relatives was to grade eggs in the basement of a Stop & Shop grocery store.

"I'm an egg candler at the moment, but I'm looking for something better," he said, as he searched his pocket for the three quarters with which to pay for the house call. Dr. Rabinovitch stopped him. "Look, why don't we just keep track of the bill for now? You can pay me when you're earning what you should be for a man of your intelligence and energy. And don't hesitate to call my office whenever you need me. Issie will be fine, but let me know if his temperature climbs again or if he has another seizure."

I was too young to appreciate the impact of Dr. R's compassion. I was puzzled when they cried after he left. From that moment on, my mother never again mentioned the legal profession to me. Her favorite expression now was "First God, then doctors." Implicit in that phrase, which she repeated time and again, was the hope and the expectation that I would one day be a doctor—no ifs, ands, or buts. Little did she know that all this brainwashing was unnecessary because I had already made up my own mind to become a doctor.

For the rest of our lives, the name "Rabinovitch" was synonymous with "doctor" to our family—a symbol of everything unselfish and virtuous. Dr. R remained our friend for life. He treated my every illness over the years: he removed my tonsils, took care of a badly infected ingrown toenail, and splinted a fractured arm. Whatever he did added to my love and respect for him and his profession.

Whenever my mind flashes back to that first encounter with Dr. Rabinovitch, I realize that such a memorable house call would be very unlikely these days—for many reasons. First of all, parents don't call a GP for a sick child; they phone their pediatricians, who don't often come to their home. The same is true for adults. When was the last time you "enjoyed" a house call? People criticize the medical profession because doctors no longer visit sick patients at home. But that's not because physicians don't care or are too busy, or that it simply doesn't pay them to do so. The truth is that patients no longer expect or ask for doctors to come to their homes. If they're really sick, they either call an ambulance or grab a cab and go to the emergency room where they can quickly get the necessary X-rays, scans, injections, or other procedures they need. Your doctor can do none of these things at your home. It's a waste of precious time having someone remove your gremlins at your bedside—except in my case!

When Dr. R visited my home that day so many years ago, he treated my illness with what was appropriate at the time for kids with an upper respiratory infection and fever—aspirin and cough medicine. Times have changed! We have since learned that in such cases, aspirin can sometimes cause Reye's syndrome, a potentially fatal neurological illness; cold medicines and decongestants can also have toxic side effects. Happily, I survived!

2

DR. R'S GP CLINIC

D r. Rabinovitch was an excellent general practitioner (GP) who not only treated colds and removed gremlins but also performed minor surgical procedures. He was not a wealthy man and had to borrow money in order to set up a small, six-bed clinic of his own in the heart of the working-class district of Montreal. There he delivered babies, fixed broken limbs, sewed up lacerations, repaired hernias, performed tonsillectomies and appendectomies, set fractures, and did other "bread-and-butter" procedures. He also maintained regular office hours and, of course, made house calls. He worked tirelessly around the clock; he had no covering doctor. He never refused to care for anyone who needed him; his fees were modest and he never asked a patient to pay more than he thought he or she could afford. He developed a wonderful reputation in Montreal because of his skill, his humanity, and his devotion to the sick.

The High School Boy-Doctor

Dr. R's house call to me was the beginning of a lifelong medical relationship with him. When I was fifteen, I started to hang out at his bustling Mount Royal Hospital where I helped in any way I could—assisting patients from the stretcher to the bed and the bedpan, running errands, and generally serving as his boy Friday. The antiseptic smell, the sight of the nurses in their starched white uniforms, the love and gratitude his patients felt for this wonderful man and his staff, were all a real-life drama for me.

I was eager to learn about health, sickness, and medicine, so in high school I took every biology course and tried to apply that knowledge in Dr. R's hospital after school. He clearly appreciated my interest in medicine and fed my voracious appetite, treating me more like a colleague than a schoolboy. After a while, he actually permitted me to remain in the operating room while he performed surgery. He let me hold a limb to which he was applying a cast; he allowed me to look on as he stitched up a deep cut, worried, I'm sure, that the sight of the blood would bother me (I was eventually able to cope, although it took some time). I often felt as if I were dreaming as I listened to the deep, regular breathing of the anesthetized patient in the otherwise silent operating room, heard the terse requests for an instrument or a sponge, watched his fingers move skillfully and without a wasted motion. I flinched as blood spurted from a severed artery, and relaxed when it was arrested by a neatly and securely tied stitch. One day, I witnessed the miracle of birth and heard the first cry of a human being; I appreciated the love and adoration on the mother's face as she cradled her newborn infant. I couldn't wait to get to school to regale my friends with *all these stories* (exaggerating my role a bit, as you might expect!).

These were overwhelming experiences for a fifteen-year-old, and they had a great impact on my future values and goals as a physician. They left me feeling like a doctor. I couldn't wait for the school holidays when I could spend whole days at the clinic and not just a few hours at the end of the afternoon.

Most of my friends worked after school and contributed what little money they made to the family coffers. I felt guilty about spending my spare time at the clinic, where I wasn't earning anything. When I mentioned to the doctor that I might have to stop coming to the hospital and get a "real" job, he offered me a small salary. He said my help was worth every penny of the two dollars he was prepared to give me each week. But I knew otherwise and did not want charity. I felt that what I saw and did at that clinic was part of my training to become a doctor. When I told my father about it, his pride showed through as usual.

"Issie, you keep working there. We don't need the money."

Of course, that wasn't true, but I was happy with his decision—and gratefully accepted it.

What we called general practitioners in those days are now mostly internists. The most complicated operation they do is remove a splinter from your finger or a foreign body from your eye. Virtually every other kind of surgery is now left to surgical specialists who limit themselves to specific operations: laparoscopic surgery, repair of broken bones, obstetrical procedures, and so on. There are even subspecialists too—orthopedic surgeons who operate only on the spine or the shoulder or the knee, surgeons who limit their work to the abdomen or the lung or the sinuses or the ears or the throat. I am in awe when I think of all the different procedures Dr. Rabinovitch could do—and do so well. But that's history. There are few if any GPs who do "everything," even in small towns with few doctors. If any of the townsfolk require a procedure, they are taken to the nearest city where it is available, Also, more and more patients are being treated remotely by telemedicine, in which specialists from distant areas perform the surgery robotically, with only a general surgeon in the actual operating room. I have witnessed such surgery performed without a hitch by doctors at the University of California at Davis. So what my idol did so many years ago is a thing of the past. The disappearance of the general practitioner is in large part the result of patients' wishes. These days, anyone who needs an operation makes careful inquiries in order to choose the most qualified doctor. They often ask which of many surgeons available in a given institution has had the most experience and the best statistical outcomes. I know of no one who would undergo even the most minor operation at a small, six-bed clinic by a GP who also makes house calls! And that's as it should be. Should anything go wrong during the surgery, such as a heart attack or stroke or hemorrhage, you want access to sophisticated emergency resuscitation. But although the changes that have taken place over the years are important and inevitable, had they occurred when I was still a teenager, I would have missed some of the most wonderful years of my life at that little clinic down the street from my home.

3

GROWING UP IN
MONTREAL

My family was poor, but we never went hungry. I appreciated so many little things that my own kids years later would take for granted. I looked forward all week to the two-cent ice cream cone my father bought my brother and me every Saturday morning. If we were good, my mother would give us a penny to buy our favorite treat at the candy store near school, two chocolate-covered coconut balls.

Although we were short on material things at home, there was a great emphasis on family ties and learning. The cramped quarters in which we lived never bothered me. I didn't know anything better or different—there was no TV to expose me to the lifestyles of the rich and famous. All my friends and neighbors "enjoyed" the same standard of living. Neither my brother nor I ever heard our parents complain or discuss their economic hardships. They loved each other, they loved us, and we loved them—and that's basically all that mattered.

My parents were nonobservant ethnic Jews who lived by the tenets of Judaism—charity and caring for those less fortunate. We only went to shul once or twice a year on the High Holidays, and then only out of respect for our friends.

The fact that I am Jewish dominated my thoughts during my formative years, and the fear and loathing of racial discrimination have stayed with me all my life. Growing up, everyone I was exposed to, except my teachers, was Jewish. That was the norm; it never occurred to me that it was a dangerous or undesirable thing to be. But then, when I was seven years old, I started hearing what Germany and the Nazis were doing to Jews. Our friends and neighbors, many of whom, like my own family, were Eastern European immigrants, talked of nothing else. Then the Second World War started, and they worried to its very end about the fate of close relatives they had left behind in Europe. In my mother's case, that meant her parents, an identical twin sister, two brothers, aunts, uncles, and a flock of children. Virtually none of them survived. (Thankfully, everyone in my father's family had emigrated from Russia to the U.S. years earlier.)

It wasn't only the Germans who posed a threat to Jews when I was growing up. Racial animosity was also a fact of life in Quebec and Montreal during those years. Most Montrealers were French Canadian, and they resented that English-speaking Protestants dominated the cultural and business life of the province. So in addition to hearing all the terrible tales of persecution in Europe, I grew up in an environment with two hostile cultures, the French and the English, neither of whom had more to do with each other—or with Jews—than was absolutely necessary.

Most Jewish immigrants in Quebec, my parents among them, identified with the English-speaking community. They tried to fit in by learning English and rarely bothered with French. As a result, French Canadians associated Jews with their resented English "exploiters." This left the Jews exposed to a double whammy of anti-Semitism: the more subtle form practiced by English-speaking Canadians, who excluded them from clubs, social circles, and senior executive positions in business, and the overt, virulent anti-Semitic outbursts from the French.

In those years, the Catholic Church fostered the anger and isolation of the French Canadians, exhorting them to "Yes, learn to speak English—but badly" and also reminding the faithful in their Sunday sermons that the Jews had killed Christ. Gangs of French Canadian kids, fresh from this weekly indoctrination, prowled the Jewish neighborhoods and beat up any stray Jewish boys they encountered; they taunted and pulled the beards of old Jews sitting on park benches. I rarely ventured alone into the French Canadian districts of eastern Montreal, and never played alone or without several friends on the slopes of beautiful Mount Royal in the center of the city.

I was thirteen years old when World War II broke out in 1939. Canada, a British dominion, immediately joined the fight. I was happy, certain that England, whose flag I saluted in school every day, and for whose all-powerful king I was prepared to give my life, would destroy Hitler. Every Jewish boy I knew volunteered for oversees service the day he turned eighteen. The majority of French Canadians, on the other hand, were opposed to Canada's entry into the war. They viewed it as a Jewish and English struggle and no business of theirs, even though France, their "mother" country, was also in the fight. Their hostility to the struggle against the Axis was so great that the Canadian government was never able to enact a nationwide draft for overseas service. The greatest concession Canada could extract from the recalcitrant province of Quebec was to conscript for service only in Canada. These "locals" (despised and referred to as "zombies" by their "active service" counterparts) performed military administrative duties at home that made it possible for others to fight the Nazis overseas.

The Quebecois did not limit their opposition to the war to speeches or politics. I will never forget the torchlight processions through the streets of the Jewish district where we lived, with hundreds of marchers chanting *"A bas les Juifs, à bas la guerre"* (Down with the Jews, down with the war), sending shivers through me. These demonstrations were almost always accompanied by some acts of violence or vandalism, but differed from what Jewish immigrants experienced on the Lower East Side in New York. There, gangs of Italian and Irish youngsters beat up Jewish kids in the neighborhood for cultural reasons. Those in Canada were usually organized and were politically and religiously inspired.

Of course, not all French Canadians felt this way. Many fought and gave their lives, especially in the "Vingt-Deux" (Royal 22nd Regiment), which was legendary in the annals of heroism in the Canadian Army.

Forget Ezra; Let's Give Our Baby Boy a Real Canadian Name, like Issie

What happened to the name I was given at birth reflected the atmosphere in which I grew up. My parents had named me Ezra, after a paternal uncle in Indiana, who was kind, intelligent, and—most important to my impecunious family—rich and generous. So I was duly registered on my birth certificate in Montreal as Ezra Rosenfeld. Several months later, however, while wheeling me in my baby carriage on a Sunday morning through the "ghetto," the area in Montreal where most Jews lived, my parents discussed how to protect my brother and me from the anti-Semitism they had experienced in Europe—the pogroms and, in my mother's case, exile to Siberia. They noticed along their walk that many stores were named Issie—Issie's ice cream parlor, Issie's delicatessen, and Issie's poolroom parlor. They concluded that Ezra was too biblical—and too Jewish. I deserved a typical Canadian name and, if possible, one that sounded a little like Ezra, so as not to offend my generous namesake. So then and there they decided henceforth to call me Issie (and my four-year-old brother, born Shachna Beryl, became John). "Ezra" was expunged from memory. My parents reveled in the hope that one day I might become Prime Minister Issie Rosenfeld of Canada.

Frankly, I never liked "Issie." It sounded like a nickname, short, perhaps, for something such as Isabel. I didn't feel comfortable with it. Don't get me wrong, I wasn't a snob: I had several friends named Issie whom I liked and respected. The name seemed to fit them . . . but not me. Then one day in my fifth-grade classroom I was sitting next to my friend Issie Lubin when the teacher called out, "Isadore, Isadore Lubin. Please come to the desk."

Isadore? He was "Issie," not "Isadore"! I couldn't wait to clear this up. Later, when we were alone, I asked him, "What's with this Isadore business?"

"That's my real name," he told me, "but I don't like it. I prefer Issie. I'm only called Isadore when my parents or teachers are angry with me."

But I liked the name Isadore (and the fact that Saint Isadore is the patron saint of wine had nothing to do with it). I decided then and there to be Isadore. My parents went along with my decision: they didn't much care what I was called, as long as it wasn't Ezra. I officially became Isadore in school, but many old friends from Montreal still call me Issie, as did my parents until the day they died.

Graduation from Baron Byng High School

May 1943: My high school graduation ceremony was rather stark, to say the least. I was sixteen years old; Canada and the Allies were locked in a war to the death. German armies had overrun Europe, penetrated deep into the Soviet Union, and were massed along the English Channel, poised to invade battle-weary Britain. We feared that the gallant English would be forced to sue for peace in the face of all their military setbacks. We worried that Churchill would be ousted by reactionary Nazi sympathizers among the landed nobility, many of whom had never made a secret of their distaste for our ally, communist Russia, nor of their admiration for the Germans. Anti-Semitism, a "tinge" of which was normal anyway in their society, didn't really bother them all that much. They dismissed the stories of mass murder in the concentration camps as Jewish propaganda. Everyone was in a deep gloom. My mother had learned from the Red Cross that her entire family—parents, identical twin sister, brothers, and all their children—were "missing." We knew what that meant, although we never admitted it. We feared for our own lives as Jews should the Allies lose the war.

Those were some of the thoughts that ran through my mind as I sat waiting for my high school diploma. Most of those attending the ceremony that afternoon were mothers, a few elderly fathers, a bevy of younger brothers and sisters, and some neighbors. There were not many men present; most able-bodied males of military age were in the service, and our fathers were at work. My own brother was away in the army. I walked to the podium in the high school gym amid a sprinkling of applause and my mother's sobs of pleasure.

After receiving my diploma, I telephoned my father at work and gave him a running account of the graduation. He didn't say much, just listened, probably vicariously graduating since he'd never attended school himself. When he came home, he brought me a gift: Queenie, a cute, little mongrel he'd found wandering the streets of the small town outside of Montreal where he now worked.

It was now time to think about my higher education. While some of my friends had looked at colleges elsewhere in Canada and the U.S., my only option was McGill University, given my family's limited finances. Much of the exhilaration I felt working in Dr. Rabinovitch's clinic had left me. I was almost seventeen and preoccupied with the war. I didn't know how long it would last or whether I would make it back if called to serve oversees. This was no time to be thinking about becoming a doctor.

4

OFF TO COLLEGE

1943: My parents beamed with pride as I set off on that September morning for the ten-minute tram ride to register in the Faculty of Arts and Science at McGill. It was very different from the excitement I shared years later with my own children when my wife and I drove them to their respective colleges—Harvard, Yale, and Williams: Unlike them, I was not destined ever to experience dorm life, fraternities, and a college social life. This was to be "bare-bones" college in a country at war. I continued to live at home, returning by tram at the end of the day's classes.

Registration was a somber scene. After we completed the enrollment formalities, we were turned over to an army recruitment officer who signed us up in the Royal Canadian Officers' Training Corps. In addition to our academic classes, we would be spending several hours a week drilling and training. In a year, at age eighteen, I would leave college for active military duty. I never felt less like a future doctor than I did that first day at McGill.

Later in the week, we were issued lieutenant's uniforms, indistinguishable from those worn by soldiers on active service. I was suddenly transformed from an awkward teenager into a suave, elegant army officer, without even firing a shot! I loved wearing that uniform. I looked so like a real officer that I saluted myself whenever I passed a mirror. I was sorry we were not given officers' pajamas too.

Even though we were only expected to don our uniforms on the days we actually trained, I saw no reason not to wear mine all the time. In the evening, after class, I'd stroll through the busy streets of downtown Montreal, looking for real soldiers to salute me. Every enlisted man, even the heroes among them who had either just returned from the battlefield or were on the way there, had to do so. After all, I was a lieutenant! I even crossed the street when I saw one or more of our gallant troops so that they could pay homage to me with a snappy salute. My classmates and I were also granted privileges at various officers' messes throughout the city where we often dined—in uniform. War was great!

I now began to fantasize, not about being a doctor but about parades, flag ceremonies—and killing Nazis. I dreamed of joining the battle overseas and returning home unscathed, my chest covered with medals, and welcomed as a hero by a grateful nation.

On the days we trained, we marched from one college building to another for our various classes, carrying World War I vintage rifles that looked like props from an old movie. Many older men and women were driven to tears at the sight of these young boys on their way to war, when, in fact, we were going from physics class to chemistry class.

I often had to remind myself that despite all this military posturing, I was still only a college student—and a freshman at that. I tried to select the courses I would be taking before being sent overseas with an eye on my potential future as a doctor, although that seemed very remote at the time. I decided to take as many premed courses as I could because if I ever did apply to medical school, I'd need to have good grades in the right subjects. So I studied hard during the winter while at college, and learned to shoot during the summer at military camp.

In 1944 the tide of war turned, and victory seemed assured. In 1945, after my second year at college, the Allies were victorious. I no longer feared ending up in a gas chamber, nor would I be a soldier or war hero—just another college student. My dream of becoming a doctor was rekindled.

The Jewish Quota for Medical School

But I now realized how difficult it would be to win a place in medical school. Thousands of men, heroes all, were coming back to resume their interrupted education. Many of them also wanted to be doctors, and they deserved to be accepted to medical school far more than I did. How could I compete with them, especially since, although I had studied hard, my grades were only high average?

After graduating from the Faculty of Arts and Science in 1947, I applied to medical school at McGill despite the unfavorable odds. My parents could not afford to send me anywhere else. McGill was, and still is, a great medical institution. I walked by the imposing, graystone anatomy building every day, very depressed because I was sure I wouldn't be accepted. How I envied those students in their white coats walking in and out of the doors! Did they know how lucky they were?

My ho-hum grades were not the only reason I didn't think I had much chance of being accepted. McGill *and virtually every other medical school in Canada and the United States* continued to enforce a "Jewish quota," usually 10 percent of the class. The year I applied to McGill, there were some 3,800 applications for 110 places; of these, 1,600 were from Jewish students. So I would be competing with 1,600 applicants for one of 11 seats.

I applied for admission to the class of 1951, although I felt it was only a formality. While waiting for the answer, I began to consider other career opportunities, such as law and journalism, neither of which excited me very much. To fire my enthusiasm for a legal career, I started reading Clarence Darrow's brilliant courtroom sagas. I found them interesting, but frankly, they did not fill me with the passion I felt for Dr. Rabinovitch's work.

About six weeks after submitting my application, I received a registered letter from the McGill Faculty of Medicine. I was terrified to open it because once I read the stark, immutable decision, my dream would evaporate—permanently. My heart racing and my mouth dry, I felt the envelope in my hands to see if I could sense the message it contained. Finally, I went into my bedroom, shut the door, sat down on my bed, took a deep breath, and opened the letter.

"I am *pleased . . .* " The minute I saw the word "pleased," I became dizzy. I shut my eyes for a moment and then resumed reading, "to tell you that your application to admission to Medicine, class of '51, has been favorably considered *subject to further refinement*" (or words to that effect). I had made the first cut and would now be competing with only 75 other Jewish applicants for those 11 places, rather than the original 1,600. One chance in 7 was better than 1 in 160, but still a long shot. However, it was enough to get me to stop reading Clarence Darrow.

The drama continued to unfold. The seventy-five Jewish applicants being considered were then subjected to something so demeaning that it would be unimaginable today. We were the only ethnic group that had to be interviewed by a "neurologist." I can understand requiring *all* applicants to medical school to undergo a psychiatric evaluation (because that's what this "neurological" exam was: no one struck our knees with little hammers to test our reflexes). But to mandate it for students of a particular faith was sheer bigotry. At the time, however, I simply viewed it as further evidence that society still considered Jews to be "different." The war hadn't changed things all that much.

I had no idea how to prepare for this interview. It was a crapshoot as far as I was concerned. What would I be asked? Would the interviewer be looking for an Oedipus complex or a fear of blood or some masochistic or sadistic qualities that might be motivating me to become a doctor? Those of us scheduled to be interviewed met for practice sessions, much like lawyers preparing their clients for cross-examination.

On the appointed day, I wore a blue blazer, white shirt, a regimental sort of tie, and black-laced shoes. A real WASP! That's what they wanted, wasn't it? Dr. Kershman's secretary showed me into his office. Sitting at a small desk was my host, a tall, well-built man in his mid-thirties wearing the loudest sport jacket and shirt I'd ever seen around McGill! He did not look up but motioned me to sit down. After what seemed like an eternity, he raised his head and stared at me. Total silence! I returned his gaze, then looked up at the ceiling, then at his diplomas on the wall, and then back at him. I finally gave in.

"Hi," I said, smiling. "I'm Isadore Rosenfeld."

"Yes. I know," he replied generously. He seemed more uncomfortable than I was.

"Is this interview hard for you?" he asked. "I mean, with so much at stake. Must be tough. But don't worry. I don't bite. It's my job just to size you up. I don't like it any more than you do. This whole thing's ridiculous."

Wow, that was something I didn't expect to hear from him! Then he asked, "What would you like to talk about?"

"That's up to you, sir," I said. "I guess the same things you've discussed with the others."

"All right. Then tell me, what do you think about socialized medicine?"

Now that was a surprise! I was nowhere even near being a doctor and, in fact, entertained precious little hope of ever becoming one, yet this guy wanted my opinion about a particular political system of providing medical care! I replied that I hadn't given it much thought, but that I was in favor of any medical delivery system that assured health care for everyone.

He nodded, then changed course. "What will you do if I don't accept you?"

I would look into some other career, I answered, possibly law. I assured him that although I would be very disappointed, I would not become seriously depressed or suicidal. Then he asked me the toughest question of the session. "How can I accept you when the next student waiting to be interviewed is the son of a professor at this medical school and the nephew of another? What does *your* father do?"

"My father is a businessman. As far as whom to accept, sir, I guess you'll have to decide who will make the better doctor regardless of his medical lineage."

He seemed to be apologizing for being forced to select someone else. We made some additional small talk, but by this time he'd obviously gotten the impression he needed. I left his office, certain I would never see Dr. John Kershman again.

After this ill-fated interview, I went directly to the Law Faculty building and picked up some of their brochures. In those days, it wasn't difficult to get into law school, and I began to convince myself that I really *did* admire Clarence Darrow almost as much as I loved Phineas Rabinovitch! I submitted my application.

While waiting for an answer from the faculties of medicine and law, I drove with my parents to visit my grandfather in Terre Haute, Indiana. Somewhere south of Chicago we stopped at a Shell station to call home and speak to my brother.

"Where have you been?" John shouted. "I've been trying to find you! You've been accepted to medical school at McGill!"

My parents and I cried in joy and disbelief. I called the medical dean's office at McGill from the gas station. His secretary confirmed that I had indeed been accepted, not as an alternate, not on a waiting list, but as a full-fledged member of the class of '51.

A few days after I started medical school, Dr. Kershman called me at home. "My wife and I don't trust babysitters," he explained, "and we rarely leave our two small children alone. But we have a very important affair to attend. Would you consider babysitting for us? We'll pay you one dollar an hour." That call was the second clue that I'd made a good impression on him. Eventually, Dr. Kershman resigned his psychiatric assignment in protest; he simply could not stomach being a handmaiden of discrimination.

There is no longer any racial or religious quota system at any medical school on this continent. And at McGill, the present dean of the medical school is Jewish, as was the last principal and vice-chancellor. And when, in 1998, McGill conferred upon me an honorary doctorate of science, I felt I'd truly come full circle, from a quota applicant subjected to psychiatric evaluation to receiving my alma mater's highest recognition.

5

MEDICAL SCHOOL

From my very first day in medical school in 1947, I was already a doctor as far as my parents were concerned. They continued to refer to me as "Issie, our son, the doctor" for the rest of their lives. And given the sacrifice they'd made so that I could become a physician, they were entitled to do so: tuition was four hundred dollars a year, a staggering sum for my family at the time. (Today, that cost is a hundredfold greater in the U.S.) The financial assistance I received from the Quebec government—a bursary of fifty dollars a year—to be repaid after graduation, made a difference.

The dean of the medical school welcomed the incoming class in the auditorium of the anatomy building. He told us how special we were, how we had been selected from among many hundreds of applicants, how hard we'd have to work, but how satisfying it would be. We men regarded the 3 women in our class of 110 as oddities. Women were supposed to be nurses and social workers, not doctors! (Today, 55 percent of all medical students in the U.S. are women.)

Unlike today's medical students, who are virtually overwhelmed almost daily by breakthroughs in some specialty of medicine or other, the pace of major advances was almost imperceptible during the four years I was studying to be a doctor. That would change dramatically as I continued my postgraduate education and practiced my profession. The most significant breakthrough was probably Alexander Fleming's accidental discovery of penicillin, the first antibiotic manufactured commercially, right after Pearl Harbor. Before antibiotics became available, a "minor" infection was simply left alone, both doctor and patient hoping it would "go away" or "run its course." More serious infections were treated with a variety of toxic substances such as strychnine and arsenic, often more harmful to the patient than the infection itself; you could lose your leg from something as trivial as the infection of a toenail spreading throughout your body. I can't even begin to estimate how many millions of lives have been saved by antibiotics. However, for many more years we remained unable to deal with a host of viral diseases—such as polio—that can now be prevented by vaccines.

As far as my own future specialty was concerned, in 1947, the diagnosis and treatment of heart disease was primitive and destined to remain so for several more years.

The Anatomy Lab

The very next morning after registering, we got right to it! We went to the anatomy lab where we were introduced to our cadaver. He may have been a "specimen" to my instructor, but he was a dead *man* to me. I wasn't emotionally prepared to see a person lying there whom I was expected to cut up in the next few weeks. None of the reading and rationalization, or the panache of being a med student, lessened my anxiety or the guilt I felt dissecting a human body. For me, it was still a human being. Mercifully, we were to start with the feet; I couldn't have handled the face, with those eyes looking at me! As it was, it took me weeks to be able to think dispassionately as I cut into this man's muscles, nerves, and organs. Several students made jokes about it that I thought were in bad taste. I soon realized that this behavior was a manifestation of their anxiety.

One day in the anatomy lab, I began to wonder about Max (the name I'd given my "body"). I set about trying to find out something about him—how he lived, and, more important, how and why he died. I wanted to personalize the process, to feel like maybe I was, in some small way, helping him, as ludicrous as that sounds. It took some research, but I was able to learn that Max was seventy-six years old when he died. He was an alcoholic who'd lived for the last sixteen months of his life in a shelter for the homeless, where he was found dead in bed one morning. Since there were no next of kin to claim the body, he ended up on my anatomy table.

From then on, whenever I looked at Max, I conjured up all kinds of scenarios as to what had really happened to him, and why his life had ended so sadly. I never came up with any answers, but knowing even the little I did about him made it easier for me to work with his remains.

Frankly, anatomy was not my favorite course, although it's something every doctor needs to know. I was very impatient those early months and years in medical school to start working with sick people. However, the wisdom at the time was that a student had first to master the basic medical sciences before seeing a patient. That's changed. Today, in most medical schools, medical students are introduced to patients and to clinical problem solving during their first year, even while they are learning the basic sciences.

So in these first two years, I went from the anatomy lab to the biochemistry lab to the histology lab to the physiology lab. I had felt more like a doctor working in Dr. Rabinovitch's clinic than I did now, where I was either studying or dissecting frogs, birds, dogs, and cats. I returned to our little hospital whenever I could because I yearned for some contact with people.

6

LET'S FACE IT: I'M A
PRACTICAL JOKER

I found medical school challenging and stressful. I studied hard for long hours and often needed to relax. But how? Some students did it by telling doctor/patient jokes, some of which I thought were in bad taste. We also played practical jokes on each other. Now that was fun! Here's one of the more successful ones by yours truly.

The Male Uterus

Our faculty was the most prestigious one on campus; doctors-to-be were the university's elite, or so we meds thought. As far as we were concerned, students of law, engineering, architecture, and others were second-raters. Those who were going to pursue careers in biochemistry took the elementary biochemistry course along with the first-year medical students, and later branched off into their specialty. We meds tolerated having these interlopers in the same classroom and lab as long as they showed the deference due future doctors. One of these biochemistry types refused to do so. Whenever the lecturer asked a difficult question, Henry was always ready to show off with the right answer. This would never do; he had to be taught his place and my classmates chose me to do it.

When I began to plan Henry's "punishment," our class was learning about sugar metabolism and how to distinguish one kind of sugar in the urine from another. Today it's done simply by putting a dipstick into the specimen and recording the color it turns. But back then, we had no dipsticks, so we put the urine into a test tube, heated it, and then noted its color. Normal urine remains yellow; pregnant women excrete lactose in their urine, which makes it turn brown when heated. (Lactose is the main sugar in milk, and pregnant and nursing females have an abundance of it in preparation for breast-feeding.) So lactose in the urine is an indicator of pregnancy. *It can mean nothing else.* A blue color indicates glucose—diabetes.

The plan in the lab was to collect our own urine as normal controls, test it, and then add to it the various reagents provided on the lab shelf, such as lactose and glucose, and note the color it turned.

After we arrived at the laboratory, the first step was to go to the john to produce our own specimens. We then returned to the lab to test them, first to see what normal urine looked like, and then to see the different colors they turned after adding a small amount of the different sugars. Again, blue meant glucose and brown indicated lactose, such as would be present in a pregnant woman. (Do you see where this is going?)

I thought of a great way to teach that smart aleck Henry his lesson. His bench in the lab was next to mine. When he returned with his urine, I had one of my classmates distract him before he could test it. I then added a liberal amount of lactose to his specimen. When Henry came back to the bench, I watched him out of the corner of my eye as he heated his own urine and waited patiently for it to retain its normal yellow color. Alas, the specimen began to turn deep brown! He was obviously puzzled.

He went back to the manual, reread the instructions on urinalysis, shook his head in disbelief, poured more of his fresh urine into another test tube, and heated it. It turned brown again. Test tube in hand, he tapped me on the shoulder.

"Isadore, what color is this urine?"

"It's brown," I answered. "Henry, you shouldn't have added the lactose yet. We're supposed to test our specimens first without putting in any of the reagents."

"That's the problem. I didn't add anything to it. This is my fresh urine."

"Come on, Henry, don't kid me. You must have put lactose in it."

"No, I swear, I didn't!"

"Well," I said, "in that case the test tube was probably contaminated with lactose from an earlier experiment. Why don't you repeat the urinalysis with a clean tube and another specimen?"

"Good idea," he said, obviously relieved.

He went off to the men's room and came back with more of his urine. I had him distracted again long enough for me to add some lactose to this second specimen as well.

"Let's do this together, Henry, to make sure there's no mistake," I graciously offered. He held the test tube under the flame, and once again, his urine turned brown!

Poor Henry was no longer a know-it-all. This was something for which, for the first time in this course, he had no answer.

"What do you think this means?" he asked me respectfully.

"Henry, we need to talk," I said, in my most serious, professional manner. "We medical students have been studying embryology. It seems that for a short time after conception, male and female embryos basically have the same anatomy; more specifically, they both have a uterus. This vestigial organ normally shrivels and disappears in the male fetus, and only females are left with a uterus. Now, Henry, listen carefully. It's very important that you understand what I'm telling you. Very rarely, there is an unfortunate developmental error as a result of which the uterus persists in a male. You wouldn't know it because it doesn't cause any symptoms. The affected man doesn't menstruate because he lacks the necessary hormones. The uterus is just there, and is rarely detected during life."

Henry was fascinated with this information and swallowed it hook, line, and sinker. "So how does this explain the lactose in my urine?"

Tricky question.

"This is embarrassing, Henry. I don't know how to tell you this, but there's a very strong possibility that you may be—how can I put it—*pregnant.*"

"You're crazy! How can I be pregnant?" he asked, as he gently moved his hand over his abdomen.

"Simple. Every normal male makes sperm. During intercourse or in some other way, you know what I mean, Henry, sperm makes its way out of the body. If one or more sperm backtrack and get into this male uterus, they can impregnate it. Now think hard. Was there a time recently when your sperm may have gone the wrong way?"

He blushed and fidgeted. "I suppose so."

"In that case, Henry, you need to see an obstetrician."

I expected him to crack up with laughter, to ask me where the eggs came from, but he didn't. He wasn't, after all, a medical student.

"Whom should I see about this, Isadore?"

"Well, we don't want it to get around. The safest thing is to see Dr. Maughn, the chief of obstetrics at the Royal Victoria Hospital."

Henry took my heartfelt advice and arranged an appointment with Dr. Maughn, a dour, no-nonsense Scot. I later learned about their conversation from Dr. Maughn's secretary, whom I occasionally dated.

"What's the problem, young man?" Maughn asked Henry. "Is your wife or girlfriend in a family way?"

"No. It's me, sir. You see, I understand that I have a . . . a male uterus and have gotten myself, well—sort of . . . *pregnant*. I need your advice. What should I do?"

Maughn didn't bat an eye. He looked at Henry coldly and said, "If this is some fraternity prank, you've had your fun. If you're by any chance serious, you need a *psychiatrist*, not an obstetrician."

I'm not sure why, but for some reason, during the rest of that academic year, Henry never again asked me for any medical advice. In fact, he studiously avoided me. When our biochemistry year together was over, he disappeared from my life and went on to become a senior biochemist in the Canadian research establishment.

I've never forgotten that male uterus episode, and apparently neither has Henry. One day, some forty years later, my brother, who resembled me somewhat, called from Montreal.

"I was at a dinner party with a fellow named Henry. When he heard my name was Rosenfeld, he asked if I had a brother. When I mentioned your name, he said to give you warm regards from the *Male Uterus*, and that you would know what that meant. He said to tell you that he miscarried and never had the baby. What was he talking about?

"I don't know," I lied. "Henry was always a little odd."

This story reflects how differently doctors and medical students are now perceived. I don't think there's any way today that a medical undergraduate could convince any *man* that he was pregnant. The lay public is much more sophisticated than it used to be. Anyone given such a strange diagnosis would immediately look up "male uterus" on Google or Yahoo! or at least get a second opinion. And that's as it should be.

The most ironic finale to this tale is—and you won't believe this—that despite my disparaging remarks about biochemical students vis-à-vis medical students, the dean of the graduate school of medicine and the executive vice dean of the Weill Cornell Medical College is not an MD. He's "merely" a professor of biochemistry!

7

PATIENTS—FINALLY!

My first two years in medical school were the longest of my life. I thought I'd never get to deal with people, but I started to as soon as I began my third year. I loved it! My very first impression after leaving all those labs with their corpses and animals was the difference in the demeanor of my teachers. They taught me not only about disease but also about the humanity in medicine. From day one, my instructors emphasized the importance of using my five senses to make a diagnosis, something that is less emphasized these days, when students and doctors tend to rely more and more on tests and technology. I learned to think of pain and suffering in human terms and not merely as symptoms of disease. I was taught, for example, how to distinguish among the different causes of a painful belly—from an acute appendix to an ectopic pregnancy—without a CT scan, MRI, or sonogram (none of which had yet been invented). I dealt with patients suffering from acute heart attacks, diabetes, drug overdoses; I learned how to detect various kinds of cancer by taking a detailed history and performing a thorough physical exam. Finally, and perhaps most importantly, I learned the importance of comforting both the dying and their distraught families.

An accurate diagnosis, then as now, requires first and foremost obtaining a detailed history and then performing a thorough physical exam. That took time then, and it does now. Unfortunately, too many doctors are taking shortcuts using only modern technology. Why should today's medical students bother to tap a chest with their fingers, or listen to breath sounds with a stethoscope, when it's so much easier, faster, and usually more accurate to fill out a requisition for a chest X-ray or CT scan? And why should they waste time listening intently to a patient's heart sounds with the stethoscope when they can get an echocardiogram and in a few minutes obtain an accurate interpretation of a heart murmur and a very good idea of the state of the heart muscle? Why depend on our five senses when machines can do it better? But do they always?

I *wanted* to be a clinical detective, and still enjoy it. I find it exciting and gratifying to be able to interpret every clue myself without the aid of all the technology. Don't get me wrong. I'm glad that all this equipment is available to me, and I never hesitate to use it if my diagnosis requires confirmation. But these fancy tests are very expensive. It's better to spare a patient the cost if I can do the job on my own. Although the old-fashioned stethoscope is a simple device, you can't imagine the diversity of sounds that pass through that diaphragm into the doctor's ears, and then to his brain for interpretation. The timing of a murmur in the heart's beating cycle—its pitch, its loudness, where it radiates in the chest—all provide a wealth of information if the doctor takes the time to listen.

I was probably more interested in the stethoscope than most because I knew, while still a student, that I wanted to be a heart doctor, and this was the sine qua non of that specialty. It's also a symbol—the badge of medicine. A stethoscope protruding from the coat pocket or worn around the neck says, "I'm a doctor." In addition to listening to the heart, my stethoscope can also tell me whether someone who is coughing has pneumonia, or whether a distended belly is due to a ruptured organ within the abdomen or to an accumulation of fluid. It can also detect a life-threatening aneurysm (ballooning) of the abdominal aorta before it ruptures fatally. So the stethoscope is great—but one has to know how to use it. I'm happy with the confidence that in a pinch, I can often do without the fancy machines, none of which is available when confronted with a sick stranger on an airplane at thirty thousand feet, or at the scene of an injury at a car accident. A doctor who knows how to use his or her five senses along with a stethoscope can do some pretty accurate clinical evaluation when necessary. That's basically what I learned in medical school, and it has stood me in good stead. Unfortunately, many of the "facts" I was taught about disease—how to prevent it and how to treat it—have turned out, sixty years later, to be wrong!

8

I WAS NOT CUT OUT
TO BE A SURGEON

I enjoyed practical jokes (giving, not receiving them). In my spare time as a student, I started making funny phone calls to people and places; I recorded them and played them for my fellow students at our parties. (I think that was legal at the time in Canada.) For example, I'd phone an emergency room and ask the nurse or doctor, in some foreign accent, exactly how to take an enema, or I'd call a radio station with a terrible stutter and apply for an announcer's job. My classmates had great fun listening to these recordings, and they made me very popular with my colleagues.

Someone must have told Dr. Gavin Miller, chairman of the department of surgery, about these tapes. Dr. Miller, known as "surgeon to the queen," was probably the most famous surgeon in Canada. He was, for me, a remote and forbidding figure. One day, he called me, *me*—a lowly, third-year medical student! "Look, Rosenfeld," he said, "I've heard that you've made some very funny tape recordings. My wife and I would love to hear them sometime. Would you come to dinner next Friday night and play some of them for us and other members of the faculty?"

Would I come to dinner at Dr. Miller's? Would I ever!

That Friday, armed with some of my funnier tapes, I arrived at Dr. Miller's house. He was a jovial, short, plump man with a touch of emphysema who wheezed every time he laughed. He loved the tapes, and he seemed to like me too. That evening was the beginning of one of the dearest friendships in my life. Years later, Dr. Miller would become my patient. I was a regular guest at his home, and the professor took a special interest in my future medical career. One evening, after dinner, he was very serious.

"Issie, where do you see yourself ten years from now?"

"I'd like to be a cardiologist and do some teaching too."

"Have you ever thought about becoming a surgeon?"

"Not really. I don't think I have the manual dexterity."

"Nonsense. Knowledge and judgment are more important for a surgeon than dexterity. Any fool can tie knots. What's really essential is to know *when* to cut. I think you'd make a great surgeon. Now listen. How does this sound to you? After you graduate, I will plan, pay for, and help you get the best surgical training possible at the finest centers in the world. When you come back, you can join me in practice, and eventually take over when I retire." (Most full-time professors practiced privately, too.)

I was speechless. I knew of no med student who'd ever had such an offer from someone of Dr. Miller's stature. I looked at my pitiful hands and fingers and wanted to crush them. How they'd let me down!

"What can I say, Dr. Miller? I'd jump at this offer if I felt I could do it."

"Why don't you go see Hans Lehmann," he said, referring to a famous McGill psychiatrist and a pioneer in the use of psychotropic drugs. "Ask him to run some aptitude tests on you. You'll see that you're wrong. You expect too much of yourself."

I agreed. It was the least I could do after such a generous offer. I saw Dr. Lehmann the next week and underwent a battery of dexterity tests, trying to put square objects into round holes, and the like. When it was all over, Lehmann took me aside. "Isadore," he said, "be a psychiatrist, be a dermatologist, be a cardiologist. Be anything, *but don't be a surgeon.*"

Relieved, I thought I had persuaded a disappointed Dr. Miller that mankind would be better off if I spent my life using a stethoscope and not a scalpel.

The Very First Time I Cut into a Living Body!

Later that year I started my surgery rotation in medical school. For the first few weeks, I simply stood at the side of the operating table as a junior member of the surgical team. My job was to hold a retractor (an instrument that pulls tissue out of the way so that the surgeon can work). Occasionally, I was allowed to put in a stitch or two. (I used to practice tying knots for hours on my bedpost because I was so much slower than my mentors.)

One occasion remains indelibly etched in my memory: I was in the OR (operating room) with Dr. Miller, who was in the process of excising a cancerous breast from a forty-five-year-old woman. (In the early 1950s, virtually all breast cancers were treated by radical mastectomy, in which the entire breast, as well as the muscles of the chest wall and every visible gland were removed. This operation is now rarely done.) As I looked on, Dr. Miller asked me to come over to his side of the table. "Here, Issie, you remove some of this breast tissue. I'll supervise you very carefully." He obviously had not accepted Dr. Lehmann's conclusions about my skill, or lack of it.

I didn't dare question the order of the chief surgeon. Until then my only "surgical" experience had been slicing a steak; at Thanksgiving dinner my mother learned never to ask me to carve the turkey! And yet, there I stood, scalpel in hand, actually cutting into the breast of a *live* woman. Blood spurted from a small artery; my professor deftly tied it off. I carefully dissected away the cancer itself, and then hesitated before turning my attention to the remaining breast tissue. By this time, Dr. Miller was convinced that Dr. Lehmann was right and took over.

"That's enough for today, Isadore. You've done very well. I'll finish the hard part: knowing when to stop cutting and leaving normal tissue alone." I then watched in awe as this great surgeon neatly cut, sewed, and stitched. That experience convinced me once and for all that I was not cut out to cut. My decision not to accept Dr. Miller's offer and become a surgeon would prove to be a boon to mankind!

My being all thumbs didn't really sadden me because I preferred to treat people with whom I can communicate rather than deal with anesthetized bodies.

9

A PATIENT DIES
IN MY ARMS

I always knew that one day I would inevitably witness a death. I expected my emotional reaction to depend on my relationship with the victim; it would obviously be more difficult for me if it was someone I knew, a family member, a loved one. But I assumed I'd be able to deal with a stranger's death in a professional manner. *Boy, was I wrong!*

During my fourth-year student rotation at the hospital, I was examining Mr. Cowan—a cardiac patient—in his room. It was late at night and we were alone. Suddenly, for no apparent reason, he turned white and started to gurgle. All I had was my stethoscope, great for diagnosis but not for treatment. It was obviously a cardiac arrest—sudden death—of which there are hundreds of thousands of cases every year. Mr. Cowan tried to say something to me, but his words were not intelligible. Suddenly, his eyes rolled up, his head dropped onto his chest, and his breath came in short, labored gasps. He was dying! And here I was, alone, and unable to do anything about it! *My mind went blank!* I pushed every call button in the room, desperate for help. No response! I tried to resuscitate Mr. Cowan by putting my lips to his and breathing rhythmically into his mouth (my own heart pounding so hard that I thought it would leave my chest), and at intervals pounding his chest with one hand while supporting his head with the other.

It wasn't working! But I didn't dare stop, not even for a moment. After what seemed like an eternity, but was probably no more than a minute or two, help finally arrived. I was never so happy to see the hospital resuscitation team—interns, residents, and nurses—rush in. They took over. I suddenly became short of breath myself and thought they might have to resuscitate me too. A resident immediately inserted a breathing tube into the patient's mouth, but the gasps stopped. Mr. Cowan's body became lifeless. He had died.

Witnessing those final moments of life—seeing someone alive and talking one moment and becoming inert the next as his soul departed, standing there and witnessing the transition from person to corpse—drained me emotionally. I blamed myself for Mr. Cowan's death. What had I done wrong? Not breathed into him often enough? Should I have concentrated on pounding his chest and left the breathing alone? Would that have saved his life? While I was torturing myself with these questions, the house staff continued its efforts. They were not in the least deterred by what was only the *apparent* death of the man. Suddenly, I heard a gasp—followed by another deep, loud rasping intake of air—and then another, and another. Unbelievably, the team had resuscitated Mr. Cowan! In those few minutes, I had seen life, death, and rebirth!

"Nice going, Rosenfeld," the chief resident said. "You saved this man's life."

I thanked him and quickly left the room. As I walked through the empty corridors, I realized that I had just experienced the ultimate reward of being a doctor. Then I raced into the nearest men's room and threw up.

10

M.D. OR M.P.?

Something happened in my third year of medical school that almost changed my life: I was asked to run for the Canadian parliament. I know it sounds incredible, but here's how and why it happened.

In 1946, while I was still a premedical student, Igor Gouzenko, a cipher clerk at the Soviet Embassy in Ottawa, defected and sought political asylum in Canada. He provided the Canadian authorities with evidence of a Soviet espionage network in Canada and implicated scores of people, including a highly respected biochemistry professor at McGill. But most important, he fingered Fred Rose, the only Communist Party member of Canada's parliament, and its only elected Jew. Rose represented Cartier, the constituency in which I had lived all my life, where I had been named Issie. Rose made no attempt to defend himself against these charges and fled to Soviet-controlled Czechoslovakia, where he later died.

This was very early in the cold war, when paranoia ran high on both sides of the iron curtain. I was ashamed and appalled that the only Jewish member of parliament had betrayed our country. I wanted desperately, as a resident of Cartier and a Jew, to make amends, to demonstrate that Rose's behavior did not reflect the beliefs in either this constituency or of Canadian Jewry. In order to do so, I decided, with the help of several friends who shared my political (really, ethnic) views, to form the Liberal Club at McGill. This project turned out to be very successful; we ran model parliaments and had many stimulating political debates. I became the de facto spokesman for Canada's Liberal Party (whose political philosophy is much like that of the U.S. Democratic Party) at McGill.

When the government called a by-election in Cartier to fill Rose's vacant seat, it was again contested by a Communist Party candidate. It was critical for the Liberals to win this election: If another Communist were sent to Ottawa, the government's credibility and foreign policy would be questioned, and the rest of the country would think that the citizens of Cartier, the great majority of whom were Jewish, were traitors sympathetic to the Soviets.

The Liberal Party selected Maurice Hartt to be its candidate in the upcoming election. He was a tough, plain-talking Jewish politician and a member of the provincial legislature in Quebec. I was asked to speak on the hustings during the campaign. This was no ordinary by-election: All the big guns came from Ottawa to campaign—Prime Minister Mackenzie King, who had led the country during the war, Lester "Mike" Pearson, the secretary of state for foreign affairs (who would later become prime minister), and most of the other cabinet ministers. I, a young premedical student, was also invited to address the audience—which I did passionately and with conviction. The press notices were very complimentary.

Maurice Hartt won the election hands down. In the next few years, he and I became friends, and frequently discussed his many political problems, positions, and ambitions. Sadly, he died from the vascular complications of diabetes, leaving the Cartier seat vacant again. I was in my third year of medical school at the time.

A few days later, I received a call from Brooke Claxton, the minister of national defense and leader of the Liberal Party. He informed me that the party elders had unanimously chosen *me* to replace Hartt! My reaction was one of shock and disbelief! I was only a medical student, not a politician! But soon my ego began to take over and on further reflection, I began to consider the offer quite seriously. After all, these guys must know what they're doing! I began to find the prospect of becoming a member of parliament at the age of twenty-three flattering and tempting. I asked my professors, family, and friends for their advice. I'm sure you can guess how my parents reacted. They were euphoric—ready and eager to add, "My son the future prime minister" to "My son, the doctor." My more rational friends warned that going into politics at this time of my life would, for all practical purposes, end my medical career.

While I was considering this incredible offer, my mind flashed back to my interview with Dr. John Kershman when I was applying for medical school. I remember him asking me, when I was not yet even a medical student, what I thought about socialized medicine! Did he have some premonition that I would one day be in a position to make such a decision for the entire country? Was I part of some grand plan for Canada? Maybe my mother was as intuitive as he in predicting the future of our country! Such were the thoughts that ran through my mind. Becoming a candidate in the upcoming election seemed entirely reasonable to me at the time. I got into my car and spent several hours driving around Cartier, whose citizens I might very well soon be representing. But on this solo tour, I was no Barack Obama; nobody knew me, nobody recognized me, and I returned home much less enthusiastic about my political career.

The following week, the prime minster himself came to Montreal on some other business. Before air travel was commonplace, cabinet ministers traveled in their own railway cars. The P.M. invited me to Montreal's Windsor Station one evening to meet on his train with him and Mr. Claxton. They told me that an opinion poll they had conducted in Cartier had shown that I could win the next election by a wide margin, and that the Liberal Party was very eager for me to accept the nomination. We discussed the mechanics of my entry into politics and how it could be coordinated with my medical career. They had it all figured out. After my election, I'd finish my last year of medical school at McGill, come home on weekends to meet with my constituents, then do an internship at the Ottawa Civic Hospital in the nation's capital. After learning the ropes as a backbencher in the House of Commons, I could expect to be named minister of health. Pretty heady stuff for a young medical student without any political or medical experience! I was on the verge of accepting this offer when Mr. Claxton invited me the next day to come to his Montreal office for a private conversation.

"I want to talk with you not as a politician, but as a friend who cares about your future. It would be very good for our party if you accepted this nomination. You're a fresh face on the political scene, and without any 'baggage.' But I worry about your future, Issie. If the Liberals remain in power, you will almost certainly become minister of health one day, given your M.D. degree. (I don't think there were any other doctors in parliament at the time.) But if we lose the election, and that's always a possibility, you'll be just another back-bencher. And what if you're not elected the next time around? What will you do then? You won't be the kind of doctor anybody will go to when they're sick, with no postgraduate training or clinical experience. So I advise you, Isadore, finish your training, become the best doctor possible, and then, if you're still interested in politics, I promise you a seat whenever you want to run."

He was right, of course, and so I reluctantly took his advice. It wasn't easy for me to turn my back on the glamour and excitement of a political career at so young an age and return to the books. But that's what I did. However, I retained my ties to the Liberal Party, and became a senior speechwriter for Mr. Claxton and various other cabinet ministers; I even wrote one radio address for the prime minister himself. My mother got the greatest kick sitting by the radio while these ministers were reading what I had written. She was especially thrilled when I anticipated, word for word, what they'd say, especially when it was the prime minister!

In the next election, the Liberal Party was defeated by the Conservatives, who remained in power for years. Had I run for office, I'd have been a politician and doctor with a useless M.D. degree.

Since that first near-taste of public life, I've maintained a great interest in public policy, especially as it relates to health care. I was proud to have been elected president of the New York County Medical Society, and later chosen to serve a four-year term as an advisor to two U.S. secretaries of health and human services—Dr. Louis Sullivan (in a Republican administration) and Donna Shalala (appointed by President Clinton). More recently, former president George W. Bush named me to the advisory panel of the White House Conference on Aging. Frankly, I don't think I've made a major impact on U.S. health policy in either capacity, but it's not for lack of trying. The longer I practice medicine, the more I am convinced that this country must provide some form of health care for all its citizens.

11

A DOCTOR AT LAST

I received my M.D. degree in June 1951, to which, for some reason, McGill also tacks on C.M. (Master of Surgery). Given how much I *didn't* know at the time, M.D. was enough of an exaggeration, but Master of Surgery was a joke. Just the thought of my operating on someone still sends shivers through my spine.

I won't bore you with the details of the ceremony and my parents' reaction to it. Let's just say that it was at least one hundred times as moving for them as either my high school or college graduation. This M.D. degree was the real McCoy, as far as they were concerned.

I was fortunate enough to have been selected for an internship at the Royal Victoria Hospital in Montreal. Affiliated with McGill, it was then, and remains to this day, a superb institution staffed by brilliant researchers and teachers. I planned to spend the first two years there as an intern and resident, then begin my specialty training at Johns Hopkins, then return to Montreal to work with the noted cardiologist Harold Segall, then spend my final year at the Mount Sinai Hospital in New York under the tutelage of Dr. Arthur Master, the father of ECG exercise testing. That last year would have the most profound effect on my life as well as my career (more about that in a later chapter).

After four years of medical school, you end up with an M.D. degree and the title "doctor," neither of which necessarily means that you are ready to treat the sick. Formal education provides little more than an overview of the major branches of medicine, after which students sign up for a residency program in the specialty they've chosen—ophthalmology, dermatology, neurology, obstetrics, and so on. But I believe that a young doctor should not make that decision immediately after graduating. Even though I had decided long ago to be a cardiologist, I thought it was important to learn a little more about other areas of medicine. A real doctor should know enough to be able to provide emergency care when needed. When there is a crisis on an airplane or at a theater or some other public place, the call is for a "doctor," not an obstetrician or dermatologist or neurologist. Those situations require a professional who can save a life, and I believe that's the responsibility of everyone with an M.D. degree.

That was the rationale behind the rotating internship policy at Royal Victoria Hospital in 1951. The first year after graduation would consist of six different two-month tours of duty—two months in general practice at a small hospital outside Montreal working with "primary care givers" and learning how to deal with medical problems of all kinds; two months in psychiatry at a hospital for the criminally insane; two months in surgery to learn how to provide effective first aid, sew up wounds, and set fractures; two months in obstetrics and gynecology to give me hands-on experience delivering babies; two months in oncology to learn the latest treatments, such as they were, for cancer and how to deal with the *total person* stricken with a fatal disease; and the final two months in a tuberculosis sanatorium learning about a disease that is now easily treated and cured.

This first year was not meant to make me a specialist in any field, but when it was over, I would feel more comfortable dealing with any emergency when there was no one around better qualified to do so.

So two days after graduation, my friend Dr. K. Royal Stewart and I were sent to a small community hospital in Sherbrooke, Quebec, about a hundred miles from Montreal. We were the first interns they'd ever had; local general practitioners and their nurses had heretofore provided whatever medical care was needed.

The First Time I Delivered a Baby

We arrived in Sherbrooke at about ten o'clock at night, wondering whether the nurses there would resent our coming. After all, they'd run the place for half a century quite efficiently without the help of kids from the big city, thank you. The hospital information desk was closed and we had no idea where to go. So we made our way to the emergency room, where we found only a clerk dozing at the reception desk.

He didn't know who we were or why we were there, so he contacted the nursing supervisor, who turned out to be quite hostile. We introduced ourselves, and she grunted what was meant to be a welcome.

"Follow me," she ordered, and showed us to our quarters. "You can choose your own rooms. I hope you brought your uniforms."

"Yes, ma'am, we have. Thank-you. Is the cafeteria open for the night shift?" I asked.

"No. We all bring our own food," she said, and reminded us, before she left, that one of us was expected to be on call starting at midnight, two hours from now.

Despite the frosty greeting, I found the whole scene exciting. Now I was a real doctor, on call, in charge, and without teachers or residents looking over my shoulder. Stewart and I flipped a coin. I won and got the first shift.

At about 2 a.m., my phone rang. "This is Sister Turnberry. One of our patients in the delivery room has just ruptured her membranes." I wondered why she hadn't called the woman's doctor. After all, she was a private patient and must certainly have expected him to deliver her. I worried that she'd resent my intrusion.

The truth is that I was rationalizing because I was terrified. Deliver a baby myself? I hadn't even *witnessed* a delivery for two years, since I was a third-year student, let alone performed one. And at the time there had been all kinds of people looking over my shoulder to make sure I didn't screw up. Now, here I was, only two days after getting my M.D. degree, out in the boondocks with no other doctor around, expected to deliver a baby on my own from a woman I had never examined!

But I had no choice, so I donned my whites and made my way to the delivery suite. I was met by two nurses, expressionless, standing like statues, arms crossed in the universal body language for hostility. I knew that if I allowed them to intimidate me, the rest of my rotation in Sherbrooke Hospital would be hell. I had to project the confidence and authority I did not feel.

The patient was lying on the delivery table, her legs in stirrups. She moaned every few minutes with each contraction. Trying to maintain my composure, I asked the head nurse about this woman's past medical history. She frowned, shrugged, and in a bored voice said, "Mrs. Eldridge is thirty-three years old and has two other children. Last one was born here about four years ago. That's the whole enchilada, doctor." ("Enchilada" in Canada? Turns out she was of Mexican origin.)

"Does she have any medical problems?"

"Everybody has medical problems."

The other nurse nodded her head in agreement.

I persisted.

"No diabetes, cardiac disorder, or bleeding tendency?"

"Look, doc. She's gonna have a baby, huh? You really think all that other stuff matters right now?"

That irritated me.

"Who delivered her other kids?"

"Dr. Randolph."

"Have you called him?" I asked, secretly hoping that he would show up at any moment.

"Of course. He said *you* should do it."

Realizing the die was cast and that I would get no useful information, I ended my interrogation and asked the nurses to drape Mrs. Eldridge with sterile sheets. But as they began to do so, I stopped them. "No, not that way. Like this," I said, and demonstrated how I wanted it done. (Actually, their way was fine, but I needed to show them who was in charge.)

"That's not the way we do it at this hospital," the head nurse asserted.

"Sorry, that's how I want patients draped when I'm doing the delivery."

They shrugged, blew out some puffs of air to show their resignation, and obliged.

I was ready to proceed.

"Fetal stethoscope, please." I'd be polite, no matter what.

The nurse placed the scope on my head and I bent down to put its bell on the mother's abdomen. I listened very carefully, ready to count the number of heartbeats per minute; too slow or too rapid a heart rate might indicate fetal distress. *Damn, I couldn't hear a thing.* I pressed on the abdomen a little harder. Total silence!

The nurses smirked at my obvious discomfiture. By this time, I had no time to solve the problem of the absent heartbeat because Mrs. Eldridge's contractions were now coming every few seconds, fast and furious. I had to get on with the delivery.

I inserted my gloved hand into the birth canal to feel for the suture lines on the baby's skull in order to determine how the head was descending. I couldn't make out any suture lines! Now I was really worried. I needed to identify them to know how to rotate the baby's head. And why hadn't I heard a fetal heartbeat? Was I forgetting something? I kept probing the contour of what was coming down in the canal and suddenly realized that *what I was feeling wasn't a head!*

"Oh my God—a breech," I thought to myself, looking to the nurses for some compassion, some reaction—anything! Their expressions remained flat. One of them commented, "It happens. No big deal. My brother was a breech."

Just my luck—my first delivery would be the most difficult obstetrical presentation there is—a breech, with the hips coming down first instead of the head. What I had mistaken for the head was obviously a knee. That's why I couldn't feel any suture lines! What would I do if she needed a Cesarean section? I had never even seen one done.

I recalled from my obstetrical lectures that when the knee presents in a breech delivery (which, incidentally, I had never even witnessed), the doctor is supposed to put a finger into its crease, flip the leg down, and then rotate the baby so that the hips come down sideways. This is known as the Pinet maneuver. Although this is all theoretical knowledge, I felt for the crease but couldn't find it. I was now drenched in perspiration, even though the temperature in the delivery room was quite cool. I asked for a pad to blot my forehead. "Damn, don't these nurses do anything on their own?" I thought. "I'm sure they wipe Dr. Randolph's head without being asked."

Suddenly there was a strong contraction of the patient's uterus, and the baby was born into my hands. It wasn't a breech at all! The baby was *dead and had no head!* What I had thought was a knee was the stump of its skull.

I had never before seen a malformed fetus, let alone one without a head. I felt guilty. Was any of this somehow my fault? Had I done something terribly wrong? Should I have confessed that I'd never delivered a baby alone before? Should I have asked for help? I was overcome by nausea. I breathed deeply and fought back the urge to be sick.

I held on to the edge of the table, fearing I might actually faint. I had visions of the nurses giggling and stepping over my prone body, saying, "Some doctor they sent us."

Slowly I regained my composure as it all became clear to me: The absent heart sounds, my inability to feel the scalp sutures, the knob I thought was a knee, and the reason the patient's doctor hadn't come to perform the delivery himself. The baby was anencephalic, a congenital abnormality incompatible with life. It must have been dead for some time—and the doctor, the patient, and the nurses all knew it! Since there was no trick to "catching" the remains, the doctor decided to get a good night's sleep at home and give me some "combat experience."

I tried to show neither surprise nor anger. I calmly removed my cap, gown, and gloves, and said, "Thank-you, ladies. I assume that everyone, including the patient, her doctor, and you, knew about this all along. Please tell Dr. Randolph that there were no complications. However, in the future, I expect you to share whatever information you have about patients with me. I'm not a veterinarian, and you are not zookeepers. Good night."

I knew very well why those nurses had given me a hard time. They resented my being there; they perceived me to be a threat to their authority and an intrusion on their turf. However, after that delivery, their behavior changed. Maybe they just felt sorry for me. They had played a rotten trick on me, and they knew it.

The rest of my stay at this community hospital turned out to be enjoyable and useful, as far as I was concerned. I got to know several of the doctors who worked there and made rounds with them. I was fascinated to see how they all differed in their approach to their patients, how their knowledge and skills varied. I also observed how men and women suffering from a wide spectrum of diseases from pneumonia to cancer to heart attacks were treated. I delivered several more babies, assisted in general surgery, applied casts to broken limbs, diagnosed and treated acute heart attacks (the only way to diagnose them in those days was clinical judgment and an electrocardiogram; therapy consisted of nothing more than bed rest and prayer, since there were few drugs and no surgery for this common disorder). Most important, during those two months in the community hospital, I learned how to comfort and communicate with sick and dying patients . . . and their loved ones.

When the time came for Stewart and me to return to Royal Victoria Hospital in Montreal, the supervisor we had met the first night shed a tear. "Why don't you two guys stay in Sherbrooke and have your own private practice here? We could sure use you." Even Mrs. Eldridge's nurses apologized for how they'd treated me that first night. "But we would never have let you get into trouble," they now assured me.

12

INTERNING
AT ROYAL VICTORIA

I spent the next two months at the Royal Victoria Hospital, helping take care of patients with every conceivable kind of illness—pneumonia, heart attacks, cancer, strokes, stomach ulcers, blood clots—you name it. I was there to learn how to deal not only with various diseases but also with the patients themselves and their families. I learned the hard way with one man. My bad judgment cost him his life.

To Tell or Not to Tell?

Matthew Ross, forty-eight years old, had been diagnosed with cancer of the rectum. His private doctor was a very knowledgeable senior attending physician who was somewhat aloof. He'd come to the patient's room for a minute or two in the morning, tell him what tests or procedures would be done that day, and leave. No sympathy, no explanation, no emotional involvement. I would not have wanted to be his patient. I was sorry for Mr. Ross and tried to make up for his doctor's "cold fish" approach by showing him some of the compassion I felt he needed.

One day Ross said he wanted to ask me a few questions. I should have been on my guard, but I wasn't.

"Everyone here is being so damned evasive, hedging about the diagnosis. I need to know exactly what's wrong with me. They keep telling me I'll be fine. That's not enough. I want to know the facts. My financial affairs are very complicated, and unless I take care of them, my family will be left in a big jam. No one has actually used the word 'cancer' but I know damn well that's what I have. I want to know what the future holds for me. Give it to me straight. I can take it. What's the bottom line?"

This request seemed so reasonable and so mature that I decided to be open and frank with him, especially since his cancer was curable. In retrospect, I realize that I had no business discussing anything substantive with him; that was his doctor's job. I was only an intern. But I wanted to raise his spirits, so I said, "Yes, Mr. Ross you have cancer of the rectum, but it's not going to kill you. As soon as all the tests are done, you will have an operation that will get rid of the cancer completely and you'll be out of here cured and as good as new." That was the absolute truth!

"Is it a tough operation, Doc?"

"Well," I replied, "no surgery is fun; you'll have a sore rear end for a couple of weeks after they remove the tumor." We both laughed.

"That's it?" he asked, seemingly relieved.

"That's it," I said.

Mr. Ross thanked me, and I left his room, feeling pretty good about myself.

The next morning I learned, to my horror, that Ross had signed himself out of the hospital during the night. I tried to rationalize his action by assuming he'd left in order to settle his affairs and that he would come back for the surgery. After all, hadn't I told him that his disease was not fatal and that the cancer could be eradicated?

Dr. Patterson, his personal physician, met me in the corridor later in the day.

"Rosenfeld, did you hear about that damn fool Ross? Checked himself out. We can't locate him anywhere. His wife doesn't know where he is and neither does his lawyer. I hope he doesn't do something foolish. You know I deliberately never used the word 'cancer' with him because I knew he had a phobia about it and wouldn't believe that we could cure it. Someone must have used that word with him."

He looked at me for a long moment, didn't pursue the matter, turned on his heel and left. This "cold fish" was a compassionate gentleman after all—and he must have had a pretty good idea who spilled the beans.

Three days later, I read in the local paper that Matthew Ross had been found dead in an Ottawa hotel room, with a self-inflicted gunshot wound to the head. He left a note saying that he didn't believe his doctors and that he could not endure the slow, painful death he was sure that all cancers cause. He had updated his will, straightened out some problems in his various accounts, provided for his wife and children, and now felt he had the right to do what he must.

Mr. Ross had suckered me. I had not been able to convince him with my optimism. His doctor knew that despite his outward appearance of "I can take it, just tell me," this man was emotionally unstable and should not, at least at that time, have been told the truth. I learned then that what a doctor tells a patient must be tailored to that patient's ability to deal with it, that a doctor must assess his or her emotional status and determine the kind of support the family can provide. Although it's been almost fifty years since this tragedy, I still regret that my naïveté and inexperience led to this man's death.

Ever since that experience, I have chosen my words very carefully when discussing cancer or any other life-threatening ailment with my patients. In my opinion, too many physicians, especially oncologists, are in too much of a hurry to deliver bad news. They usually do so under the guise of honesty and forthrightness. While everyone has a right to know the nature of his or her problem, exactly when and how it's explained to them can make a tremendous difference to the quality of life left for them.

I never use the word "cancer" with my patients; I always say "tumor" or "growth." I emphasize that the speed with which a malignant tumor progresses varies from person to person, that response to medication may be surprisingly good. In short, I *never remove hope*, for despair is worse than the most severe pain. Many patients who demand to know the whole truth deep down expect to be shielded from bad news. As my experience with Mr. Ross years ago taught me, telling someone the "truth" can be the wrong thing to do.

Even Bad Cancers May Not Kill!

Let me fast-forward for a moment to describe an experience I had when I was already in practice because it is so relevant to the question about what doctors should tell their cancer patients. We'll return to my next rotation after this story.

I'd been in private practice little more than a year when a woman in her early twenties came to see me about an enlarged gland in her neck that she'd noted only in the past week or so. It was small and hard, didn't hurt, she had no fever, and she felt perfectly well. She wouldn't have bothered me about it except that her husband insisted she have it checked out.

Enlarged lymph glands are very common and not always detected by the patient. Doctors routinely look for them anyway, in the neck, the armpits, the groin; in the space above the clavicles (collarbones); and around the elbows and the groin. X-rays, CT scans, and MRIs can detect others inside the chest or belly. They are most often enlarged by an infection. These glands are like sieves; they filter the lymphatic fluid that flows through them, trapping any bacteria it may contain, thus reducing the chance of the infection spreading to other parts of the body. The bacteria cause the glands to become inflamed, painful, and swollen.

Doctors search the area from which the fluid that reached the gland has come in order to determine the source of the infection. Painful, enlarged glands in the neck may be due to a sore throat or an infected tooth; when your cat scratches your arm and it becomes even slightly infected, glands in your armpit may swell and hurt.

These lymph glands not only snare bacteria and viruses; they also trap cancer cells. When they do, however, although the gland is enlarged, it is not usually inflamed or painful. So cancerous lymph nodes do not, as a rule, hurt, which is why this patient waved a red flag when she told me she could feel this gland in her neck but it was not painful.

When I examined her, she looked healthy, and had not obviously lost any weight, as patients with advanced cancer often do. When I examined her neck, I felt a lump the size of an almond. It was rock hard! My pushing and pulling on it did not seem to bother her. I then examined her thyroid for the presence of any nodules. There were none. I looked for other enlarged glands in her armpits and groin. Nothing. I then felt her liver and spleen. They were normal too. I now needed to have the gland biopsied; it was small enough for the surgeon to remove completely while doing so. That would tell me not only if it was a cancer but also what kind and where it came from (the primary site). Malignant cells that metastasize (travel from their original site) usually retain their appearance so that, for example, a lung cancer that had somehow migrated to this woman's neck would show up as such under the microscope.

The gland was sent to the lab; a few days later the pathologist called with bad news. The biopsy showed it to be cancer. Worse still, it was so highly malignant that he was unable to identify the organ in which it originated. Such cancers are referred to as "undifferentiated," meaning that they are growing so wildly that their original cells have lost their identity. I sent the biopsy slides to pathologists at other hospitals, including those at the Armed Forces Institute in Bethesda, in the hope that someone might identify its cell type. No one was able to.

Although this young woman's outlook was grave (wildly growing cancers that have already spread are very hard to cure), there was an outside chance that if we discovered what kind of cancer it was and where it had originated, we could remove it, radiate it, or administer the appropriate chemotherapy. That might at least buy her some time. We'd have to embark on a total body investigation. All we had then were X-rays because this was before the days of MRIs, PET, and CT scans.

The problem in launching such an extensive search was that this woman had no idea how gravely ill she was: as far as she was concerned, all she had was a little lump in her neck that wasn't giving her any trouble, and we had removed it. What was all the fuss about? How could I justify doing all those X-rays and other uncomfortable tests without alarming her? If I were to tell her that she had cancer, feeling as well as she did, she'd think I was crazy and go to another doctor.

I told her that I wanted to have some other tests done and that I hoped she would humor me. She agreed without asking other questions. (Many such patients suspect deep down what's happening, but they don't admit it either to themselves or to their doctors. They just go along with whatever recommendations are made.)

During the next several days, we ran scores of blood tests; we X-rayed the patient's bones, her bowel, her upper intestinal tract; we studied the liver, the pancreas, the spleen; we evaluated her lungs, her head, and her neck. Every test came back normal! Where could this devastating cancer have come from?

I met with several cancer specialists from Sloan-Kettering Memorial Hospital in New York. There is no better cancer center anywhere. The head and neck oncologists there were convinced that the primary tumor was somewhere in her head or neck. In their opinion, we had been unable to locate the exact site because it was probably still microscopic in size. All it takes are a few tiny cells to travel to a nearby gland and multiply there. My consultants emphasized that unless we found and removed this cancer's site of origin, it would spread throughout this young woman's body and kill her. And if this search was not successful, they believed there was no alternative but to remove every lymph gland in the chain that runs along either side of the neck up to the ears. If a thorough analysis of all this tissue didn't come up with the answer, then the tumor was probably in her tongue and we might have to remove it!

How could I recommend so drastic a procedure to this beautiful young woman who had no symptoms whatsoever? After we were done with her, her face would be an ugly caricature. I met with her husband and told him what I had been advised to do, that according to the greatest experts in the field, this was her only chance of survival. He was shocked. He asked for time to think it over, and begged me not to mention anything to his wife. While this drama, of which she was totally unaware, was unfolding, she had begun to resume her normal life, relieved that her "checkup" was over and nothing had been found.

The next day her husband came to see me. "I've spent every waking moment agonizing about what to do," he said. "I even went to see our pastor this morning. I honestly believe that if we subject my wife to this drastic, mutilating surgery, her life will not be worth living. She's always taken such pride in her appearance. She'll never agree to it. Please, let's not even tell her. She's happy; she feels well. Let her enjoy what time she has left. I know her better than anyone. If she learns the truth, she'll kill herself."

As a man, a husband—and also as a doctor—I agreed with him. But I had an ethical dilemma. *He and I* concluded that the proposed extensive surgery would disfigure her to such an extent that she would rather die, but *she* hadn't told me that. How did I know that given the option between a hideous appearance and death she wouldn't choose life—under any circumstances? How much did her husband's own feelings enter into his decision—his revulsion at being married to a grotesque-looking woman he would feel too guilty to abandon? Although he claimed the legal right to make that decision, he was wrong. My first responsibility was to my patient.

I agonized over what to do. I went back to my consultants. "I need some data, some statistics," I told them. "I know that if we do nothing, she will surely die. But how long could she go on feeling as well as she does now?" I asked. They weren't sure—months, maybe even a year or two. "And what are the chances of a complete cure if we operate?"

"Maybe 10 percent."

That was enough for me. Given those numbers, and knowing this woman as I did, I decided to tell her nothing. I discharged her from my care with a "clean bill of health." I said, and it was true, that although the gland we'd removed was "diseased," we could find absolutely nothing else wrong with her. There was nothing more that could reasonably and safely be done. I urged her to let me know if she developed any other symptoms or if any other glands became enlarged.

That was almost fifty years ago! She has never been sick since! She had a baby, became a very successful career woman, and is now in her early seventies. We never did determine the source of that malignant gland—and nothing else ever acted up anywhere in her body!

The irony of it is that if we'd told this woman the truth and she had rejected the extensive surgical approach we recommended but instead had gone to Lourdes, or taken some herb or other, or seen some faith healer, or checked in to a clinic in Tijuana, she (and I) might have credited any of them with "curing" her fatal disease.

13

RIDING THE AMBULANCE— ROSENFELD ON THE WAY!

Interns at the Royal Victoria Hospital rode the ambulance three days a week; paramedics had not yet been "invented." Frankly, I loved going out on these emergency calls. The flashing red lights and the siren, then as now, meant that help was on the way. During my internship, ambulances were equipped only with splints to secure broken limbs, oxygen for people with heart attacks, and morphine to control pain. We didn't even have an ECG machine! The ambulance staff consisted of an orderly, a driver, and an intern in charge.

The days I was on ambulance duty, I might be working in a clinic or rounding on the wards when a voice on the overhead speaker would announce: "Dr. Rosenfeld, two-three, two-three." (Pagers had not yet been invented.) The message would be repeated every few seconds until I responded. I'd then race down to the emergency room and board the waiting lifesaving vehicle. If the ambulance would be going by my house, I'd quickly telephone my mother to alert her. She and all her neighbors would then stand by their open windows and watch for "Mrs. Rosenfeld's son, the doctor." As I drove by, they waved and shouted, "Good luck!" I maintained a determined, grim expression, and looked straight ahead. *It was Rosenfeld to the rescue.* Ta-dah!

Most of the calls we received were to transport people with strokes and heart attacks to the hospital. Unfortunately, the only treatment I could offer on the ambulance was oxygen. One of these calls is vividly etched in my memory. A skier on Mount Royal, in the center of Montreal, had been injured and was lying at the bottom of one of the slopes. I arrived at the scene to find a small crowd and two police officers. The patient, a man who looked to be in his early forties, was lying on the ground, eyes closed—and his body motionless. It was hard to tell, at first glance, whether he was breathing. He did not respond to my questions. I thought it might be a language problem, so I tried again, in French.

"Ou avez vous le douleur?" I asked. (Where does it hurt?)

Still no answer. It never occurred to me that this guy might actually be dead. After all, the police had lots more experience with death than I did, and they wouldn't have called an ambulance for a dead man. My job was with life, not death! I was there to splint a broken limb, not to bring back a corpse!

Montreal, in the dead of winter, is a cold place. The temperature that day must have been −10°F. Everyone, including the man on the snow-covered ground, was bundled up. I removed my gloves and tried to open his eyes. They were glazed over. When I shone my penlight into them, his pupils did not react. At this point, he looked dead to me, but I didn't dare say that unless I was absolutely sure, what with the crowd of onlookers and the police standing there. Also, the hospital did not like us to bring a corpse back in the ambulance; doing so would earn me a demerit. Corpses were for the coroner and the police, not for the Royal Victoria Hospital.

I looked desperately for other signs of life. His breath was not visible although the temperature was below freezing. Wait. Was that a short wisp of air coming out of his mouth? I looked again. Nothing. I felt for a pulse in the neck. There was something . . . *maybe*, but it was so faint I couldn't be sure. It could have been my own muscles contracting. Or had rigor mortis set in? Maybe this guy was really dead!

"Well, doc, what's the verdict?" the police sergeant asked, "We can't just have him lying here forever. Are we taking him to the hospital or the morgue?"

"Let's put him in the ambulance for a few minutes where I can examine him more carefully," I suggested. I climbed in to the back of the ambulance and continued my examination. The fingers on my own hands were so cold that I wasn't sure I could really trust what I was feeling. The cop stuck his head in.

"If you're headed for the hospital we'll escort you. If it's to the morgue, there's no rush. We can stop for coffee and warm up, huh?"

The cop may have thought that was funny. I certainly didn't. I had a life in my hands. Although every instinct told me the man was dead, I said: "I'll take the escort. Let's go."

"You're the doctor," he said.

To hell with my worries, I thought as we sped off. So what if the emergency room staff laughs at me? Deep down I knew what I couldn't say to the sergeant: "I just don't have the confidence, the guts, or the experience to make this decision."

Fortunately, our medical team at the hospital knew how to deal with severely frozen victims. They quickly removed the man's clothes and hooked him up to an ECG. The tracing revealed a heart rate of twenty or twenty-five beats a minute. There were only four or five respirations a minute. (So there *had* been a short wisp of breath, after all.) They immediately immersed him in a warm bath (yes, *warm*; the best way to avoid gangrene and tissue damage), and gave him oxygen and intravenous fluids to support his blood pressure. After a little while, my "corpse" slowly returned to life before my very eyes! What if I had pronounced him dead? Would somebody at the morgue have checked? Maybe not. After all, a *doctor* had pronounced him dead. I would have made a horrendous mistake, and no one would have been any the wiser—not even I.

Interns no longer ride the ambulance—a good thing! They have been replaced by paramedics who have been trained to deal with virtually every type of emergency—heart attacks, shock, broken bones, hemorrhaging, or seizures. These days, there would never have been any question whether a frozen, unconscious skier was still alive. Not only would a paramedic have known how to handle the situation, but there would have been an electrocardiograph machine in the ambulance to tell whether the heart was beating. Perhaps most important, paramedics can now communicate instantly by radio and portable phones with emergency room physicians who provide them with whatever further instructions they need. All ambulances have oxygen, as well as every conceivable type of emergency medication to raise or lower abnormal blood pressure, regularize heart rhythm, control pain—you name it.

The paramedic phenomenon is one of the major advances in emergency care in this country. If there is any question in your mind about the urgency of your symptoms, wherever you may be, don't waste your time dressing and finding a cab, or asking a friend to drive you to the emergency room. Call 911 and wait for the ambulance. Chances are, however, I won't be on it.

14

WORKING IN A MENTAL HOSPITAL

My next two-month rotation was in a mental hospital, not primarily as a psychiatrist but to provide medical care for any psychiatric patient who developed physical problems. It was assumed, of course, that I would also develop some experience in dealing with disturbed individuals unfortunate enough to have been incarcerated—sometimes for life.

Everyone is familiar with the courtroom defense of "legally insane," when a person is deemed not to be responsible for his or her actions because of permanent or temporary mental instability. We often think this is just a clever move on the part of a defense attorney to spare a client from imprisonment. I often wonder how a jury of laymen can decide such a complex issue when it hears diametrically opposite opinions from prosecution and defense psychiatrists. Too often, someone committed to a mental hospital has not been given a neurological examination to rule out an organic, or physical, cause of "insanity." I learned this the hard way during my rotation at this hospital for the mentally ill.

The senior psychiatrist at the Verdun Hospital for the Insane welcomed me when I arrived. Frankly, I was not nuts about going there.

(Don't you love my puns?) After leaving the entrance hall, he unlocked a reinforced door to the ward through which he had planned to escort and "introduce" me to some of the demented souls whose medical doctor I would be for the next two months. Before he could completely open the door, he was hit in the face by a handful of excrement hurled by one of the patients. Surprisingly, he didn't seem the least bit angry; he didn't charge into the room looking for the perpetrator, as I might have done. He calmly suggested that we go downstairs to clean up and then try again to enter the ward. He washed his face, and we went back upstairs. He opened the door again (I was careful to stand directly behind him). We entered uneventfully this time. There were scores of patients doing various things—some were reading, others were exercising, and many were just sitting looking into space. I greeted a few, after which we returned to the staff quarters.

One evening a week or so later, the psychiatrist usually on duty in this hospital's emergency room had a personal emergency and asked me to take over for a few hours. I was sitting in his small office when I suddenly heard a man screaming at the top of his lungs:

"You'll all be sorry. You won't get away with this!" he shouted. "My wife and this quack shrink are in cahoots."

Although shouting and screaming were not unusual at this mental hospital, I nevertheless rushed into the admitting office to see what this was all about. A very angry man wearing a straitjacket over a rumpled blue suit was struggling with three attendants. Another man stood nearby with his arm around a woman with bruises on her face and arms, her dress torn, and her hair disheveled. He was the psychiatrist who had called the ambulance; the woman was the restrained man's wife.

"I want my lawyer. You'll be sorry. You won't get away with this!" he yelled. "This phony shrink has been screwing my wife and they are planning to kill me. I was only defending myself when I hit her. I want my lawyer. Who the hell are *you?*" he spat out at me.

I had worked at other hospital emergency rooms receiving injured, bleeding, drugged, comatose people, as well as those in pain—all of whom were happy to have made it to the hospital alive. I had no idea what to do in this situation.

After the attendants put the patient in a soundproof examining room, his psychiatrist briefed me about him. Mr. Kastor was fifty-one years old. He and his wife had been married for almost thirty years; they were childhood sweethearts. He was not a wealthy man but made a good living at the taxi company that he owned in a suburb of Montreal. His behavior had been normal until a few weeks ago, when he started coming home unexpectedly in the middle of the day, sneaking quietly into his house, convinced that he would find his wife in bed with another man. He would telephone her from his office every hour to see if she was home. When she answered, he hung up without a word. Matters gradually worsened; more recently he accused his wife of trying to poison him, refusing to eat any meals she prepared, insisting that she taste them first—from his plate, not hers. However, there were other days when he was completely normal— even euphoric; and then, for no apparent reason, he suddenly became moody, depressed, angry, and paranoid. He repeatedly told his wife that the dispatcher at his company was a thief and that he'd hired detectives to "monitor" him. Things finally got so bad that he moved out of the bedroom that he and Mrs. Kastor had shared since they were married, and spent the night in his library behind a locked door.

During one of his calmer moods, he agreed to see a psychiatrist only if his wife came along. At first the psychiatrist felt that perhaps his strange behavior was due to stress at work and that it would pass. He gave Mr. Kastor some tranquilizers at this first appointment and scheduled a second one. But the irrational behavior continued. One moment he was calm, almost like his old self, and the next he had delusions that his wife was planning to slit his throat while he was watching television. He wouldn't let her sit behind him.

Earlier that evening, he attacked her after she had walked over to his chair and was gently brushing the hair from his forehead. He pummeled her face, neck, and arms. Unable to defend herself, she tore away, ran to a neighbor's house, and phoned the psychiatrist. He told her to stay where she was and immediately called our hospital for an ambulance.

I treated Mrs. Kastor's cuts and bruises, left her with a nurse, and went back to the struggling, screaming patient who was now strapped to an examining table in a secure room. I had him sedated and waited for the drug to take effect so that I could examine him physically, which was all I was qualified and supposed to do. I wasn't a psychiatrist.

A half hour later, I returned to find that Mr. Kastor had quieted down. I asked the attendants to remove his restraining straps so that I could do my physical exam. They stood by, just in case the sedatives I'd given wore off and he turned violent again.

"Hello, Mr. Kastor. I'm Dr. Rosenfeld, the medical intern here. I want to make sure you're OK. Looks like you and your wife had a little misunderstanding. Now, just relax and we'll have you out of here by the morning."

There was no point trying to tell him that he was deranged and paranoid; that was up to the psychiatrists. My job was to perform the physical, and I could only do that if he didn't feel threatened by me.

"Thank-you, doc. You look like the only normal person here," he said, and actually smiled at me. The drug had taken full effect—but I knew it wouldn't last very long.

"Do you mind if I give you a quick going over? I want to make sure you're OK."

"Of course. Thanks. But let's make sure that door is locked."

I had the attendant lock the door, and motioned for him to stay in the room with me. I was in no mood for physical combat. I then performed a routine physical and found nothing abnormal. Mr. Kastor's blood pressure, heart, lungs, and a routine neurological examination were all normal. I drew some blood and was about to leave when he asked me, "Why the bars on the window? Do you think they may try to kidnap me?"

I took the easy way out. "You never know," I said. "They're for your safety," which was true.

I didn't see Mr. Kastor again for several days. He was admitted to the ward after our psychiatrists had diagnosed him as a *classic paranoid schizophrenic.*

"Can it just develop like that out of the blue," I asked, "in a man who's been entirely normal for more than fifty years?"

My psychiatric colleagues assured me that it could.

Despite the various drugs the psychiatrists gave Mr. Kastor, including Thorazine—which had just been developed—his persecution complex continued unabated. He refused to see his wife, his children, or any of his employees.

Some three weeks later I received a call from one of the hospital psychiatrists. "I wonder if you'd take a look at Kastor. I noticed the other day that he's developed a tremor of his right hand, and he doesn't appear to be walking normally—veering a bit to one side. I think you should check him out for Parkinson's."

I had Mr. Kastor brought to my examining room. He was quiet and appeared depressed. His right hand was indeed shaking, and he was unsteady on his feet. I performed a more careful neurological exam than I had when he was admitted and noticed that the big toe in his right foot moved upward when I stroked the sole. It should normally bend forward. This indicated that there might be something abnormal going on in his brain—physically. Had this abnormality been there all along, and had it been missed? I had no idea. When I asked him how he felt, he answered:

"How's a guy supposed to feel in a cuckoo's nest like this? It gives me a headache. I've had one ever since they stuck me in here. Can you give me something for it? And when do I get out? I'm a working stiff, you know. Can't afford vacations like this."

I called the staff psychiatrist and said I didn't know exactly what was wrong, but I recommended that a neurologist examine Mr. Kastor as soon as possible. I suggested a skull X-ray and a lumbar puncture (in which the fluid bathing the brain and flowing in the spinal canal is analyzed).

His reply startled me: "You medical guys see stroke and tumor in every one of these nut cases. But OK, I'll call and set it up."

The neurological exam I suggested was scheduled for the following week. That would prove to be too late. Three days later Mr. Kastor was found dead in his bed.

The autopsy report shocked and surprised me. The pathologist found a large, encapsulated *benign* tumor pressing on the frontal lobe of the brain—the area that controls higher intellectual function. It could have been completely removed in a fairly straightforward, virtually risk-free operation.

This brain tumor had caused Mr. Kastor's paranoia and violent behavior. Had he killed his wife, a court of law might well have declared him criminally insane and remanded him to a hospital such as ours—or they may have chalked it up to a marital dispute and sentenced him for murder.

I am certain that a more sophisticated neurological exam than I or anyone else had ever done would have detected the tumor and prevented his hospitalization and his death. He could have returned to a normal life. If only I had detected that up-going toe the night he was admitted, I might have saved his life! If, if, if . . . might, might, might.

I had many sleepless nights and nightmares after I heard the autopsy findings. I could hear Mr. Kastor pleading: "Doc, there's something wrong. Help me."

As a result of that experience so early in my career, I have throughout my entire professional life looked for every reasonable *physical* explanation in *any* patient at *any* age who manifests abnormal behavior before referring him or her to a psychiatrist.

My experience in those two months of working with the mentally ill would help me deal with several other unexpected psychiatric problems that would arise in the years to come.

15

ALONE IN A CAR WITH
A MADMAN

For my last two-month rotation, I was assigned to the Royal Edward Laurentian Hospital, in the heart of the beautiful mountains north of Montreal. I loved the place and considered it a reward and a place to rest after my hard work during the preceding ten months. A cure for tuberculosis had not yet been discovered in 1952, and patients with this terrible infection, especially those who did not respond to the primitive therapy then available, were sent to this hospital for rest, fresh air, and more aggressive treatments such as collapsing the affected lung and other surgical procedures (none of which are used anymore). To protect the staff from contracting this very contagious disease and maintain our resistance, the administration made sure we did not work too hard. I was on call for only six hours a day, five days a week—a far cry from the 24/7 schedules of previous and later house-staff assignments. I had lots of time to hike in the woods and fish in the lakes. The medical staff met daily for a few hours to review patients' chest X-rays and to discuss our patients' medical progress and problems.

One afternoon, while at one such conference, I was called away to take a phone call from the chief psychiatrist at the mental hospital I had just left.

"Isadore, you remember Bob Golden, don't you?" I did indeed: Bob was a young man in his mid-twenties who'd been a college football player. Tragically, he had become schizophrenic while at school and needed to be hospitalized because of frequent outbursts of violent behavior. I couldn't imagine why my former chief was calling me here in paradise about demented Bob, whom I hadn't seen for weeks.

"Yes, of course. What's the problem?"

"He had been doing very well, without any symptoms of paranoia or aggressive behavior. At their last visit to the hospital, his parents had found him so well that they asked for permission to take him to their summer cottage in the Laurentians for the weekend. I guess we were wrong to give him that pass because he's gone on a rampage up there, smashing all the windows and furniture at home. His family has fled in terror and called us for help."

"Gosh, I'm really sorry, but what can I do about it now?" I asked, as I prepared my fishing rod.

"Bring him back."

"Bring him back? Just like that? He's violently mad, and you want *me* to bring him back? Why don't you call the cops? They're better equipped to handle such cases than I am. Or better still, just send an ambulance with a couple of orderlies for him."

"If he gives the police a hard time, or resists, they may hurt him. Remember how strong he is. And by the time an ambulance gets up there he might be gone, and who knows what he'll do next? I think you can handle him. He liked you. What do you say?"

What could I say? "OK, wish me luck." I armed myself with a pocketful of small glass syringes vacuum-filled with morphine. When the syringe is crushed, the morphine is injected under pressure.

I drove my green Pontiac coupe to the Golden home in the town of Val Morin some twenty miles away. I'd have had no trouble finding the house even without an address. It looked like something in a war zone: windows were shattered, glass strewn everywhere, shutters askew—and there was total silence. I tapped gently on the door with one hand, my other in my pocket holding a morphine syringe. A moment later, Bob, a handsome big hulk of a man, opened the door. He recognized me and smiled happily.

"Hi, Dr. Rosenfeld. I'm so glad to see you. What are you doing here?"

I never deliberately lie to my patients, even those who are mad, so I said, "After I left our hospital, I came to work at the TB hospital, a few miles away. They told me you were here, so I came to see you."

I looked around at the devastation. Dishes were broken; the furniture was in shambles. "Hey, Bob, it's good to see you too." Now *that* was a lie. "What happened here?"

"It's my family, doc! Would you believe that they actually expected me to make my bed! I never make my bed in the hospital. Why should I do it here? I got really mad."

"Bob, I don't believe it! I don't blame you for getting mad. You're not a maid! What a nerve! I wouldn't stay in this house another minute if I were you. They'll probably ask you to do it again tomorrow morning." I figured there was no point in telling him that there was no more furniture to smash and that no one in his right mind would set foot in the place while he was still there. "Look, I have a great idea. My car's right outside. Why don't we drive back to the hospital together? I'll buy you a malted milk on the way. What do you say?"

"Wow, would you really do that? Would you really drive me back? Gee, thanks."

So off we went, Bob and I, back to the Verdun Hospital for the Criminally Insane, the longest seventy minutes I'd ever spent—alone at the wheel with a violent schizophrenic sitting beside me. Anything in his purview might have set him off. Although our relationship had always been a good one, it was still a risk, but I was prepared to take it. Without prior experience working with such patients, I would never have been able to rescue Bob. There's no telling what might have happened to him. We got to the hospital safely—where no one dared ask him to make his own bed.

A House Call with My German Shepherd

I'm going to fast-forward here to describe a similar experience several years later when I was in private practice in New York.

Patients of mine had a troubled son, Mark. I didn't know his formal psychiatric diagnosis, but he had an uncontrollable temper. One day, Mark stabbed someone during an altercation in Greenwich Village in New York. He was arrested and taken to the holding pen of the neighborhood police station. He'd have been hauled off to jail, but his influential parents arranged to have him transferred instead to the psychiatric division at Bellevue Hospital.

Mark let it be known that he was furious at being locked up in the "booby hatch," as he called it. He preferred the macho alternative of being imprisoned with other tough guys rather than holed up with loonies. "I'll kill you for this," he shouted at his mother and father, as the doors to his room were shut and locked.

A week or so later, my wife and I were at home fast asleep when the phone rang at about eleven o'clock. It was Mark's parents, who lived in a penthouse in our apartment building. They told me they were coming home from the theater when our smiling doorman greeted them with the news. "Good evening. I'm so happy for you. Mark is home. He's upstairs waiting for you."

Panic-stricken, they turned and fled, and called me from the first telephone booth they could find. (This was before the days of the cell phone.)

"Doctor, the doorman tells us that Mark is in our apartment. He's escaped from Bellevue! We can't go home. He said he'd kill us! We called his psychiatrist but can't reach him. Please help us."

The same old story. Why me? I'm a cardiologist, not a psychiatrist. "I think you ought to call the police or the hospital. They'll come for Mark and bring him back," I replied.

"No, no. We can't do that! They'll hurt him. You know how cops are. Please go to our apartment and try to take him back to Bellevue."

"Why would he go back with me after going to all the trouble to escape?"

"We don't know. We're desperate. What else is there to do?" they asked.

"Let me think about it. Call me back in five minutes."

I hung up the phone and consulted with my wife. "What's the problem?" she asked. "You're a doctor; you've got to go." My Camilla, a doctor's daughter, has always been imbued with the nobility and self-sacrifice of medicine. "I'll get dressed and go with you," she volunteered. "And we can take Christopher," a beautiful German shepherd that I'd gotten as a puppy a couple of years earlier from the kennels of Scotland Yard.

Christopher was as close to human in intelligence as a dog can be, and fiercely protective of those he loved. For example, he never permitted me to spank any of my kids when they were naughty; he'd growl and gently seize my wrist in his jaws until I calmed down. Taking Christopher along was a great idea, but there was no need for Camilla to come. I dressed, and with Christopher in tow, I went to Mark's apartment after telling the doorman to call the police if I wasn't down in fifteen minutes.

The Franklins' apartment opened directly into their foyer from the elevator. The door was open. Unlike what happened with Bob many years earlier, there was no carnage. I didn't want my police dog to provoke Mark, who'd probably had enough of cops and their trappings, so I ordered him to lie down and "stay" in the little hall outside the elevator door. He would not move until I released him from that command. I went into the apartment and left the door slightly ajar.

There was Mark wearing a spiffy sports jacket and slacks. He looked, for all intents and purposes, like an Armani model.

I must have a way with violent schizophrenics because his face broke out into a smile as soon as he saw me: He had been to my office in the past for the occasional flu shot. "Gee, doctor, I'm so glad to see you. What are you doing here?"

Again, I told him the truth. "I live in this building, and the doorman told me you were home, so I came to see you. What's up? You look great."

"Aw, you know, I got into a fight with this creep, and he pulled a gun on me. So I knicked him in self-defense. Big deal. The cops are making a federal case out of it. They locked me up in that booby hatch, and I didn't like it, so I left. Security at that place is a joke."

"Mark, listen to me. This is serious. I'm sure you were acting in self-defense. A good lawyer your parents will be glad to hire will probably get you off. But if you don't go back to Bellevue right now, the cops will come after you and maybe shoot you. Take my advice. Let me drive you back to Bellevue. Don't worry. I'll explain everything to them. I don't think they've sent out the alarm yet. There's still time, but we've got to hurry. I'll phone them. OK?"

I had no idea what I would do if he declined my offer.

"Yeah, I think you're right. OK, I'll go back with you. I can't wait to see their faces when they realize that I outsmarted them and escaped from their locked facility."

"Let me change my clothes, Mark. I'll come back for you in a couple of minutes." I didn't want him to see my police dog waiting outside. I took Christopher back to our apartment, returned to Mark, and took him in a cab back to Bellevue, where he was diagnosed as a paranoid schizophrenic and committed.

This is another example of why I believe that every graduating M.D. should have the kind of varied basic training that I did before specializing.

16

BEGINNING MY RESIDENCY

After I completed my rotating internship, my training as a cardiologist began in earnest as a first-year resident at my "home base," the Royal Victoria Hospital. In this first year, I spent three mornings a week in the cardiac clinic, trying to make heads or tails of what at first looked like wiggles on the electrocardiogram. I worked on the public wards where, along with my senior residents, I helped look after people who had no private doctor of their own. I spent twelve hours a week in the emergency room sorting out all kinds of problems, many of them cardiac, in the scores of people who came in at all hours of the day and night. The rest of the time I assisted the attending physicians with their private patients. Then, as today, one's personal physician made the diagnosis, prescribed treatment, and came to see the patient for a few minutes every morning and again at the end of the day if the patient was seriously ill. But as the resident, I was the real caregiver for the remaining twenty-three hours and ten minutes of the day—and night.

I followed the course of disease in many cardiac patients that year. Any man with a heart attack on a stretcher brought by ambulance to the emergency room reminded me of my father. It was 1953, and I soon realized how little I could do for such patients. Heart-attack patients, then as now, received priority in the emergency room. The moment they arrived, they were quickly hooked up to an ECG machine. Oxygen was routinely given, usually in a tent because neither nasal prongs nor masks were yet widely used. Nitroglycerine was never given to anyone during an acute attack, as we do today. We know today that nitro is critical in the early minutes and hours of a heart attack. Doctors were not yet aware of the benefits of aspirin and anticoagulants; there were no drugs other than digitalis to control cardiac rhythm; there were no pacemakers or defibrillators; there were none of the many medications we now use to strengthen heart muscle (other than digitalis); there were no catheterization labs, and stenting and open-heart surgery were still years away. There weren't even coronary care units to which to send patients who were lucky enough to survive a heart attack. Sometimes I even wondered why we bothered admitting these "acute cardiac" patients to the hospital; they could have had the same bed rest at home.

But in the ER we watched these patients, gave them painkillers, provided tender loving care, and wished them well. Those lucky enough to survive were sent from the emergency room to the medical ward. There were no monitors then, and many patients died from serious, undetected arrhythmias as they lay unsupervised in their beds. The death rate from heart attacks was close to 25 percent.

Patients usually were kept at complete bed rest in the hospital for a full six weeks, during which time many developed clots in their veins from just lying around. When these clots traveled to the lungs, as they often did, the unfortunate victim often died of a pulmonary embolism. After six weeks of bed rest, they were sent home to vegetate, grow fat, and become depressed. Exercise was strictly forbidden, diet was unregulated, there were few effective medications, and return to work was usually discouraged.

Compare all that with what happens today. If you call for an ambulance because of chest pain or pressure, a well-trained paramedic will attend you en route. He or she will immediately give you an aspirin, take an ECG, and transmit it by radio to the doctor in the ER. You will then be given whatever medication you need—while you are still in transit. If your heart stops or develops a life-threatening arrhythmia, the paramedic can shock it back to normal electrically with the equipment on board. When you arrive in the emergency room, there is not a second wasted. You will be hooked up to an ECG machine and then pounced on by a team of doctors. An intravenous nitroglycerine drip will be started to widen the narrowed arteries, along with a blood thinner such as heparin to prevent the fresh clot in the coronary artery from getting bigger or breaking off; blood is drawn for immediate enzyme analysis to see if there has been any heart damage and, if so, how much; blood pressure and heart rhythm are continuously monitored and any abnormalities corrected by one or more potent drugs. And, of course, oxygen is administered via prongs in the nose.

But that's only the beginning. Other critical decisions are made depending on the severity of the attack, when your symptoms started, your age and general condition, and your response to the treatment you've been given. The doctor may choose to administer a drug (tPA) that dissolves the fresh clot blocking your coronary artery or may immediately send you to the catheterization lab for a coronary angiogram to determine whether the closed artery can be opened with a balloon and kept open with a stent. If you don't respond to any of these steps, an emergency bypass operation may be performed. The possibilities are endless. If you don't die before reaching the hospital, you will almost certainly survive after you get there.

Back in 1953, I began to have second thoughts about continuing in this field. But what other specialties were more effective than cardiology back then? Antibiotics were not yet widely available, so infections were treated "supportively"; arthritis was managed with painkillers much as it is today; neurology consisted essentially of prescribing exercises to stroke patients. The truth is that in the early 1950s, there was little if any effective therapy for most of mankind's afflictions— and we knew even less about what caused them. So doctors-in-training like me focused on learning how to *diagnose* disease, not to prevent or treat it.

So I decided to stay in cardiology, trying to keep abreast of new developments and to become an expert electrocardiographer. I never expected the tremendous advances that would be made in the next few years while I was still training.

During this year at the Royal Victoria Hospital, I saw the first glimmer of that revolution in the offing. One of my surgery professors, Dr. Arthur Vineberg, believed that he could improve the blood supply to cardiac muscle by taking an artery out of a patient's chest wall and implanting it directly into the heart. That was a revolutionary concept at the time and one for which I think he should have received the Nobel Prize. After showing that it could be done in animals, he began performing the "Vineberg procedure" on selected patients. He opened the chest, exposed the heart, and dug a little tunnel into the cardiac muscle into which he then inserted a small artery (the internal mammary) taken from the chest wall. The pressure of blood flowing through that artery into the heart muscle formed new blood vessels within it! The Vineberg procedure was performed around the world for several years before it was replaced by the now ubiquitous bypass operation, in which the internal mammary artery or veins from the leg are grafted onto one or more diseased coronary arteries rather than digging a tunnel into the heart muscle. The concept, however, is the same, and it was *my* teacher who first thought of it!

17

HOPKINS, BALTIMORE, CARDIOLOGY— AND RACISM

1953: My next year of cardiology training was at Johns Hopkins Medical Service at Baltimore City Hospital. My main focus was cardiology, but I was expected to help out with other serious illnesses. During these twelve months, I witnessed some dramatic medical progress, along with a kind of racial prejudice that was not entirely new to me as a Canadian.

Polio was then a major killer and crippler of the young; the Salk vaccine was still two years away. It broke my heart to see so many kids whose muscles of respiration were paralyzed by the polio virus and who were doomed to spend the rest of their lives incarcerated in "iron lungs," respirators without which they could not breathe. I can still hear the constant hum of the motors that resembled tin-can sarcophagi. I found it very stressful to examine these poor children, to feed and comfort them—and to try to give them and their families hope when none existed. I *never* imagined that medical science would eradicate this terrible disease in my lifetime. But it has, and iron lungs are nowhere to be found in any hospital anywhere. Whenever I am depressed by the toll of cancer or AIDS or Alzheimer's, my spirits are lifted and my hope restored when I remind myself of how we conquered polio.

Any Volunteers?

One day a little girl was brought to the hospital with meningococcal meningitis, an infection of the lining of the brain. Meningitis is extremely contagious and is easily spread to anyone in close contact with the patient despite the most stringent precautions. In 1953, penicillin was the only antibiotic available to treat this deadly disease. If the bug that caused the meningitis happened to be resistant to penicillin, the patient almost always died. Unfortunately, there was no way to predict who would respond to treatment and who wouldn't.

When this child was admitted to our hospital, the physician-in-chief, a wonderful man named George Mirick, called a meeting of the resident staff. He explained to us the risk of treating this little girl. "It's not likely to happen," he told us, "but this case can cost you your life. I don't feel I can assign anyone to it, so I'm asking for volunteers."

All eight members of the house staff, seven men and a woman, volunteered. Since only three were needed, we drew straws for the "privilege" of caring for that little girl. I was one of them. Because her life was at stake, none of us gave any thought to our own health or survival. Doctors are often criticized when they refuse to make house calls, or ask to be paid up front for their services, or always seem to be playing golf when they're needed. The list of our "failings" is endless. This opprobrium, though sometimes valid, pales in comparison to the self-sacrifice that doctors have made throughout the ages, and continue to make, when the chips are down and there is a life at stake. Of course, there are bad apples in every profession: surgeons who won't operate on someone who is HIV positive and doctors who won't treat unless you pay in advance. However, the great majority of my profession adheres fervently to the Hippocratic oath. This sick little girl in Baltimore fifty-five years ago is a case in point. Happily, her infecting organism was not penicillin resistant. She was cured of the meningitis, and none of the treating physicians became ill.

Aside from brief visits to New York, Terre Haute, and Miami Beach, I had not spent much time in the United States before moving to Baltimore. But wherever I had gone, the melting-pot concept of America seemed much more civilized to me than the neverending racial conflicts I had experienced growing up in Quebec. I was in for a surprise in Baltimore.

My chief resident was one of the best doctors I'd ever met. He made rounds with us every single day of the week and was available for any emergency, day or night. He taught me more medicine and cardiology than anyone ever had. I was impressed not only by his vast knowledge but also by his compassion for the sick, regardless of race or creed. He *really* cared. He winced when someone cried out in pain; he was saddened by the despair of others and uplifted when he was able to heal.

Our hospital served the poorer districts of Baltimore and cared for many African American patients. In 1953, black patients were admitted to segregated wards and looked after by black nurses. Although Caucasian patients also had black nurses, white nurses did not normally attend blacks. Doctors, however, crossed color lines . . . largely because there were so few black physicians.

The head nurse on one of these black wards, an African American named Mary, was a gem. She was about thirty years old, good-looking, smart, hard-working, and had a great sense of humor. The patients loved her, and so did the house staff. She and my chief resident worked closely together to run one of the best wards in the hospital. They enjoyed their professional relationship, and their mutual respect was evident. My chief and I would stand by her desk after rounds each day, review all the problems, and kibitz.

One day, my resident and I were going out for dinner. As we left the parking lot in my car and were about to pass by the hospital entrance, I saw Mary standing on the steps, waiting for a cab. I slowed down to offer her a lift. My resident, a southerner, said icily to me, "Don't you dare stop. If she gets in, I get out."

I couldn't believe it! My friend explained to me that working with "them" was one thing, socializing was quite another. He would never ride in a car with any black, and that included the nurse whom he respected so much professionally. It wasn't personal, he pointed out; it was just her color. Interestingly enough, as we went by Mary, she smiled and waved at us. She no more expected me to stop for her than did my resident. At that moment, Quebec didn't look so bad after all!

That situation has changed in Baltimore and throughout the country, almost as dramatically as the disappearance of the iron lung. There is no question in my mind that today my resident would give President Obama a lift if he needed one. Unfortunately, we still have a way to go. The virus of racial and religious discrimination lingers in the hearts and minds of too many people everywhere.

The revolution in the diagnosis and treatment of heart disease was now in full swing. The rapid advances in cardiology that were just beginning to take place in Montreal the previous year were already being widely used at the medical mecca of Johns Hopkins. I attended every conference that dealt with new cardiac drugs, procedures, and theories. I would have liked to spend at least one more year in Baltimore, but I was due back for my fourth year of training in Montreal.

18

BACK TO MONTREAL

954: I had mixed feelings about returning to Montreal to spend a year at the Jewish General Hospital. I had just been exposed to new and exciting diagnostic techniques and treatments. I had always worked at major universities where these advances were being made, and so I had some trepidation about returning to what was then essentially a community hospital. But I had chosen to do so because this was the home base of the very famous cardiologist Dr. Harold Segall, a recognized authority on the clinical examination of the heart. He had made a science of interpreting the various murmurs and heart sounds that a doctor could hear with a stethoscope, and few could teach it as well as he. Remember, this was decades before the invention of the echocardiogram that now provides those answers immediately.

Many years earlier, when my father took sick, Dr. Rabinovitch had called Dr. Segall for consultation. He was a short man, with a bow tie and pince-nez, and one of the few specialists who made house calls. My initial impression was that he was imperious and behaved like a snob to Dr. R, to my father, and to me. He arrived at our apartment more like a nobleman than a healer. He was one of the few doctors who owned a portable ECG machine, as primitive as they were at the time, and he was able to interpret the tracings it provided with great expertise. After he examined my father, he opened his portable unit as tenderly as a fortune-teller with a crystal ball and recorded the tracing. He left the impression that his little machine held the answer to all of my father's and mankind's ills.

Although I was only a college student at the time, I had read a great deal on the subject of heart disease. I asked Dr. Segall several reasonable questions in order to help me understand my dad's illness and assuage my own anxiety. He seemed to resent my asking them, as if it was none of my business and beyond my intellect to understand what was going on. He was distant, arrogant, supercilious, and cold. He directed the answers to my questions to Dr. Rabinovitch, as if I wasn't there. So I was curious to see whether his teaching was any better than his bedside manner.

Once I started working with him, however, I came to appreciate how cultured and caring Dr. Segall really was. When I introduced myself to him shortly after I arrived at the Jewish General, his first question to me was, "How's your father doing? I was very moved by your love for him, and I had a feeling that you might one day be a cardiologist. So it's the full turn of the wheel for you to be working with me. I'll bet he's proud of you." He remembered! My animosity evaporated.

In the following months I marveled at the diagnoses this man could make just by listening carefully to the patient's story and using only his stethoscope. He was able to imitate the heart sounds and murmurs he heard, sort of like a medical Donald Duck. What I learned from him has stood me in good stead, because I have since been called to evaluate cardiac patients in remote areas without any fancy machines. It's a pity so few medical students now appreciate the potential of the stethoscope; medical costs would be much lower if they did.

Dr. Segall instilled in me a greater curiosity about medicine than I had ever had before. And although we focused on maximizing my clinical acumen, we were both also interested in the evolving cardiovascular technological research. One day I read that Dr. Paul Zoll, in Boston, had invented an external cardiac pacemaker that restored the heartbeat after a cardiac arrest (a condition called heart block in which the heart either stops completely or slows so much that the patient dies). Zoll's device shocked the heart through electrodes placed on the surface of the chest. It was effective, but painful: the patient's body would convulse with every zap from this external pacemaker, the forerunner of the modern internally implanted unit that does the job often without the patient even being aware of it. But Zoll's unit did keep people alive for several days who would otherwise have died.

Dr. Segall and I went to Boston to meet Dr. Zoll and learn how to use his pacemaker. We were impressed and brought one back to Montreal. We later were the first Canadian doctors to publish a paper about its use. So even a community hospital can make or develop advances.

My year with Dr. Segall went by quickly, and in 1955 I was anxious to return to mainstream cardiology. My next stop was Mount Sinai Hospital in New York.

19

THE BEST YEAR OF MY LIFE

1955: My fifth and last year of postgraduate training was a fellowship in cardiology at Mount Sinai Hospital in New York. I would be working with its famous chief of cardiology, Dr. Arthur Master, best known for his pioneering work in "exercise electrocardiography." The ECG, when taken at rest, is often normal even in persons with active angina pectoris. Master had standardized a stress test designed to elicit diagnostic electrocardiographic changes in the ECG after the patient walked up and down a specially designed staircase. This was a major contribution to clinical cardiology and the forerunner of modern stress testing. Master defined the criteria to interpret changes in the postexercise electrocardiogram and to distinguish the innocent from the significant ones. I was also interested in learning vectorcardiography, a seemingly promising new diagnostic approach to supplement the ECG. It had been pioneered by Dr. Arthur Grishman, a member of the Mount Sinai staff.

A Mount Sinai appointment was so prestigious and hard to get that its fellows *were not paid*, not a nickel. (Such a fellowship anywhere these days, even at Mount Sinai, pays about $25,000 to $35,000 a year.) Things were now going well enough in his new grain business for my Dad to foot the bill for my going to New York. Fortunately, I also won a scholarship of $75 a month that helped pay for my meals and accommodations.

I rented a one-bedroom suite at the Wyndham Hotel on W. Fifty-eighth Street near Fifth Avenue for an unbelievable $125 a month! (That same apartment now costs at least three times as much for just *one day*!) The Wyndham was very much the "in" place at the time. It was comfortable and well situated across the street from the famous Plaza Hotel and the home of such Broadway and movie stars as Cyril Ritchard, Richard Burton, and many other celebrities. For me, it was New York City at its most exciting.

Mount Sinai was a great place to work. Its doctors were brilliant, hardworking, imaginative, and energetic. The work was interesting and arduous, and I was able to complete my thesis that year. I eventually became one of the few experts in vectorcardiography and wrote a thesis on this technique. Unfortunately, it proved to have little practical value and has since been abandoned by cardiologists, including me.

Dr. Master was constantly urging his fellows to engage in research and write scientific papers, in keeping with his motto, "Publish or perish." Since he worked as hard as he pushed us to, I couldn't complain. I ended up coauthoring more than forty scientific papers with him, as well as a textbook, *The Electrocardiogram and Chest X-Ray in Diseases of the Heart.*

I Fall in Love!

Even if I had learned *nothing* at Mount Sinai, that year would turn out to be the most important one of my life. Although I had made a few friends, I didn't have much of a social life in New York. One day, Mrs. Master phoned to invite me for Thanksgiving dinner: her husband had told her that I was from out of town and alone. I had never been to their home before. I accepted with pleasure and did not expect that it would lead to the most daunting challenge of my life.

The Pursuit and Capture of My Camilla

I arrived at the Master apartment at about one o'clock. While we were sipping cocktails and talking about the weather, my life suddenly changed. For as I sat nursing a Bloody Mary, the most beautiful girl I had ever seen walked into the room. It was Camilla, their younger daughter. I had always thought "love at first sight" was a cliché; I never believed it would happen to me. But it did—in an instant!

Camilla was a statuesque, tall, slender brunette with beautiful skin and sensitive, hazel eyes. She was wearing a navy blue woolen dress with a high neck and a simple gold pin. I remember every detail of what she looked like, down to the color of her lipstick and the fact that she wore no nail polish.

However, there was one minor complication interfering with my total eclipse of the heart: *Camilla was there with her boyfriend!* Surely, she deserved someone better—like me. I anxiously watched the two of them eating their Thanksgiving turkey. When they weren't holding knives, forks, or spoons, they were holding hands (ugh!). I thought this was very insensitive of her. Couldn't she tell how I felt? Surely, she must have had some of those same vibes. Alas, she did not, and as soon as dinner was over, she and Ronald excused themselves and went off to the movies (to see *The Tender Trap,* ironically enough!).

So there I was, stuck with the rest of the family. I have no idea what we talked about, because I was fantasizing about this beautiful, spoken-for woman. When the meal was over, Dr. Master asked me to go for a walk to discuss my future medical career, but I was more interested in how deeply my Camilla was involved with that chap (who would later become a very distinguished and internationally famous law professor). A few minutes into our walk, I casually asked Dr. Master whether he thought his daughter would have dinner with me sometime.

"Oh, I doubt it, Isadore. Ronald has been her boyfriend for several months, and she hasn't been dating anyone else."

I probed a little further, trying not to seem pushy.

"But she's not engaged or anything like that. Is she?"

"No, not actually engaged, but going steady, I guess you'd call it. In my day that was usually a pretty solid commitment. Today, who knows?"

Was he leaving the door open just a crack?

He went on to say that Ronald was studying at Harvard. Aha! Not living in New York. That made it easier for me to end his relationship with *my* girl.

The following Monday, after my rival had returned to Cambridge, I struck! I telephoned Camilla, told her how much I enjoyed meeting her, and asked if she'd have dinner with me sometime.

"I'm sorry," she said. "I'm really not dating. But I did enjoy meeting you and hope to see you again sometime." On that happy note, she said a very definite good night.

I couldn't get her out of my mind. I analyzed every intonation and inflection of that conversation and concluded that she liked me. (Years later I learned that, in fact, she did not!)

I called her again three or four days later. This time, I told her about a restaurant that had just opened to great reviews, and would she like to go? No, she wouldn't. There were no inflections this time from which I could draw any hopeful conclusions.

I let another week go by and called again. This continual rejection was very frustrating! Why was she delaying what I thought (prayed) to be inevitable? This time I stopped beating around the bush, took the bull by the horns, and said, midway through our very short exchange: "Oh, by the way, I'll be sending you some material about Montreal—its history, climate, culture, that sort of thing." She sounded puzzled.

"Why on earth would you do that?"

"Because I'm going back to Montreal in June, and that's where we will be living after we're married," I replied.

Click.

Luckily for me, she didn't tell her father about any of this. I might well have lost my job on the grounds of sexual harassment. It was no such thing. It was l-o-v-e, *love*.

Christmas week: I bought my Camilla a gift at Bergdorf Goodman. (Remember, I hadn't seen her since Thanksgiving Day.) As it turned out, what I thought was a beautiful pair of leather gloves proved not to be Camilla's taste. (She didn't like bright yellow and still doesn't.) I enclosed a card saying that the *Farmer's Almanac* was predicting a cold winter, and I didn't want her hands to be cold. She sent me a polite, short thank-you note, suggesting that this gift was unexpected and unnecessary. It could have been worse. She could have said it was "inappropriate." Not to be deterred, I called again a few days later and invited her out for New Year's Eve. Fat chance. She declined and told me she had other plans (with Ronald, no doubt).

You'd think, wouldn't you, that by this time any rational man would have called it quits? Not I. During the next three months, I called her virtually every week. The answer was always the same. She was busy, indisposed, or going out of town. Then, one day, I got my lucky break. Her brother called me. I had initially befriended Arthur with ulterior motives, but had grown to like him a great deal, and we became real friends. During one of our conversations, I had confided to him my feelings for his sister.

"I don't think the Ronald thing is going too well. Don't let on that I told you, but try asking Camilla out again."

As soon as I could get to a phone (there were no cell phones then), I called her. But I had learned my lesson; I wasn't the least bit aggressive or pushy this time. I started the conversation by telling her that I'd just finished a wonderful book I wanted to send to her. I thought she'd enjoy it.

"What is it?" she asked.

"You probably haven't heard of it," I replied disingenuously. "It's called *I and Thou*, by Martin Buber. He's a theologian born in Germany who is now living in Israel."

The truth is that her brother had told me that Camilla was studying comparative religion at Sarah Lawrence College and that she was very much taken with Buber's work. I hadn't even heard of Dr. Buber, but after Arthur tipped me off, I hit the books. I spent hours in the public library reading about him (this was before the days of the Internet and Wikipedia).

Camilla didn't let on that she was a student of Buber.

"What's the book about?" she asked.

She'd taken the bait!

I pressed on. "It's all about our relationship with God and with each other. The *Thou* in the title refers to God. Quite fascinating, really. I'd love to discuss it with you sometime, if you're interested in that sort of thing."

"Well, I must say, this is a great coincidence," she said, "because I happen to be studying Buber at Sarah Lawrence. I'd like to hear what you think about his concepts."

"I don't believe it! Why don't we have dinner and talk about it?" I asked.

I have blessed Arthur ever since then for clueing me in.

A long pause—during which my heart stopped. (You say that's only a figure of speech? Nonsense! I'm a cardiologist and I assure you it actually stopped!) She agreed, and we went out the next night, and the night after that, and virtually every night thereafter. That was in March 1956. We were engaged on June 30, and married on

August 19 that same year! And guess where we spent our honeymoon—in Montreal and touring the province of Quebec!

How I wooed and won Camilla was very much like my father's courtship of my mother half a century earlier (see chapter 41). The times and the circumstances were different, but as you will see, my dad and I shared several similar frustrations and obstacles.

20

PRIVATE PRACTICE

Camilla and I were married in New York on August 19, 1956, and after our honeymoon, we moved to Montreal. I introduced her to my friends and family, and we found an apartment and an office. I was no longer an intern, resident, or fellow. I was a certified specialist about to start my own practice. Everything had finally come together for me.

There's one story I would like to share with you about Camilla that says so much about her. Unlike me, she comes from a well-to-do family and her parents had provided her with a modest nest egg. While we were discussing my future practice of medicine, she told me that she had opened a special bank account from which I could draw money whenever I had a patient who could not afford to pay my bill. She did not want me ever to turn anyone away who was poor. She was twenty-one at the time! In all my years as a doctor, I've never refused to care for anyone because they couldn't pay my fee. P.S. I never used her money.

I started to build a modest practice specializing in cardiology, and nine months after we settled in Montreal, our first child, Arthur, was born. I would never have predicted what happened next. After living in Canada for fewer than two years, we decided to move back to New York. I was sad to leave my parents and my friends, but there were several reasons for our decision, not the least of which was the uncertain political situation in Quebec at the time. The separatists in Quebec, who were committed to breaking away from the rest of Canada, seemed to be very popular. Were this to happen, I could not live there. Also, both Camilla and I felt there were more opportunities for us in the United States. We have never regretted the move, despite many moments of nostalgia for my life, family, and friends in Montreal.

When we returned to New York, my former chief and now father-in-law invited me to join his cardiology staff at Mount Sinai Hospital. I chose not to, even though I had enjoyed my year there. I did not want any accomplishments I might achieve in the future attributed to nepotism. I also felt that if I stayed with Dr. Master, I would have less control over my professional career. My parents-in-law weren't happy with this decision, but they and Camilla respected it.

I applied for a staff appointment at New York Hospital and was accepted provisionally, without admitting privileges, for one year. ("Let's see if you like us and we like you," I was told by the physician-in-chief.) Until I had those privileges, I had to turn over to another doctor any patients who needed to be hospitalized. I eked out a living doing house calls at night and on weekends for my father-in-law and any other doctor who asked me to. This dearth of patients left me lots of spare time, which I filled by doing clinical research. Several of the papers I wrote at that time were published in academic medical journals, giving me a small reputation in the world of cardiology.

Office practice when I started was much different than it is now. Medicare had not yet been enacted, fees were low, there weren't many expensive machines and tests, employers did not provide health care coverage, and few patients had or needed health insurance. Those who were employed usually earned enough to pay for their visits to the doctor. My fees were flexible; I charged wealthy patients more than those who were poor, and often waived the fee for those who could not afford it. The really indigent received their medical care at hospital clinics. When someone was sick at home and couldn't easily come to my office, I made a house call. Today I would have you go to the emergency room because hospitals can do so much for you when you're seriously ill.

My practice began to grow, especially after I received full staff privileges at New York Hospital–Cornell Medical Center. My hospital colleagues began referring patients to me for cardiological consultation. It was a slow, gradual process—until the day I received a phone call from Paris.

A Call from the Bolivian Tin King

1968: "Dr. Rosenfeld, there's a Mr. Patiño calling," my receptionist announced on the intercom. Patiño, Patiño—a familiar name. Where had I heard it? Of course, there was the prominent and wealthy Bolivian tin king, Antenor Patiño, but I had never met him and he surely would not be calling a young, unknown cardiologist in New York. I took the call. It was the tin king himself calling me! He must have been trying to reach a Rosenberg or Rosenblatt or Rosenman, but certainly not me.

"Dr. Rosenfeld, this is Antenor Patiño. We haven't met, but Perla Mattison tells me you are a very good cardiologist." (Perla was the wife of Graham Mattison, a successful banker and financial advisor to Barbara Hutton, the Woolworth heiress. She had taken a liking to me and made a point of telling all her friends what a good doctor I was; I had treated her for a cold!) "My wife has had a heart attack. Will you come to Paris to see her?"

Me? Come to Paris? For Mrs. Patiño? There were many famous heart specialists throughout the U.S., including one just a few feet away from me in the office next door—my own father-in-law, Dr. Arthur Master.

"Who is your wife's doctor?" I asked.

He mentioned the name of a famous French cardiologist—the French equivalent of Michael DeBakey or Arthur Master in this country: a man with a big reputation whose name it would not be appropriate for me to mention.

"Mr. Patiño, I'm sure you know that your wife has the best cardiologist in France. He's world famous. You certainly don't need me."

This irritated Patiño, who was not accustomed to being questioned. "Why don't you want to come? Why are you making excuses? Is it the money? If so, you can be sure I will pay your fee. I'm 95 percent sure that our doctor is right, but that's not good enough for me. I want a second opinion—from you."

Frankly, I couldn't imagine that there'd be any difference of opinion between this patient's physician and me—but, as they say, "it's your nickel," or, in this case, *tin*. That night I was on my way to Paris. As I sat in the first-class compartment of the Air France jet (where I had never sat before), I mused, "Suddenly, in one phone call, Isadore, you're in the big league—in the international medical arena." I was intrigued by what lay ahead. Who wouldn't have been?

I was met at the airport by a chauffeured Rolls Royce, another first for me, and driven to the Patiño apartment; *palace* would be a more appropriate description. I had never seen anything quite as opulent—or furnished in better taste. The walls of the huge rooms were hung with great paintings, the likes of which I had heretofore only seen in museums and books. I hoped that the weeping El Greco in the entrance hall did not portend things to come.

Mr. Patiño greeted me at the door. He was a short man with a warm smile. He led me up a winding staircase to the second floor where the distinguished French professor was waiting for me. He was dressed in a formal morning coat and flanked by a coterie of assistants, all waiting impatiently to be done with this nobody from New York. Mr. Patiño left us alone to deliberate.

"I'm very proud to meet you, professor. I want you to know that it was not my idea to come here. But Mr. Patiño can be very insistent, as you know."

"Yes, yes," he replied impatiently, the implication being: "Let's get on with it. I have more important things to do than make small talk with you."

He had one of his assistants recount Mrs. Patiño's history to me: She was in her early fifties and had always enjoyed good health. Three or four days earlier she had experienced some discomfort in the left side of her chest; it lasted for about an hour and then gradually subsided. The pain had come on for no apparent reason; she had not been exerting herself. Nevertheless, because she felt weak, she called the doctor.

Her symptoms had abated by the time he arrived. He immediately took an electrocardiogram, and it was abnormal. He diagnosed a heart attack and prescribed complete bed rest, oxygen, and other medications used at the time. It was as simple as that. Cut and dried.

"Do you have any questions?" he asked.

"No," I replied, "it all sounds perfectly straightforward. May I see her electrocardiogram?" Her tracing showed some minor abnormalities that one would expect in someone with coronary artery disease. "And, if you don't mind, I'd like to examine her for a few minutes."

With a classic Gallic shrug, he led me to Mrs. Patiño's bedroom. She was beautiful and elegant, lying comfortably in bed—wearing an oxygen mask. The professor left us alone.

She smiled at me and said, "Perla has told me such nice things about you. I appreciate your coming all this way, but I don't know what more you can do for me. They tell me I've had a heart attack. I can only follow their advice and pray that I will be well soon."

We had instant chemistry; I liked this modest, beautiful lady. I asked her some relevant questions about her lifestyle and possible risk factors. She was not a smoker, she watched her weight, her blood pressure had always been normal, she was not diabetic, she exercised regularly, and there was no major history of heart disease in her family.

"Please," I asked, "describe the pain you felt as precisely as you can, Madame Patiño. Show me exactly where it was. Was it sharp like a knife, or pressing, or burning?"

She said that it was sharp, and definitely not a pressure.

"Have you ever had it before?"

"Oh, yes," she said, "many times, especially after exercising too much, but it never lasted this long."

"Was it worse when you took a deep breath?"

"No."

"When you swallowed?"

"No."

"When you moved about the bed?"

"Maybe a little."

"When you turned your neck?"

"Yes, I think so, but I'm not sure," she replied.

"Do you have the pain right now?"

"No."

As I listened to her story, I began to suspect that this woman had *not* had a heart attack, and that her symptoms had very likely originated in her neck. The pain fibers that supply the arms, the jaw, and the chest all exit from the cervical spine. As a result, different diseases in that part of the spine, such as a protruding disc, can mimic the symptoms of a heart attack. To help confirm my diagnostic impression, I asked Mrs. Patiño to move her neck in various positions, one of which reproduced her pain exactly!

I was not very worried about the ECG "abnormalities" either; they might well have been a normal female variant. One of my major

interests in electrocardiography was the difference between the tracings of healthy men and women. I had found, and previously published
my findings, that certain ECG patterns that are clearly abnormal in
men may well be a normal variant in women. Given her history and
the results of my physical exam, I was convinced that the changes in
Mrs. Patiño's tracing were not indicators of disease and were *not* due
to a heart attack. But how could I tell that to her famous doctor?

Le professeur was waiting impatiently for me with his coterie in
the anteroom. *Merde alors!* This was *très difficile.* What was I to do
now? How could I disagree with my important French colleagues?
For a nanosecond, I considered that it might be more politic just to
go along with everyone and not stir up an international medical
hornet's nest. But it was an ill-considered option, and one I was not
prepared to exercise.

I was asked to come here for my opinion; I would give it and go
home.

"Well, doctor?" the French physician asked, as he started to put
on his coat.

My mouth was dry; I licked my lips. I had too much wine on the
plane and eaten more than my share of caviar; I was parched and jet
lagged. I wanted to get this over with as quickly as possible.

"Professor, let me say first that I agree completely with your man-
agement of this case," I said in French. (All those years in Montreal
had stood me in good stead.) He smiled, no longer threatened by this
young interloper from abroad. I then continued in English. "You
were naturally obliged to put Mrs. Patiño to complete bed rest while
you were evaluating her symptoms. However, I am happy to tell you
what, in my opinion, you have probably suspected yourself. She did
not have a heart attack; her symptoms are due to cervical radiculopa-
thy (pressure on the nerves leaving the spine), and I believe that her
minor electrocardiographic changes are a normal female variant."

I was giving him a way out. I hoped that he would take it and
congratulate me on my perspicacity. It was not meant to be.

"I see," he replied. "And how long would you continue to keep
her in bed?"

"Frankly, I'd get her up as soon as possible and encourage her to
resume a normal life. I suggest we get an X-ray of her neck and then
have her see a good physiotherapist. But as far as her heart is concerned, I don't believe she has any problem. *Il n'y a pas de prob-
leme.*" My French was tinged with a Canadian accent, but it was
French nevertheless.

The Frenchman was livid.

"Do you realize what you're saying? Do you know who these people are? Do you understand that your reputation will be destroyed if you are wrong—if something happens to her because of your, your—ill-considered opinion? *C'est fou!*"

Now *I* was getting annoyed.

"Doctor (to hell with the nicety of *Professeur*), it was not my idea to come here in the first place. Let me repeat: I am not even slightly critical of how you've managed this case so far . . . and I intend to tell that to Mr. Patiño. I'm not here to argue with you."

At this point, the door to the anteroom opened, and Mr. Patiño came in.

"So, gentleman, what have you decided?"

My "colleague" drew himself up to his full height, and with a combination of ridicule and indignation, said: "*Your* Doctor Rosenfeld does not believe your wife has heart trouble. My associates and I are unanimous in our opinion to the contrary. I advise continuing the same treatment. I shall return here tomorrow afternoon."

And with that, he left.

Mr. Patiño and I were alone.

"You really don't think that my wife has had a heart attack?" he asked.

I repeated to him what I had told the French gentlemen. I explained my interpretation of his wife's pain and her ECG changes. I said that it had been prudent to confine his wife to bed until the picture was clarified, but it was now time for her to resume her normal activities. I assured him that I would fully understand if he preferred to disregard my advice and perhaps obtain yet another opinion.

"How sure are you of your diagnosis?" he asked.

"As sure as I can be," I answered, "but I'm only human."

What a tough decision for this poor man to make, faced with diametrically opposite opinions and his wife's life at stake. He adored her. He knew nothing of my credentials or my training, just what he had heard from Perla Mattison. In his place, I would probably have stayed with the "establishment" recommendation.

"Doctor, my wife and I had planned a formal dinner party tonight at Maxim's. I was intending to go there without her, just with our daughters. Do you really believe it's safe for her to come with us?"

"Well," I replied, "she'll be a little weak in the legs from all that bed rest, but there's no reason for her to stay home . . . none whatsoever, in my opinion."

"My instincts tell me that you're right," he said. "I wondered all along why a young woman would suddenly get a heart attack without warning. Her mother lived to a ripe old age, and her father was also very old when he died. I called you because I am not in a position to question her *former* doctor, but you've done that for me, and I thank you. All right, enough of this. We're all going to Maxim's!"

With that, he rushed into his wife's room and said, "Good news, Beatriz. There's nothing wrong with you. So, enough. Get up and get dressed. We don't have much time. We're giving a party tonight!"

Beatriz was dumbfounded—but very happy to comply.

Then he turned to me. "You'll come too, of course."

"I'd love to, Mr. Patiño, but I didn't bring a dinner jacket with me."

He laughed. "Don't worry. I'll take care of that," he said. An hour later, his tailor had fitted me with a very nice tuxedo.

That evening we all went to Maxim's. I escorted Mrs. Patiño's lovely daughter, Countess Rovasenda. It was a great party, but I watched my new patient like a hawk. Although I was confident with my diagnosis, I suddenly broke out in a cold sweat. What if something happened? Do they still use the guillotine in France?

Mrs. Patiño not only survived the party, she is now in her nineties and still going strong, as beautiful as ever. That visit to Paris was the start of a relationship that has continued to this day!

The news of my surprise diagnosis spread like wildfire through Patiño's circle of friends, and it wasn't long before some of the other people you'll read about in this book began to consult me professionally.

There's a lesson in this story for any young doctor just starting out: Had I played it safe and not heeded my conscience, I probably wouldn't have the practice I do today. But even worse, Mrs. Patiño might have mistakenly been labeled a cardiac patient early in life.

21

ARISTOTLE ONASSIS

After my Paris adventure with the Patiños, my name spread among their friends in Europe. Aristotle Onassis was the first to call. He was having palpitations and had heard about me from the Patiños. He was perfectly frank and told me that he had checked me out with Dr. Michael DeBakey in Houston, who had told him I was a good cardiologist.

I didn't need a *Who's Who* to know who Onassis was. A newcomer to shipping who had started from scratch, he'd become a legend, parlaying a few war-surplus U.S. naval vessels bought at bargain-basement prices into a huge fleet of oil tankers. Unlike Greek shipping magnates of an earlier generation, who had avoided media attention and treasured their anonymity, he was often featured in gossip columns, for reasons usually related to romance, not shipping. Many of the stories were about his relationship with the leading diva of world opera at the time, Maria Callas, and later his marriage to the former first lady, Jacqueline Kennedy.

I arranged to see Onassis in my office the next day. He was a short, swarthy gentleman. Given his wealth, prominence, and notoriety, I found him to be surprisingly modest, unassuming, without airs, and, frankly, without charisma. He was just a regular guy. We made small talk for a while to see if we had chemistry—and we apparently did. During that first visit, Onassis told me about his son, Alexander, who had died in an airplane accident a few months earlier. He confided in me (and the rest of the world) that he remained certain it was foul play, but had never been able to prove it. He told me how he had pinned all his hopes on his son to perpetuate the Onassis legacy and how Alexander's death had emotionally devastated him.

Onassis told me that shortly after Alexander's accident, he began to notice some shortness of breath, palpitations, and an uncomfortable awareness of his heartbeat. None of this surprised me— bereavement can have a profound physical and emotional impact; the mind and the body are inseparable.

I took a detailed medical history and examined him carefully. The ECG revealed a rhythm disturbance due to an electrical problem in the heart. I decided his heart function, valves, and coronary circulation were normal. I ruled out other noncardiac causes of this arrhythmia, such as an overactive thyroid.

There are many different kinds of abnormal cardiac rhythm, most of which are harmless, but some can have serious consequences, such as sudden death. Onassis' premature contractions, or "extra beats," were potentially serious because they originated in the ventricle or pump of the heart. If many of these occur sequentially—that is, one after the other—for a sustained period of just a very few minutes, the consequences can be life threatening. Today, this problem is treated effectively with several anti-arrhythmic drugs, pacemakers, and implanted defibrillators. I prescribed for him what was the state-of-the-art therapy at the time and asked him to remain in New York for a couple of weeks so that I could see if the medication was working.

Onassis phoned me a few days later; his palpitations were much less frequent and he felt better. I had him come in and wear a twenty-four-hour cardiac monitor. It showed a significant decrease in the number of these "extra" beats. He told me that his depression over Alexander's death was also beginning to lighten a little, and overall, he was feeling better.

One day he called me, and asked, "Isidoro, would you and Camilla join Jackie and me for dinner tonight? Let's go to the Chinese place you've been telling me about."

My wife and I used to eat at Uncle Tai's, our favorite Chinese restaurant in New York. It was around the corner from our apartment, and we loved the food. I called David Keh, the owner, and told him that Mr. and Mrs. Onassis would be joining us for dinner that night. I warned him not to alert the press; I didn't want Jackie attacked by a swarm of paparazzi.

When Camilla and I arrived at Uncle Tai's just before eight o'clock, there were no photographers in sight. We waited for our hosts at a table in a secluded area of the room. Ari and Jackie joined us a few minutes later. When our former first lady walked in to the room, I felt as if I had known her all my life. Over the years, while she was in the White House and after her husband's assassination, her picture was everywhere. She was the cultural icon of our time— her clothes, her taste in art, and her comments about life in general all came together as we greeted each other. She was as elegant as I had expected—and very warm. There were no airs about her. I was immediately drawn to her, and we remained good friends for many years, through thick and thin.

David's star chef, Uncle Tai, after whom the restaurant was named, prepared a sumptuous banquet. After dessert, Onassis signaled for the check. David graciously insisted that we be his guests. After a pro forma protest by Onassis, we left. Outside, to my dismay, a bunch of paparazzi pounced on us. For the first time in my life, I understood what a horrendous experience that can be. We had to fight to get into the car, and once we did, photographers kept us from shutting the door, pushing their cameras with flashbulbs popping into our very faces. We finally escaped. One of the other diners had tipped off the press. I thought all this fuss was about me, but my wife said that it was probably Jackie O in whom the press was interested.

He Couldn't Keep His Eyes Open!

Feeling better, and with his palpitations under control, Onassis returned to Greece. I didn't hear from him again for several months— no news was good news. Then one day, he reappeared. He'd come back to New York to see me, but this time it wasn't his heart. He was now having trouble keeping his eyes open. It wasn't because he was sleepy; he just physically couldn't raise his eyelids. It sounded like myasthenia gravis.

Myasthenia gravis (the name is of Latin and Greek origin meaning "grave muscle weakness") is basically a disease of the immune system in which the body mistakenly produces antibodies against its own muscles and nerves. It is characterized by weakness of the muscles normally under one's control, most commonly those that move the eyelids or control facial expression or are involved in chewing, talking, and swallowing. Sometimes, however, muscles responsible for breathing and limb movement are also affected, and that can be life threatening. Although myasthenia gravis can now be accurately diagnosed by a variety of tests that detect immune molecules and antibodies, the diagnosis can be made clinically by injecting Tensilon, a medication that briefly relieves the symptoms of the disease.

To confirm my diagnosis, I escorted Onassis across the hall to the office of my friend Robert Coles, an excellent ophthalmologist. After examining him and doing the Tensilon test, Coles said to me, "This is myasthenia gravis. He's got *tsuris.*"

Onassis said nothing, but when we got back to my office, he asked, "What's tsuris?"

"It's Yiddish for 'worries' or 'problems'."

Myasthenia gravis occurs more frequently in younger women and is uncommon in men in their sixties. It often follows a severe illness or emotional upset. I was convinced that Onassis' emotional shock over his son's untimely death was the cause of his disease.

Having confirmed the diagnosis, I started him on Mestinon, a drug that prevents the breakdown of acetylcholine, a neurotransmitter that transmits nerve impulses to muscles so that they can contract. Onassis' muscle strength improved dramatically after taking the pill, but only briefly. There are now several new therapies, including plasmapheresis, in which the patient's blood is filtered to remove harmful substances that cause the disease; removing the thymus gland (located in the front of the chest below the neck) can also help. As a result of these and several other new approaches, most patients with myasthenia gravis now have a normal life expectancy. But not back then.

Onassis continued to suffer from generalized muscle weakness. His eyelids were now constantly half-closed, and he had to raise them with his fingers in order to be able to see. He began to use strips of adhesive tape to keep his eyelids open, an ingenious solution that became his sad trademark. The press had a field day, photographing him whenever they could.

"Sorry, Ari, I Can't Do It!"

On one of my visits to Scorpios, Onassis' private island in Greece, while we were sitting at the beach chatting, he told me that he had been reading about myasthenia gravis and learned that it can sometimes affect the muscles of respiration as well as the eyes.

"Isidoro, my friend," he said, *"I don't want to die gasping for breath.* I don't want to go out suffering. Do you understand what I'm saying?"

Of course I did.

"I want you to give me a pill that will end my suffering. I promise you I won't take it unless my condition becomes unbearable . . . and no one will ever know you gave it to me."

I was devastated by his request for a suicide pill. My training, my background, my emotional makeup, not to mention the law, all made it impossible for me to give it to him. The best I could do was to leave him with a loaded syringe of a drug that would improve his breathing should such an emergency arise. He was not happy with my decision.

On that same visit, I had another, more lighthearted experience. Scorpios is in the Ionian Sea, a few miles from the mainland. After breakfast one day, Jackie suggested she and I visit a charming Greek town across the water. We boarded a small tender for the fifteen-minute ride. There, at the dock, lying in wait for Mrs. Onassis, was the usual horde of paparazzi. She and I strolled along the main street, trying our best to ignore the six photographers in front of us, snapping pictures nonstop as they walked backward. After some window-shopping, we returned to the island on the tender.

Three months later, one of my patients brought me a clipping from the German magazine *Der Spiegel.* There were Jackie and I, walking side by side in that little Greek town. The photo bore a very interesting caption: *New romantic interest for Jackie O'? Mr. Martini from New York, pictured here, is said to be her new "friend."* I thought it was funny . . . my wife was not amused (and Mrs. Martini, whoever that was, probably wasn't either).

Onassis' myasthenia gravis continued to worsen. I consulted every specialist in this disorder I knew, either personally or by reputation. None of them had anything more to offer. Then, after an intensive search of the medical literature on the subject (remember, this was before the days of Google and WebMD), I read that researchers at

Johns Hopkins University had had some success with high doses of steroids (drugs in the cortisone family). After discussing the case with the lead investigator of the study, I started Onassis on a course of that therapy, with impressive results. His strength slowly returned and he was able to get rid of the eye tapes. He was a new man!

"You SOB, why didn't you give me this medicine before?"

I thought he was joking—but he was dead serious. Why had I kept him waiting with this new therapy? Why hadn't his ability to pay any fee brought him these new research results sooner? I didn't allow this outburst to diminish my affection for him. The steroid therapy worked wonders. Uplifted by his renewed sense of well-being, Onassis resumed an active business life. He began to spend more time in Greece, where he dealt with the financial problems of his airline, Olympic. I did not hear from him for several weeks until he telephoned from Athens one day to tell me that his myasthenia had become much worse again and that he was coming to New York for me to reevaluate him.

When he returned, he was again wearing his eye tapes. I asked him if he had any clue as to why he had suddenly deteriorated.

Onassis' "Miracle" Cure

It seems that Jackie had been reading about a miraculous medication being promoted by a European physician. The substance, procaine, which is still marketed throughout Europe as a miraculous rejuvenator, is a 2 percent solution of lidocaine, a commonly used local anesthetic. It had been researched and evaluated by scientists in this country who were unable to document any of the benefits it was claimed to have. Nevertheless, in response to Jackie's request, this "miracle" drug's proponent was flown to Scorpios, where she administered it to my patient. (No one bothered to tell me about it.) Shortly after the treatments started, Onassis' muscles became weak again—the myasthenia symptoms had returned to square one.

Experts in this disease know that certain chemicals and medications can worsen myasthenia. These include several antibiotics, such as erythromycin and oxytetracycline (Terramycin), but also procaine! I insisted that Onassis discontinue this medication, and I immediately increased the dosage of the steroids he was taking. This improved his strength somewhat but not as dramatically as before, and for the rest of his life, Onassis remained incapacitated by his myasthenia.

One day, several months later, I received a call from Onassis' daughter, Christina, in Athens. "Daddy is very sick. He has pneumonia and isn't getting any better—even with the antibiotics the doctors are giving him. Would you come as soon as possible? I'll have tickets sent to you for TWA, not Olympic, because if the press sees you on one of our planes, they'll know there's a problem with Daddy."

I told her I would leave that night. A few minutes later, Jackie called me. She was in New York. "I've heard Ari is sick. I'm coming to Greece with you." And so the wife of the owner of Olympic Airlines and I flew to Athens together on a TWA plane.

Patients with Pneumonia Don't Turn Yellow

The following morning I went directly to Onassis' home in Glyfada, on the outskirts of Athens. He was in bed; the room was dark, the shades were drawn, and the air was musty. He appeared weak and drawn. There were at least seven doctors in attendance. I asked Onassis about his pneumonia. Did it hurt when he took a deep breath? No. How high was his temperature? He didn't know, but he hadn't felt feverish. How bad was his cough? It wasn't bad at all. Had he spit up any blood? No. I expected a few "yes" answers from someone with pneumonia.

I asked to see the chest X-ray. The doctors told me they hadn't taken one because Onassis refused to be hospitalized, and it was too difficult to bring a machine to his house. In any event, they said the diagnosis of pneumonia was obvious from their physical exam.

Onassis was irritated at Christina for having called me. He thought he was beginning to feel better. "I don't know why she had you come all the way from New York," he said.

I listened to his chest carefully; his breath sounds were loud and clear. Clinically, I found *no evidence* of pneumonia. His doctors explained that his infection had probably cleared after the antibiotic treatment. There was something about all this that made me wary of the diagnosis. The whole picture just didn't "smell" right. I insisted that the shades be raised so that I could assess Onassis' color and complexion.

He complained. "The sun hurts my eyes. Can't you just turn on more lights?"

"No," I explained none too pleasantly. After a long overnight flight from New York, I was not about to have the patient tell me how to examine him. Incandescent light is not ideal for examining a sick patient; daylight, when possible, can be much more revealing.

"Please raise the shades," I asked one of the nurses. Onassis muttered something and waved a hand weakly. The shades were lifted, and as the bright morning light flooded the room, I observed a *jaundiced* Onassis! The yellow color of his skin and eyes had not been evident in the darkened room under inadequate artificial light.

The rest was easy. What we doctors call a "differential diagnosis" of jaundice basically boils down to three main possibilities: liver disease, obstruction of bile passing from the liver or gallbladder into the gut (when anything interferes with the flow of bile it backs up into the liver and into the bloodstream, causing jaundice), or a rapid, abnormal breakdown of red blood cells releasing pigment that makes one look yellow. Simple blood tests can distinguish among these various causes. I had them done, and in Onassis' case, they indicated that he had obstructive jaundice, probably from a stone lodged in one of the bile ducts. The problem would have to be corrected surgically.

A Very Serious Mistake

What happened next is public knowledge and has been revealed in other books about Onassis and Jackie O. I discussed the options with my patient. Because of his myasthenia and his longtime use of cortisone-type medication, I thought Onassis was a high risk for *any* operation, and strongly recommended that he come to New York Hospital to be treated by a world-famous gallbladder surgical team headed by the late Dr. Frank Glenn. He reluctantly agreed. I alerted Dr. Glenn, and Olympic Airlines prepared one of its planes to fly us there in the morning.

A few hours later, after I returned to my hotel, Onassis phoned me:

"Isidoro, I've been thinking it over. I hope you don't take this personally, but you're a heart specialist, and this is not a heart problem. My doctor in Paris, a famous gastroenterologist at the American Hospital, suggests that I come there for the surgery."

Not take it personally? Was he kidding? I took it very personally because I felt he was making a very serious mistake.

The plane that was to have flown Onassis to New York took off the next morning for Paris instead. Jackie accompanied her husband; I returned to New York.

A few days later, a French surgeon called me.

"You were right, Dr. Rosenfeld. Mr. Onassis has a stone in his common bile duct, and we will operate to remove it tomorrow."

"What procedure do you plan to do?" I asked, worried that Onassis would not be able to withstand prolonged anesthesia. He had been on substantial doses of cortisone that can interfere with healing and scar formation and also make one vulnerable to infection.

"We will open the abdomen, explore the bile ducts, remove the stone, and take out the gallbladder," the doctor explained.

I tried to be diplomatic but simply blurted out: "Forgive me, but I think that's a mistake. I suggest you do a local procedure. Remove the stone, put a drain in the duct, and leave the gallbladder alone for now. He may have a hard time recovering from more extensive surgery than that because he's been on steroids. Later on, after you've tapered and discontinued the steroids, you can take out the gallbladder. I feel strongly that, at this time, you should *only* remove the stone." I'll never forget his answer: "That's not how we do it in France."

I was shocked into silence. I may have been less than diplomatic but I strongly believed that what I told the surgeon was in Onassis' best interests. I was so sure of it that I called Jackie and begged her to intervene. She was of little help. She said that she had met the French surgeons and had complete confidence in them. The die was cast.

Onassis underwent the operation and appeared to make an uneventful recovery. Jackie phoned to tell me the good news—and maybe to gloat a little? I was relieved by her message, but I didn't think Ari was out of the woods yet. I didn't tell her that and shared her happiness for the moment.

The next week, a contrite, worried Jackie called again. "We're having a problem. Ari is running a fever and not responding to any of the antibiotics they're giving him. Who's the best infectious disease expert in the States?"

"Dr. Louis Weinstein in Boston," I told her.

"Can you call him and explain the situation?"

"Of course," I said.

I called Dr. Weinstein and briefed him about the case. He left for Paris that night and called me the next day. He concurred that the steroids had made the infection difficult to treat. The French doctors in charge had done all they could. Dr. Weinstein said there was little more he could do at such a late date and was pessimistic about ever controlling the infection.

It gave me no satisfaction to know that I had been right. I was terribly upset that after all these years Onassis was destined to die *unnecessarily*. Jackie remained at Onassis' bedside for a few more days and then returned to her children in New York. A couple of weeks later, Onassis died. There was no question in my mind that he would have survived had a limited procedure been done rather than the extensive surgery he underwent.

Onassis left the bulk of his vast estate to a foundation that continues to fund many educational and health programs, but its major focus is to improve health care in Greece. I like to think that my making him aware of the inadequate facilities there for treating pediatric cardiac patients played a role in his decision to build and maintain the Onassis Heart Center in Athens. Today, that institution is among the foremost in Greece and has made unnecessary the program I helped establish in the early 1970s to repair the hearts of children with congenital cardiac disease (see chapter 23).

22

NIARCHOS—
ANOTHER GREEK TYCOON

Manna from Heaven

Stavros Niarchos and Aristotle Onassis were both extremely successful, self-made men with high media profiles. I knew them very well, and I was their physician for years. They were extremely loyal and generous to their friends and families.

Niarchos and Onassis never publicly announced or acknowledged any animosity toward each other, but anyone in the know did not usually invite them both to the same party. In 1973, after my first trip to the Soviet Union as a member of the National Institutes of Health Task Force on Sudden Cardiac Death (chapter 46), Gerald Van der Kemp, curator of the Château de Versailles, was planning to give a dinner in my honor in Paris. Was there anyone special I'd like him to invite? I wanted both Onassis and Niarchos to attend, but that clearly was not feasible. I literally tossed a coin—and Onassis won.

The media had an ongoing field day with Onassis and Niarchos. Although I spent hundreds of hours with both men, they never discussed or demeaned each other in my presence. Whatever private vendetta they may have had, I honestly believe they'd have missed one another if anything happened to either of them. I considered them to be competitors, not enemies.

A short time after Onassis became my patient, Niarchos asked me to come to the South of France as soon as possible to see his fiancée, Lady Blandford. (This was Tina, Onassis' former wife, who was then married to Lord Blandford, now the Duke of Marlborough, whom she was planning to divorce in order to marry Niarchos.) She was at her home in Villefranche in France and complaining of pain in her legs. Niarchos was worried about her. I left for Europe the next day.

Niarchos met me at the Nice airport, and we drove to Lady Blandford's home on the bay. In the car, he told me about the tragic death of his last wife (who just happened to be Tina's older sister) and how much he loved Tina, whom he was hoping to marry after her divorce from Lord Blandford.

Lady Blandford, an attractive, slightly built blond, greeted us at the door. She thanked me for coming and insisted I call her Tina. Pretty soon, all three of us were on a first-name basis—Stavros, Tina, and Issie (whoops, Isadore!). I examined Tina and found that nothing more than a few innocent varicose veins were responsible for the discomfort in her legs. We celebrated the good news with a couple of drinks, and since I'd flown all night from New York and was tired, I went to my hotel to get some rest.

The next morning, Niarchos invited me to have lunch on the *Creole*, his legendary sleek, black, sailing yacht anchored in Villefranche harbor. As we approached the boat on a tender, I realized why it was reputed to be the most beautiful ship afloat. The lines were flawless; it was a breathtaking sight. The wood everywhere on the ship was handcrafted and of the finest quality. We dined outdoors on the deck, just the two of us, served by stewards in formal attire. The wine was a '49 Château Haut-Brion, which, I later learned, was Niarchos' favorite label.

That evening, as we drove back to the airport, Niarchos asked me to be his doctor. And that was the start of a wonderful relationship. For the next quarter of a century, Niarchos and I remained very close. Unlike Onassis, he never had much wrong with him physically, and I reassured him over the years about his minor complaints. But for my family and me it meant great vacations to wonderful parts of the world. He was extremely generous and devoted to us.

The Largest Gift Cornell Had Ever Received!

One day in 1979, several years after we'd met, Niarchos and I were having dinner together in New York. He was in a pensive mood. "You know, I really appreciate all you've done for me. I know that I haven't always been easy to deal with. I'm demanding; I have a bad temper; I can be a pain in the neck—for all of which I'm very sorry. But I'd like to do something for you. How about a Rolls Royce? I know, I know, you're worried about paying tax on it. I'll pay the tax. The car won't cost you anything."

I was overcome by his generosity. "Stavros, you're wonderful to offer me such a gift. Of course, I'd love a Rolls. Who wouldn't? But frankly, I'd be embarrassed to be seen driving it. I'm not sure it's appropriate for a doctor, even one who has such rich patients, to be driving a Rolls Royce. But if you really want to do something for me, which is, of course, not necessary because I enjoy being your doctor and your friend, why don't you donate some money to Cornell Medical School? We need to recruit new professors, and some of our buildings are old and desperately need renovation. You'd get more mileage for your money giving it to our medical school than providing me with a luxury car."

"OK, what do they need most, and how much will it cost?" he asked.

"An endowed professorship, which we would name for you, would be a million and a quarter dollars." (That same chair today costs two million, and the price is going up all the time, so if any of you have been thinking about endowing a chair, hurry up and let me know.)

"In what field?"

"I don't know. Let me call the dean and find out."

The nanomoment I got home, I called Ted Cooper, our dean of medicine, and told him the exciting news. There's nothing that makes a university official happier than the prospect of a big contribution. "Niarchos wants to know where we need the money most."

"Well," said Ted, "we could use a chair in pediatric cardiology, and with people traveling to so many exotic places these days, I'd like to set up a division of international medicine at Cornell. Then, of course, our anatomy building is falling apart. That alone will cost about two and a half million to renovate. Why don't you offer him these options and see which one he wants?"

The next morning, Niarchos and I had breakfast at his apartment in the Waldorf. I showed him the dean's list, which added up to a total of five million dollars. He studied it carefully, and then said, "Let me think about this. I'll let you know which one I want."

A few days later, he left for Europe without giving me his decision. Weeks went by and then months. Still no word from Niarchos, but lots of calls from the dean. "What's the matter with your friend? Where are the big bucks he promised?"

"I don't know. Maybe he lost one of his oil tankers."

Some four months later, Niarchos called me from Paris. "I haven't been feeling quite right. Can you come over this weekend and take a look at me?" I left that Friday morning. After I arrived, he invited me to dinner at Maxim's, his favorite French restaurant. Those were the days when terrorists were kidnapping rich people for ransom and Niarchos was trying to keep a low profile. So instead of his Rolls, we drove to Maxim's in a Volkswagen station wagon. As we sat beside each other in the back seat, Niarchos suddenly turned to me and asked, "Do you remember my promise to do something for Cornell?"

Did I remember? How could I forget? "Well, I've been considering all the needs you have, and I've decided what to do." (Hurray, I'd be in the dean's good graces again.) "Which chair would you like?" I asked.

"Oh, listen, I can't make up my mind. Why don't I give you five million dollars for the whole package?" If I had been in the Rolls, there'd have been a place for me to faint, but this little car was too small. I was astounded, overwhelmed, and so very grateful.

There are now two chairs that bear Niarchos' name, as well as the large building that houses the Anatomy Department.

A short time after Niarchos made this very generous gift to our medical center (at the time, it was the largest private contribution ever to that institution), he required back surgery. Given his generosity, you can imagine the kind of treatment (which is excellent, anyway) he'd get at our hospital. But he loved his comfort, so he chose, instead, to go to Baylor in Houston, where he could have a suite rather than just a nice room. Niarchos wanted the best of both worlds—Houston for comfort, Cornell for expertise—and he got it. I asked the chief of orthopedic surgery at Cornell to operate on Niarchos in Houston—and he agreed. We were flown there on Niarchos' Boeing 737, which waited for us a couple of days after the operation and then brought us home. The surgery was successful. Niarchos ended up both comfortable and healthy.

Several months later, Tina, whom he had married, died suddenly. She'd apparently had a blood clot to her lung. Niarchos was devastated. He never remarried, although he was courted by a variety of international beauties.

A few months later, Niarchos called me with a special request. He was on his beautiful private island in Greece and having chest pain. The local doctors weren't sure what it was, and he was very worried. Would I please come over? I told him I was expected at a very important meeting in Moscow two days hence. "Look," he said, "take the Concorde to Paris. It arrives in the early evening. My plane will fly you to Athens, and my chopper will bring you to Spetsopoula."

"But helicopters don't fly at night there, do they?" I asked.

"Not usually, but I'll send an engineer along so that it's safe. The next day, my plane will fly you to Frankfurt, where you can connect to Moscow. You'll arrive there on schedule." It sounded a bit tiring, but I agreed.

After a long day and night of travel, I arrived at Spetsopoula at 2 a.m. and went directly to Niarchos' bedroom. Without even changing my clothes, I took a brief history and looked at the chest X-rays and ECG that had been done. "Nobody can figure out why I have this pain in the left side of my chest," he complained.

As it turns out, I didn't even need to do a physical on him, because there, as plain as day, on his chest X-ray I could see a hairline fracture on one of his ribs that his doctors had missed. He had cracked it in an injury that was so slight he couldn't remember when it happened.

Niarchos was happy with my diagnosis and relieved that his problem was not cardiac. I went to bed for three hours and took his chopper back to Athens airport early in the morning. His plane flew me to Frankfurt, where I made the connection that brought me to Moscow later that day—right on schedule, as Niarchos had promised.

In the last six months of his life, Niarchos developed some serious problems. He had apparently suffered a toxic reaction to a medication he'd been given, and his kidneys began to fail. He ended up in an excellent hospital in Zurich, where his condition was clearly terminal. His sons and daughter, of whom I was very fond and had literally seen grow up, asked me to come. When I arrived, he was in a coma. Dr. DeBakey was there too. After a desperate attempt to save his life with a surgical procedure that Dr. DeBakey had recommended, Stavros Niarchos died. Niarchos' children, deep in bereavement, were comforted by the fact that no stone had been left unturned to save their father.

This man enriched my life and that of my family like no other. My wife, children, and I have only the fondest memories of him and will never forget the wonderful times we spent together. But he also made a great difference to our institution which, like many others, never has enough money to fulfill all the dreams of its teachers and scientists.

We tend to think in vague terms about fundraising. Most institutions such as ours operate at a loss and depend on private gifts to maintain high teaching and research standards. I realized after Mr. Niarchos' generous gift to Cornell in 1978 what a difference it made to our private, nongovernment-supported teaching institution. Because of his generosity, we could afford to hire several new teachers and researchers who were able to devote themselves full time to the education of medical students and the pursuit of original ideas that led to important discoveries—free from the pressure and diversion of "earning their keep." Niarchos' gift inspired me to set up my own foundation, which over the years has made it possible for my donors and me to help not only Cornell but also researchers in other centers here and abroad.

Before he died, Stavros Niarchos established a foundation that has been generously supporting a host of charitable organizations throughout the world, including ours. His loving children are perpetuating their father's memory by devoting themselves to overseeing the work of the Stavros Niarchos Foundation.

23

SAVING CHILDREN'S LIVES

1974: Dr. Mary Allen Engle, a superb and caring doctor who was chief of pediatric cardiology at New York Hospital–Cornell Medical Center called to tell me how upset she was about what she had heard at a recent international heart conference on the island of Rhodes. A Greek physician there reported that some thirty infants in Greece born with "fixable" congenital heart abnormalities were dying every year for lack of medical care. There were no centers in Greece where their cardiac defects could be repaired. Their families could not afford to take them abroad to have the necessary surgery. Dr. Engle knew that I was the doctor of several Greek shipowners and wondered whether I could persuade them to help save these youngsters.

She and I met the next day to consider how we could arrange to bring these children to our hospital, which was staffed and equipped to take care of them. We determined that the cost would include airfare from Athens to New York for at least one parent, expensive diagnostic tests, consultations with the appropriate specialists, surgical fees if surgery was indicated and feasible, and hospitalization for about two weeks. The parents accompanying the children would also need some place to stay, and New York is an expensive city. We calculated that this would add up to a couple hundred thousand dollars per child.

I called Onassis and told him of my conversation with Dr. Engle. He was shocked. He had no idea that his native country of Greece could not care for its own children nor how urgent the problem was. He was obviously distressed.

I told him that we would like to start saving these young lives as soon as possible and that we have excellent and experienced surgeons as well as a superb staff and facilities to do so. "But this is going to cost money, Ari. Can you help?"

"What do you need?" Onassis said.

"Transportation, to begin with," I replied.

"Done." he exclaimed. "As many children as you want—and their parents. I'll fly them all to New York on my airline. No charge. I'll set it up. It is shameful that Greece cannot care for its own. *Shameful.*"

My words had wounded his pride in his country . . . the country of history's most important physician, Hippocrates, who revolutionized medical thinking.

I flew to Athens a few days later to meet with Niarchos and George S. Livanos, the two other shipowners who were my friends. When I made them aware of the plight of these Greek children, and informed them of Onassis' offer, they too immediately and without hesitation agreed to pay all the hospital costs. The hospital was prepared to reduce its charges as much as possible. (Then as now, hospitals, especially those that teach and conduct research, were constantly struggling to make ends meet.) We contacted the Greek archbishop, who offered to find accommodations in New York City for the families of the children. The final step was to provide for the medical care itself. Every one of the doctors we contacted—physicians, anesthesiologists, and surgeons—volunteered their services free-of-charge.

Our next step was to arrange for the Greek cardiological community to identify the children who needed the heart surgery. Dr. John Nihoyanopolis, a distinguished pediatric cardiologist, volunteered to do so. We were all set.

Within a couple of months, the first patients started arriving, and soon we were operating on at least one child every three or four weeks. The results were spectacular! More than 95 percent of them returned home cured!

After Mr. Onassis died in 1975, the foundation he had established before his death began to plan and build the Onassis Hospital in Athens, a first-class medical center. It was the realization of his dream. After it was up and running in 1992, there was no further need to bring Greek children to New York for open heart surgery. They were able to be treated in their own country.

24

AN UNWELCOME
DECORATION

A bout two years after we started this program, Mr. Petronakis, the Greek consul in New York, called to inform me that his government had decided to reward me with its highest decoration, the Order of the Phoenix. When could I come to Greece with my wife and four children to receive this honor?

"The colonels," who were generally viewed as dictatorial and anti–human rights, ran the government of Greece at that time. I had no sympathy with them and was uncomfortable being decorated by them. I told this to a stunned Mr. Petronakis.

"This is most embarrassing. If I convey your sentiments and your refusal to my government, they will construe it as a slap in the face to Greece, and they will no doubt terminate this children's program."

I told the consul I'd get back to him. Camilla and I thought long and hard about it, and decided that the welfare of these youngsters was more important than our political views. I called Mr. Petronakis and informed him that we would be "happy" to come to Greece.

A few weeks later, my wife, my four children, and I left New York for Athens. We arrived on a beautiful sunny day and were put up in a lovely suite at the Athens Hilton. Since the ceremony was scheduled a few days later, Mr. Petronakis, who had come to Greece for the occasion, suggested that after seeing the Parthenon, the Acropolis, and other sites in Athens, we should visit several beautiful Greek islands. The next morning, we went to the Athens airport.

As I stood in line waiting to buy the plane tickets, the clerk suddenly closed the counter. I looked around and saw that all the other counters were also being shut. Suddenly, the terminal was filled with police and armed troops. I couldn't find anyone who would tell me what was happening. I finally accosted a police officer who informed me that there had been a political coup, a revolution, that all the colonels had been arrested and imprisoned, and that Constantine Caramanlis was returning from exile to form a new government.

I didn't dare tell anyone that we were here as guests of the toppled government. We had given up our rooms at the Hilton. Where to go? What to do? I'd have to try to get our hotel rooms back. I phoned the Hilton from the airport, and fortunately, our suite hadn't even been made up yet. Yes, they'd hold it for us. Relieved, the six of us went to the entrance of the terminal to return to Athens by taxi. There wasn't one in sight. After half an hour of mounting anxiety, I took a twenty dollar bill from my wallet and waved it frantically on the airport steps. After a few minutes, a man driving a Volkswagen stopped and agreed to take us to the Hilton. Nothing is impossible until you've tried it! I couldn't imagine six of us, plus the driver, and five bags, fitting into a tiny four-seater Volkswagen. But where there's a will, there's a way, so we did it and returned to the hotel.

From the balcony of our room we watched the jubilant crowds shouting "Caramanlis! Caramanlis!" My kids (and I) were terrified by the jets swooping by low in the skies, as well as the tanks and armored cars in the streets. Camilla, an incurable romantic, thrilled by the downfall of a dictatorship, loved to see all the happy people milling about, laughing, and congratulating each other. She insisted we all go down to the lobby so that our kids could get the feeling of what it was like for oppressed people to be liberated! Frankly, I don't like mobs of any political persuasion. This revolution would have given me more pleasure if I could have watched it on TV in my living room in New York. However, my parental responsibilities, plus the fact that Camilla is the boss, obliged me to accompany her and our children downstairs. We were all, yes, I too, swept up in the happiness of the crowd. My children have never forgotten that day!

Now, how to get home? All flights to and from Athens had been cancelled. No one was leaving Greece. I phoned my Greek friends who had made our children's program possible (and therefore were responsible for my being decorated and in this mess) to see whether they could get us out of the country, or at least make sure we were safe. I learned that they had all left the country. I didn't bother calling Onassis because I was sure that he was gone, too. Rich and prominent people are never sure how a revolution will affect them. To my chagrin, I later learned that he had never budged from his island, Scorpios.

So we were stuck for a while. Thank goodness I was an American and could count on our embassy for help. Read this next part carefully because you never know when you will be stuck in a foreign country in turmoil and need help from our embassy.

I dialed our embassy number for an hour. There was no answer. Finally, a clerk picked up the phone and asked what our problem was. It was as if he was totally unaware of what was going on in the streets! When I explained to him why we were concerned—the possibility of violence, the inability to get home—he told me not to panic, and to keep tuned to the armed forces radio station for further instructions. We sat by the radio for hours, waiting for that information. All we heard were baseball games being broadcast from the U.S.! I have never forgotten this failure of our consular corps to help Americans in distress, real or imagined.

I then called Mary Lasker, who was very close to President Johnson. She told me not to worry. She would contact the State Department and if there was any real danger, she'd see that we got out of Greece one way or another, even if it meant sending a submarine from our Mediterranean fleet. I'm not nuts about submarines either, so I called my friend Hushang Ansary, then Minister of Finance in the Shah's government in Iran. There was nothing he could do. So we just waited.

I soon realized that despite all the false rumors, such as the one that the supporters of exiled King Constantine were marching on Athens, we were in no danger. Some other Greek friends who hadn't left the country invited us to their homes and kept in touch with us. While waiting to go home, I ran into Mr. Petronakis, who had made all this possible, in the Hilton lobby. Ever the diplomat, he greeted me, I presume facetiously, with, "Oh, so you're still alive!"

Four days later, we boarded the first commercial flight to New York. On the plane with us was the new Greek government's ambas-

My parents
Vera and Mischa

Age 15, in uniform—
Royal Canadian
Air Force cadet, 1941.

With my bride Camilla cutting
our wedding cake, August 1956.

Captain, Royal Canadian
Army Medical Corps, 1951.

Danny Kaye presenting award from the American Physicians Fellowship for Israel, 1979.

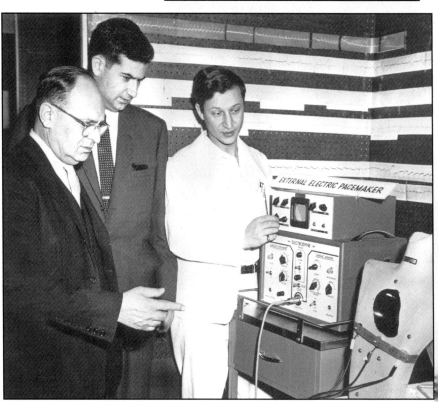

With Drs. Harold Segall and Irving Yachnin,
viewing the first external cardiac pacemaker used in Canada, 1954.

Healthy Heart Day
March 17, 1987
10 a.m. – 2 p.m.

Celebrating Camilla's 70th birthday.

Addressing Healthy Heart Day national seminar. (Photo courtesy of Research! America.)

Receiving Research! America's award for Impact on Public Opinion in Medicine in Washington D.C., 2001. (l-r) Mary Woolley, Research! America president; Louis Sullivan M.D., U.S. Secretary of Health and Human Services and founding Dean of Morehouse School of Medicine; Hon. Paul G. Rogers, Chairman, Research! America's Board of Directors; Isadore and Camilla. (Photo courtesy of Heather Jameson.)

Photographer Richard Avedon,
longstanding friend and patient,
2003.

With good friend
Walter Matthau on the set
of *Grumpier Old Men*, 1995.

With longtime friend, actress Sophia Loren, 2004.

"Snaking around" with Gary Collins and my son, Arthur Rosenfeld, on
The Gary Collins Show, 1982.

Olympic Gold Medalist Scott Hamilton receives Research! America's Isadore Rosenfeld Award for Impact on Public Opinion in Medicine, 2004. (Photo Courtesy of Research! America.)

Marlo Thomas—actress, producer, and advocate for children's research as National Outreach Director for St. Jude's Children's Research Hospital which was founded by her father Danny Thomas—receives the Isadore Rosenfeld Award for Impact on Public Opinion in Medicine, 2005. (Photo Courtesy of Research! America.)

Research! America awarded California Governor Arnold Schwarzenegger with the Isadore Rosenfeld Award for Impact on Public Opinion in Medicine for his steadfast support of health and medical research. George Vrandenberg accepted the award on his behalf, 2008. (Photo Courtesy of Mike Gatty, DC Event Photos.)

Presenting Research! America's Isadore Rosenfeld Award for Impact on Public Opinion in Medicine to actor Michael J. Fox.

Bob Woodruff
receives the
Isadore Rosenfeld
Award for
Impact on Public
Opinion in
Medicine, 2009.
(Photo Courtesy
of Mike Gatty, DC
Event Photos.)

With President
Reagan at the
White House,
1984.

Receiving award as
Cofounder and
President, Foundation for
iomedical Research, from
Dr. Michael DeBakey and
Sam Donaldson.

On the set of Fox news TV show *Sunday Housecall* with anchors Jamie Colby and Eric Shawn, 2009.

Kitty Carlisle Hart a
New York Governo
Averell Harriman
celebrating my
50th birthday, 1976.

sador to the UN, who, interestingly enough, would later become my patient.

I never did get the Order of the Phoenix, although the Greek children's program continued for several more years. I guess no future government wants to have anything to do with someone the colonels wanted to honor. However, I have not abandoned hope that someday I will proudly wear that decoration. At a small dinner party given by one of our friends, I had the pleasure of sitting next to King Constantine of Greece. When I told him my Order of the Phoenix story, he said, "I'm glad you never got that decoration from them. I promise you that one of the first things I will do when I return to my throne is to bestow it on you."

I'm still waiting.

25

Probably the Most Dramatic Experience of My Career

979: I was at Uncle Tai's, my favorite Chinese restaurant in New York City, having dinner with several of my Cornell medical students. They were in their final year, and we were celebrating the end of the course in bedside medicine I had taught them. At about eight o'clock, while we were enjoying our shark's fin soup, spring rolls, and Peking duck, I was called to the phone. It was my close friend George Livanos, calling from Paris.

George is a Greek shipowner who, unlike his more visible former brothers-in-laws, Stavros Niarchos and Aristotle Onassis, is a very private person. (He has permitted me to write this account of his mother's illness.) He was calling because he was concerned about his mother. In her midseventies, she had several days earlier developed severe chest pain and been admitted to the American Hospital in Paris. The doctors there were unable to control her angina with the drugs then available—intravenous nitroglycerine, oxygen, and morphine. He was told that her outlook was poor, and that she was either in the throes of a heart attack or about to have one. He asked if I would come to see her right away. I agreed.

I told him I'd take the first plane the next day, since all the flights to Paris had already left.

"Would you leave tonight if I can arrange it?" he asked anxiously.

"Of course, but how's that possible?"

"A friend has offered to lend me his G-2 jet. How soon can you be ready to leave?"

"I'll go home right now, pack, and get my passport. I'll be ready within the hour."

"Good. I'll have a car pick you up."

I rushed home, packed some clothes, and was driven to Teterboro airport, where I boarded the waiting plane. We left at eleven o'clock that night for Paris and I was at Mrs. Livanos' bedside at the American Hospital a few hours later. I had known this woman for several years. The matriarch of a shipping empire, she was an unassuming, wonderful, quiet woman—a widow—passionately devoted to her family.

She was in bed, attached to a bank of monitors that displayed her pulse rate, blood pressure, and electrocardiogram. There were oxygen prongs in her nose and intravenous needles in her arms. She was propped up on two pillows to help her breathe because her lungs were congested. She was pale and moaning.

Her ECG revealed evidence of serious ischemia; that is, her heart muscle was not getting enough blood because one or more of her coronary arteries were blocked. Bypass surgery was rarely being performed in France in 1979. The American Hospital was not then the sophisticated medical facility it is today, and I was not aware of any other place in France where this kind of surgery was being performed, especially on such high-risk patients. To move her to my hospital in New York or anyplace else would be extremely risky. This was a catch-22 situation: whatever decision I made might turn out to be a disaster.

I met with Mrs. Livanos' family and doctors, and explained the gravity of her condition. There seemed no choice but to leave her where she was and try to optimize her medications. The French doctors agreed to the medical regimen I proposed, and I returned to New York the next day, less than optimistic about her chances for survival.

I remained in constant touch with Mrs. Livanos' doctors and her son several times a day. They told me she was not responding to the drug regimen I had prescribed, and her condition was deteriorating.

She was now in almost constant pain and her ECG had worsened. I rushed back to Paris. My worst fears were confirmed when I reviewed her situation again. Her heart muscle was weakening, and she was more short of breath. I suspected that at least one major coronary artery was slowly closing and that she was heading for a massive heart attack. The *only* solution, in my opinion, was bypass surgery. But where should it be done? Did I dare suggest moving such a sick woman?

Her son and I discussed the matter privately. "George, I'll be very candid. Your mother may not make it, not here, anyway. Her only chance, and it's a small one, is to be moved to some facility where she can have an angiogram and a bypass operation. The closest place I can think of is London, but getting her to the airport, flying her there, and transporting her by ambulance may be more than she can handle. And, quite frankly, I'm not sure how much experience the doctors there have had with such high-risk, unstable angina patients. Let me call Dr. Michael DeBakey and ask him what he knows about the English surgeons and whether he can suggest some other place in Europe."

I called Dr. DeBakey and described the situation to him.

"Look, Isadore," he said. "As long as you've decided to bite the bullet and move her, she might as well come to the States. I'd be happy to set up everything and operate on her myself at the Methodist Hospital here in Houston."

I thanked him and said I'd call him back. George and I again discussed our options. What Dr. DeBakey had advised made sense. There was no point in taking the enormous chance of moving this very sick woman to a facility that did not have the experience necessary to save her life. If we were going to move her, then the extra few hours flying to the States would not make a difference.

I weighed DeBakey's generous offer to operate on Mrs. Livanos in Houston, but I decided that it was best to bring her to New York where I could oversee her care and where we had a superb surgical team headed by Dr. V. Subramanian. He had operated on many of my high-risk patients with great success.

I called Dr. DeBakey and told him of my decision. He understood completely and wished me the best of luck—saying not to hesitate to contact him if there was anything further he could do.

I told Mrs. Livanos' son that I thought she had only a 50 percent chance of surviving the move, let alone the surgery. However, I emphasized that I was recommending that we chance it because I believed she would die unless we did.

George asked me only one question. "What would you do if it were your mother?"

I swallowed hard. "I'd move her," I answered.

"OK," he said, holding back tears, "then that's it. Let's do it."

Time was of the essence. Every minute brought my patient closer to a heart attack and possible death. We'd need our own plane and George arranged for one to leave from Le Bourget airport near Paris. In order to protect his mother on the long transatlantic flight, I planned to equip the plane with every conceivable technological tool we might need en route and the personnel to use it. I contacted our cardiosurgical team in New York. Dr. Subramanian agreed to leave for Paris that night, and so did Dr. Jeffrey Borer, the chief of our cardiac catheterization team. I asked them to bring along an anesthesiologist, two surgical residents, and two cardiac surgical nurses, together with whatever emergency equipment they might need on the plane. I wanted to be prepared for any eventuality on that flight, even emergency surgical intervention. I telephoned the Philips Company in Belgium that makes the extracorporeal balloon pump, which could be inserted into the aorta if the patient went into shock. They agreed to provide this equipment along with a technician to operate it.

Later that day, George and I went to the airport to check out the plane and to have some of the seats removed to make room for a stretcher. We ordered other changes in the interior configuration to accommodate the support team and its equipment.

We were all set. My "task force" was on its way from New York, the balloon pump and technician would soon be in Paris, and the patient was psychologically prepared for the flight. Key members of Mrs. Livanos' family would accompany us—George's wife, Lita (George would take a commercial carrier because he and his wife never flew on the same plane without their children), and Mrs. Livanos' granddaughter, Christina Onassis.

The following morning, I met the New York team at Orly airport in Paris, and we went to Le Bourget, the airport used by private planes. We spent the next few hours setting up all the equipment. I then returned to the American Hospital and arranged for the ambulance to bring my patient and me to the airport. We arrived at Le Bourget thirty minutes later. Mrs. Livanos' stretcher was hoisted onto the rear of the plane by an elevator platform. The entire medical team boarded and the doors were shut. We were ready to leave . . . *on the flight of her life—and mine.*

I waited impatiently for the plane to taxi to the runway. Every minute counted, but for some reason we were not taking off. I went to the cockpit to find out what was delaying our departure, and the pilot explained that the president of France was leaving Paris, and the airspace in the area had been "neutralized." He had no idea how long we would have to wait.

"Get on the radio," I said, "and tell them we have a serious emergency and need to take off immediately."

"OK," he replied, "but it won't work. Presidential security always takes priority."

"Do it anyway," I insisted.

He did and was told in no uncertain terms that if we had an emergency, we should take our patient to one of the many excellent hospitals in Paris. There was no way they would open the skies for us.

So we sat parked there for almost two hours. Subramanian, Borer, and I kept Mrs. Livanos under close surveillance. We adjusted the oxygen, gave her medication for her pain, and sedated her. The wait was agonizing. Nervously, I checked my own pulse. It was edging over one hundred beats per minute . . . even though I was sitting perfectly still. Finally, we were cleared for takeoff and taxied down the runway.

When we reached cruising altitude, I called the state police in New York from the plane to request they escort the ambulance from Westchester airport, where we would be landing, to the city limits. There, I'd have New York's finest waiting to ease our way through traffic to the New York Hospital on Manhattan's east side.

The Atlantic crossing was unremarkable. A tailwind helped make up for some of the delay on the ground. Thankfully, there was no turbulence. My patient's ECG did not worsen, although she frequently complained of painful chest pressure. We repeatedly adjusted the dosage of her intravenous medication, but there was no need for any of the heroic surgical intervention I feared might be necessary and for which we were prepared.

As we approached Westchester airport seven hours later, we ran into another problem. The weather had turned nasty; no planes were being permitted to land in the New York area! The last thing we needed was to circle endlessly with the nitroglycerine dripping. Worse, what if we were diverted to another city? Where would I take Mrs. Livanos and my entire team? I asked the pilot to inform air traffic control that we had a prime emergency on board and *must* be given permission to land if at all possible. After a few minutes, they made an exception for us. Ours was the only plane to descend into the New York area that afternoon!

As we taxied to the gate at Westchester airport in White Plains, I could see my wife's station wagon, the New York Hospital ambulance with its flashing lights, and three state police cars waiting on the tarmac. The plane pulled up to the gate, and the hydraulic lift holding the stretcher with Mrs. Livanos and Dr. Borer, standing beside her, was gradually lowered to the ground. Suddenly, the entire platform dropped several feet. Dr. Borer lost his balance and hurtled some ten feet to the ground. I rushed to help him. Miraculously he was not seriously hurt; just some bruises. He shrugged me off and said, "Take care of your patient." I turned to Mrs. Livanos. Fortunately, her stretcher had been well secured to the platform, and she withstood the fall without harm. Actually, she thought it all quite amusing. "We fly across the Atlantic without any trouble—and then *this* happens!" Suddenly, I realized that my pulse was racing again. I had to relax because there would soon be many decisions for me to make.

I rode with the patient in the ambulance, and we made the thirty-five-mile trip in nothing flat. The emergency team at the hospital was ready for us. Bruised and battered, Dr. Borer prepared to perform the cardiac catheterization. Mrs. Livanos' fearful odyssey was over. We would now do whatever was necessary to save her life.

The coronary angiogram, done thirty minutes after we arrived, clearly showed what I had expected: the left main coronary artery, from which two of the three other coronary arteries branch off, was about to close. Dr. Subramanian prepared to operate immediately.

Mrs. Livanos was wheeled to the operating room within the hour. Dr. Subramanian successfully bypassed the left main coronary artery, and two other less severely occluded vessels for good measure. Miraculously, her heart had not been permanently damaged even though it had been deprived of much of its blood supply for so long. I was exhilarated to see the pale heart muscle turn a healthy pink after normal flow was restored to it.

A few days later, a reassured and relieved George Livanos flew back to his home in Greece, leaving his mother to convalesce under my care.

Good News, Bad News

Mrs. Livanos made an uncomplicated recovery. Two weeks later, I called George and told him that his mother was ready to be discharged. He was overcome with joy and invited Camilla, our four children, and me to escort her back to Greece and spend a week's holiday with him.

On the plane trip to Europe, I suddenly had a terrible premonition. I turned to my wife and said, "I've been thinking about my father. For some reason, and I can't explain it, I feel I will never see him again." My dad lived in Montreal, and although he'd had heart trouble for as long as I could remember, there had been nothing new in his condition to warrant this premonition.

Camilla tried to reassure me that my worry was simply the result of the drama and stress of the past few weeks. She was obviously right, and I tried to put it from my mind and enjoy the rest of the flight to Athens.

After we arrived, we were helicoptered from Athens airport to George's home. We landed twenty minutes later; the chopper's doors opened and George saw his smiling mother holding out her arms to him.

Then, George turned to me, his tears flowing. I knew at once that what he would have to say would not be good. He embraced me and whispered, "Isadore, my friend, I'm so sorry to tell you this. We received a phone call a few minutes ago . . . your father has died at home in Montreal."

Shifting Emotional Gears

It took a moment or two for my mind to switch gears. I had been on a high for weeks, celebrating life and the return of George's mother from the brink of disaster. I was in the very midst, the culmination, and the fulfillment of that event. The words, "*Your father has died*" did not penetrate for a moment. I stared, puzzled, at my friend. And then it hit me! *My father was dead.*

My family and I immediately returned to Athens airport and boarded a plane to Montreal to attend my dad's funeral and to be of some comfort to my mother.

Remembering My Father

I had grown up in a small family. There were just my parents and my brother. Despite all the emotional support I had given to countless patients and friends over the years, this was the first time in my fifty-two years that I, myself, had lost a loved one. The deep grief I felt was compounded by the fact that my father was very special to me.

He had suffered from angina pectoris (pain in the chest due to blocked coronary arteries in the heart) since his late forties. I always lived with the fear that one day, while clutching his chest in agony, he would die of a heart attack. Today was that day. He died within hours after it started. I later learned that in his last moments, he kept asking, "Where's Issie?"

As I've said so often in these pages, my main motivation in becoming a cardiologist was to be able to care for my father. Ironically, when he needed me most, I was helping rescue someone else's parent from the brink of death.

I learned from my mother that the day I was flying to Greece, my dad complained of his usual chest pain, except that this time it continued despite his taking several nitroglycerine tablets. My mother called the ambulance, but by the time it arrived, my dad was dead. He was eighty-three. He'd lived a long, sad life, brightened only by the devotion of his wife, sons, and grandchildren. I loved him very much.

26

A VERY IMPORTANT
DISCOVERY

In the 1950s, patients who'd had a heart attack were usually admitted directly to the ward or a private room. There was no way to monitor them while they were convalescing other than keeping them hooked up to an ECG machine. And that wasn't practical for someone who was already ambulating. It was not uncommon for such patients to die suddenly because we could not always predict or detect a potentially fatal rhythm disturbance after they had been unhooked from their ECG machine.

I always worried about that, and was always on the lookout for some way to monitor the electrocardiogram in a post–heart attack patient who was walking about.

One day I read that scientists at the National Aeronautics and Space Administration (NASA) had attached to one of the monkeys they'd sent into space a portable ECG that could transmit a tracing by means of an FM radio signal. There was no wiring and no tethering—exactly what I had in mind to monitor ambulatory cardiac patients. I contacted NASA about it and was put in touch with William Thornton, a young engineer involved in this project. He and I discussed his work on the phone, and he agreed to come to New York for more in-depth discussions. Our goal was to design a device to transmit the ECG of in-hospital ambulatory patients by means of an FM radio signal so that they could be monitored without being attached to an ECG machine.

Thornton arrived shortly thereafter to discuss the details of our project. After a few days, he then went back to his lab to work on it and came back two weeks later with prototype equipment similar to what the space monkeys had worn. We began testing these transmitters on some in-hospital patients. Our early FM models had problems with drifting, similar to what sometimes happens when you're listening to music on an FM radio station. This made it very difficult to interpret the electrocardiogram. Thornton went back to work on the problem and returned once more with a new and improved unit. It worked perfectly, and since then, hospitals everywhere have been able to monitor patients while they are walking about. Any arrhythmia they develop is instantly seen at the nursing station and treated then and there. The original equipment has been refined over the years, but to the best of my knowledge, ours was the initial prototype. Its use has dramatically reduced the postcoronary death rate.

Bill Thornton is, in my opinion, one of the outstanding medical technology scientists of my generation and deserves all the credit for this advance. He was in his early thirties when I met him, a shy, balding, gangling young man. After working together in the hospital all day, we'd go back to my apartment, where Bill would spend the night. The day he was returning to Houston, he'd leave at the crack of dawn and walk on tiptoes to our front door in order not to wake my wife and me, or any of our children. The problem was that this great scientist invariably lost his way in my apartment. Our bedroom was at the end of a long corridor in the opposite direction from the elevator. Bill almost always ended up in our bedroom. I found his difficulty finding his way in my home of particular interest in view of the nature of his future career.

One day I gave Bill some important advice. "I'm not the key man in our project, Bill. It's your engineering skill that's making it happen; my job is simply to tell you what doctors need. But when we publish our work, I'll get most of the credit, not you, because I have an M.D. behind my name, and you don't. Bill, you're going to make many great contributions to medical technology in the years to come, and I'd like to see you, not some hanger-on doctor like me, get the credit for it. You're still in your thirties. It's not too late for you to study medicine. Take my advice. Invest four years of your life and get an M.D. degree."

He listened. That very year he entered the School of Medicine at the University of North Carolina and four years later received his M.D. degree. Dr. William Thornton had no burning desire to treat the sick. He was first and foremost an engineer, and his interest and expertise was in devising tools to help other doctors. After graduation, he remained in the air force and continued his research on various monitoring and other devices at Lackland Air Force Base. He made fundamental contributions to the development of the Holter machine (the unit that records your ECG during a twenty-four-hour period while you're going about your business), even though it doesn't bear his name.

Bill Thornton, who couldn't find his way out of my dark apartment, later became the first medical astronaut and actually orbited the Earth—not once, but three times. And to my surprise, he always landed back on Earth in the right place at the right time!

In the course of his brilliant and daring career, Bill made many major discoveries; he invented equipment that's used not only in cardiology, but also in many other areas of medicine. Here's just one example: Have you ever wondered what happens when astronauts move their bowels in space, given the absence of gravity? Don't ask me how he did it, but Bill Thornton figured it out and designed a commode that makes it possible.

One of the most thrilling experiences in my life was watching Bill Thornton launched into space. And I will always cherish the memento he sent me of his first flight. It's a framed photograph of his shuttle, with a view of the Earth below, and the actual arm patch that he wore on his uniform. The picture is inscribed "To Dr. Rosenfeld, Thanks for the knowledge I took with me into space."

Recently the medical school where I have taught for years, Weill Cornell, named Thornton, whom I had persuaded to become a doctor in the first place, the Rosenfeld Visiting Professor in Cardiology. What a great climax to a wonderful relationship that started between two young men so many years ago! Bill is now retired from the air force, but is not spending his time reminiscing in a rocking chair: he's teaching medical students in Texas. Thanks to him, we can look forward to a whole new generation of doctors whom he will surely inspire, as he did me.

There's an interesting twist to this monitor story. When the first remote ECG unit became available, my wife and I demonstrated it at a meeting of the American Heart Association. I was hooked up to the transmitter, and Camilla handled the screen on which my ECG tracing would be displayed as I walked around the huge auditorium. Doctors crowded around, excited to see a tracing from someone hundreds of yards away. Suddenly, one physician asked my wife who was wearing the monitor. When she asked him why he wanted to know, he pointed to the many ventricular premature contractions (extra beats) on the screen. "Whoever is wearing the monitor has got a problem," he told her. "It's my husband!" she said. "Well, you'd better get him over here and show him his arrhythmia." She found me and brought me back to the screen. I was smoking a cigarette, and every time I inhaled, more of these extra beats appeared. I was shocked (scared is more accurate)! I took the cigarette out of my mouth, removed the package from my shirt pocket, and threw them both away. I have not smoked a single cigarette since! That was 12:30 p.m. on April 12, 1960. I never expected that a device I helped introduce would one day add years to my own life.

27

SWEET DREAMS

I often hear some of my colleagues who also teach at my medical school warning their students not to become emotionally involved with their patients' illnesses, presumably in order to maintain their objectivity. That may be true theoretically, but I don't know how any doctor who really cares for his or her patients can shield himself in that way. A recent experience of mine convinced me that worrying about a patient also means thinking what more you can do. That's a good thing—for everyone concerned—as this next story illustrates.

Noel was in his early eighties, a good friend of mine, and not my patient. He seemed to be in good health. He called me one day in August to tell me that he had some aches and pains, nothing very serious, and that his own doctor was on vacation. Would I help him with this problem? Dealing with such nonspecific symptoms is not my forte, so I referred him to one of my rheumatology friends, who examined Noel and reported to me that he thought his symptoms were due to muscle spasm. He was sure they would respond to massage, exercise, any of the over-the-counter painkillers—and time. Noel would feel better in a few days. He didn't, and called me about ten days later to say that he was feeling much worse. His legs were now so weak he could barely get out of a chair; he had no appetite, and he was losing weight. I called his doctor's office and had the secretary forward Noel's chart to me, hoping that I'd find some clue in his earlier workups. His doctor had done complete routine evaluations over the years, the last one only a couple of months ago. All his blood tests—liver, sugar, kidney function, thyroid—were completely normal. Noel had also had a colonoscopy fairly recently, and it was normal too, as were his chest film and electrocardiogram.

I thought I ought to see Noel myself to try to put things together. A thorough physical examination was unremarkable except for the loss of seven or eight pounds since he'd last been weighed by his own physician. His blood pressure, electrocardiogram, routine screening blood tests, blood count, and urine were all normal. There was no blood in his stool specimen.

I couldn't quite put my finger on it, but he looked sick, and I was uneasy about it. However, I reassured him and arranged for him to see a gastroenterologist about his poor appetite and weight loss. That specialist did not find any abnormalities either.

As the weeks went by, Noel's condition continued to deteriorate. His aches and pains had now spread throughout his body; he was down almost forty pounds and weaker than ever. He now even had to be helped off the toilet. I had him consult a cancer specialist to rule out an underlying malignancy. Every single test came back negative. Finally, his condition deteriorated so much that I admitted him to the hospital for a complete evaluation by all the doctors involved in his care. We found nothing. After six days, it was the consensus that he must have an underlying cancer somewhere and that there was no point in keeping him in the hospital. We sent him home with twenty-four-hour nursing care, convinced that at some point the malignancy everyone was sure he had would declare itself in some recognizable way.

After he was discharged from the hospital, I visited Noel at his home every couple of days. These visits took a toll on me, too; I couldn't bear seeing him so sick while I stood by helplessly. Every time I came to his home, he was weaker and thinner. He was now bedridden and had lost some eighty-five pounds. I couldn't get him out of my mind. Believe it or not, I even dreamt about him.

One night, while tossing, turning, and thinking about Noel, a thought suddenly entered my mind! I remembered reading about a condition called "formefruste hyperthyroidism," overactivity of the thyroid gland without the typical telltale signs and symptoms of this disorder—a rapid heart rate, heat intolerance, an enlarged thyroid gland, bulging eyes, and nervousness. Could this be Noel's problem? I got out of bed at 3 a.m. and went to my library to look up this condition. Everything I read suggested that Noel might have this form of hyperthyroidism that often presents with weight loss and diffuse muscle aches and pains.

It was a long shot, but at 9:01 that morning, I called my office and asked my technician to go to Noel's home immediately, draw a complete thyroid blood profile, and send it to the lab with a request that the analysis be done as soon as possible. That afternoon, at four o'clock, I learned that Noel's thyroid numbers were off the wall! I personally took him to the hospital to see the one doctor we had not consulted—a thyroid specialist. He examined the thyroid gland and found it to be physically normal. However, the blood tests were incontrovertible. We immediately started antithyroid medication—and the rest is history. Within two weeks, Noel had regained twenty-five pounds, his aches and pains had cleared, and all his other puzzling symptoms disappeared. Within six weeks, he was back to his old self.

I suppose that ultimately the right diagnosis might have been made without my "dream." It's much more likely, however, that Noel would have died because he had been written off until his cancer declared itself. The message from this experience is that I would not have dreamed about this patient if I hadn't cared about him.

And by the way, you can be sure I will never miss a diagnosis of formefruste hyperthyroidism again—and neither will any of the many doctors involved in this case.

28

A Psychiatrist
with Two Hats

Erich Fromm was, in my opinion, one of the great psychiatrists, philosophers, and thinkers of the twentieth century. He was also my friend and patient. He lived mostly in Mexico and Switzerland and spent two months every year in New York. When he was in New York, he would come to our apartment every Sunday morning just to talk about the "world." What a treat it was for me to listen to him—his wisdom and knowledge were awesome.

Fromm had grown up in an orthodox Jewish family in Frankfurt, Germany, and was smart and lucky enough to flee the Third Reich in 1933. Early in life he had studied the Talmud and could recite it chapter and verse, but later became disenchanted with organized religion. However, even though he was a confirmed atheist when I met him, I found him almost godlike in his love and caring for mankind. Although he did embrace some aspects of Marxism, he was powerfully antiauthoritarian and an outspoken opponent of the Soviet regime. He earned his living both as an analyst and author.

In 1956, Fromm published his most popular book, *The Art of Loving,* which can still be found in most bookstores. His later work *The Anatomy of Human Destructiveness* reflects his attempt to cope with and understand the impact of the Second World War on the world's psychology. He published several other best sellers that fused politics, psychology, religion, history, and philosophy into a seamless humanist perspective of life. He also authored a trenchant critique of Sigmund Freud, provided ardent support for "secular humanism," and cofounded SANE, an international peace organization. He was an intellectual hero to millions around the world, and remains one thirty years after his death at the age of eighty.

In his later years, Fromm became skeptical about psychoanalysis, just as he had with formal religion. He felt that many practicing psychiatrists and psychologists do not have the knowledge, motivation, or training to guide those in emotional distress. He believed that for most people with behavioral problems, pharmacological agents are more effective than psychotherapy—which makes the following story all the more interesting.

When our oldest son was twelve years old, we began to make preparations for his bar mitzvah—his coming of age as a Jewish adult. The bar mitzvah is an inviolable Jewish tradition. My brother and I both had one, as did my father and my wife's father. In fact, every male Rosenfeld in recorded history has had a bar mitzvah. My wife and I never expected that our son Arthur would be the first exception. However, one day he announced to us, "I'm not going to have a bar mitzvah because I've learned your secret."

"Oh? And what is it?" I asked.

"Our family is not Jewish."

"Really? How so?" I asked, somewhat shocked, to say the least. Had all my tormentors in Quebec and those who applied the Jewish quota to me when I applied to medical school been mistaken?

"Because we never go to temple; mother never lights the Sabbath candles, we never pray together—all the things that my Jewish friends do."

He had a point. We are ethnic Jews, but do not pursue the trappings of religion. "So I don't see any point in my having a bar mitzvah."

Camilla and I never forced our children to do anything against their will. All four have grown up to be happy and successful men and women. But when Arthur revolted that day, I was sorely tempted to lay down the law. Although neither my ancestors nor I understood any of the Hebrew chants that we performed during our bar mitzvah rituals, we accepted the fact that Jewish boys had to do this in order to officially become men.

Arthur did not agree. As far as he was concerned, he had become a man at eleven or twelve and didn't have to wait until he was thirteen for a rabbi to confirm it.

During one of our Sunday discussion sessions, I asked Dr. Fromm how to handle this crisis. I fully expected that, given his own atheistic bent, he would sympathize with Arthur. He thought for a moment and then said, "I have a solution for you. I know a man who used to be a rabbi. He gave it up because he could not accept the dogma that went along with his job. But he knows a great deal about Jewish history and ritual and is perfectly competent to prepare Arthur for his bar mitzvah. Your son might find him more acceptable than someone who is a religious professional. I know how you feel, so I'll have this man call you to arrange to meet Arthur and perhaps persuade him to go through with the ceremony."

The Rabbi Is a Postal Clerk!

I was very grateful that Dr. Fromm did not launch into a discourse about why bar mitzvahs are a waste of time. He went out of his way to help me, and a few days later, Arthur's mentor-to-be called me. "Dr. Fromm has told me of your situation, and I would like to help."

"Thank-you very much, Rabbi. This means a great deal to my wife and me. By the way, what are you doing now that you're no longer in the rabbinate?"

His answer floored me. "Oh ho, you'll never guess," he bellowed with glee. "I have the most exciting and satisfying job imaginable. Every morning, after I wake up, I can't wait to go to work in the main post office! I get there by six o'clock, sort the mail, and put it in bags. Then I tag each sack with its destination—Chicago, New York, Pittsburgh, to every city in the world! Then I haul them all out to the platform and personally throw them directly onto the trucks. No one helps me! It's all me! I say good-bye to each and every sack and wish it a happy journey. You can't believe the satisfaction this gives me, how wonderful it is to know that I'm doing something that will give pleasure to thousands of people. That platform with its sacks of mail is my threshold to the world. I have fulfilled my destiny!"

I listened incredulously. Could this sack-throwing rabbinical postman be the same man whom the famous Dr. Fromm recommended to prepare my son for his bar mitzvah?

"Thanks for calling, Rabbi," I said. "Our plans have changed. I'll get back to you. Don't bother calling us. I know how busy you are."

I hung up and let him continue to fulfill his destiny on the post office platform. I then phoned Fromm. "Erich, were you kidding about that so-called rabbi?" I figured that maybe my analyst friend was paying me back for some of the practical jokes I had played on him over the years.

"What do you mean 'kidding'?" he asked. "Did you speak to him?"

"Erich, the guy's a nut—a schizophrenic!"

"What do you mean 'schizophrenic'? I've known him for years. He's as sane as you or I."

"Look Erich, you're the analyst. I'm just a doctor, but take it from me, that guy's got a screw loose. He's fulfilling his destiny by throwing sacks of mail onto the back of a truck!"

"He must have been kidding you," Fromm said.

"Erich, if he was kidding me, he should have his own TV talk show. The guy's mentally sick." I had the temerity to tell the world-famous analyst I was right and he was wrong about a psychiatric patient! And that's where we left it.

A few days later, Fromm called me. "You know, you were right. I had lunch with the rabbi. He's schizophrenic all right."

"Erich, how could you, of all people, miss recognizing that?"

He was chagrined. "There's no excuse except that I had only met him on social occasions—cocktail parties or a dinner at someone's house. It was never apparent to me."

"But wouldn't you have been tipped off just talking to him? It wouldn't have taken much."

Here was Fromm's classic answer, one that I'll never forget. "When I'm not in my office in my professional capacity, I don't wear my analyst's hat!"

That surprised me because, like most people, I've always thought that psychiatrists could see right through you. I've always been careful, sometimes even uncomfortable in their presence, assuming they are analyzing my every word—and drawing the wrong conclusions. I'm relieved to be able to tell you that that's apparently not so, at least if Erich Fromm is any example.

When I'm at a party, I can spot someone with emphysema or Parkinson's disease. I can even recognize a skin cancer on the face or some other exposed part of the body. They're as obvious to me as that schizophrenic man should have been to Erich Fromm. Do psychiatrists then have a different mind-set than "physical" doctors like myself, who always wear their "doctor's" hat? I don't think so. Frankly, I think the great Dr. Fromm simply missed the diagnosis. But that is something we *all* do, now and then.

29

YOU LOSE SOME, YOU WIN SOME

One of my patients, whom I shall refer to as Alfred (his family does not want me to use his name), was a brilliant TV personality. He was attractive, worldly, intelligent, and a good friend. He often included me among the guests he frequently interviewed—politicians, journalists, authors, and doctors—anyone making news. Alfred and I had mutual respect and affection for each other. One of his passionate interests was how hospitals cared for patients. He believed fervently in patients' rights; he was angry at the system and convinced that people were pushed around and often neglected in hospitals. I thought he was right about some of his complaints but that his ire was exaggerated. Whenever the subject came up, he reminded me that he, personally, would *never* agree to be hospitalized, no matter how sick he was.

Fortunately, Alfred remained in relatively good health for many years. However, as he grew older, he began to develop vascular problems in his heart and legs which I was able to treat without hospitalization.

One evening, I received a call from a doctor in Montreal, where Alfred had gone to make a film. While on the set, he had suddenly developed chest pain and was taken by ambulance to a very good hospital. The doctor informed me that Alfred had suffered a heart attack, but there were no complications and he was in stable condition. If all went well, he expected to discharge him in a week or so.

The right treatment during the first few days after a heart attack is very important, not only for survival but also to reduce permanent damage to the cardiac muscle.

When the doctor had finished speaking with me, he passed the phone to Alfred and left the room.

"Listen, if this guy thinks I'm going to stay here, he's crazy. I feel fine. I have no more pain, and there's no reason for me not to come home," Alfred said.

I warned my friend that it would be very dangerous for him to leave the hospital, and especially to fly back to New York, within hours of having had a heart attack. I told him that he might as well stay where he was because I'd put him right back in the hospital if and when he got here. The "if" was not lost on Alfred.

"Well, that's something we can negotiate when I get back. In the meantime, I'm signing myself out of here in a few minutes. I'll stay in a hotel tonight and get the first plane back to New York in the morning. I'll be in your office before noon."

I started to protest, but the line went dead. I didn't even know where he was spending the night. There was no way for me to stop his folly.

Shortly before noon the next day, a cheerful Alfred arrived at my office as promised. He was all smiles. "I told you," he taunted, "you doctors are all Cassandras. I had a little pain, it cleared up, and I'm fine. Never thought I'd make it, did you? OK, what now?"

I listened to his description of the painful chest pressure he had experienced the day before; I looked at the ECGs and all the other data he'd brought with him from the hospital in Montreal; I examined him carefully and took another tracing. "Alfred, you're playing with fire," I told him. And then I issued a warning, something I rarely do, "Unless you listen to me, Alfred, you're going to die. I don't want that to happen. You're not only my patient, you're also my friend. Please come to the hospital with me right now. I'll take you there myself. I'll get you the best room with the best nurses. I'll send you home the minute it's safe to do so. We'll either get an angiogram or observe you very carefully for a while. Please, Alfred, do it for me."

He smiled. "I love you, doctor, but you're making a mountain out of a molehill. Don't worry, we'll remain friends, but I've got to find another doctor. I can't be your patient anymore. You just don't seem to understand what makes me tick."

"Alfred," I remonstrated, "it's because I want to keep you ticking that I'm telling you this." It was no use. He said good-bye, we shook hands, and he left. I believe he did see another doctor the next day, but I don't know who it was or what he was told. The bottom line is that two days later, Alfred was found dead in the elevator of his apartment house.

I think of this man very often. What a pity that he was so conditioned by fear that he rejected what a man of his intelligence must have known was the only right course for him to follow.

Alfred didn't have to die. All too often patients erect a barrier that even the most conscientious doctor cannot penetrate. Despite Alfred's sad story, superstition and fear can be overcome and reason can prevail. Thankfully, for every stubborn friend that I could not help, there have been many I could.

A Similar Story with a Different Ending

After Alfred's death I promised myself that I would try to communicate more effectively with patients who were still well but whose lives were threatened by fear and superstition so that they would do the right thing in an emergency. This resolve was soon tested by a man I'll call Martin. A psychiatrist in his sixties, he'd had a heart attack several years earlier, but was now feeling fine and working hard without any symptoms. This is the case with most people who've survived a heart attack. Martin wanted to be my patient; he wanted me to advise him about lifestyle, medication, and anything else that might prevent another heart attack. He continued to enjoy good health for several years, and stopped practicing medicine in order to pursue a business opportunity. Bright, ambitious, and energetic, he became extremely successful and very rich.

He remained perfectly well for about ten years after his first visit to me, but then developed some minor abnormalities in his ECG. Even a slight change in someone who's had a heart attack is worrisome. I scheduled his office visits at more frequent intervals to monitor the progress of his disease. One day he complained of some shortness of breath that he attributed to the eight pounds he'd gained since his last visit. He promised to lose them before his next scheduled appointment. He came back a few weeks later, looking noticeably thinner, but told me that he was still short of breath when he "did a little too much." He was now also experiencing an "awareness" in his chest when he walked briskly outdoors. I had him do a stress test, which had previously always been normal. This one was not. It was time to intervene more aggressively. "Martin," I told him, "I think you ought to have an angiogram so that we can look at your arteries to see if anything needs to be done. I'm worried about these symptoms, especially now that your stress test is abnormal."

That's when Martin dropped his Alfred-like bombshell. "I will never have an angiogram," he told me in no uncertain terms. "There's no point in doing it because no matter what you find, I will never, ever consider heart surgery." (This was before the days of angioplasty.)

"Why not?" I asked. "You know how successful bypass operations are when performed by experienced surgeons. And I'll have the best one do yours if it turns out to be necessary."

"I know all that. Surgery may be good for the rest of the world, but not for me. You see, I know that I will never survive the operation."

"What the devil are you talking about?" I asked. I couldn't believe what he was telling me.

He replied, "Ever since the prospect of surgery became a possibility, I've had a strong intuition, premonition, call it what you will, that I would die on the operating table. That conviction has grown stronger with every passing year. I simply will not have an operation—under any circumstances. And you'd better accept that fact. It's not negotiable."

No one looks forward to having heart surgery, but most patients who need it eventually accept it. Not Martin. I was amazed. Here was an educated patient, and a doctor to boot, who simply would not listen to reason. He was convinced he would die and that's all there was to it. It was entirely irrational. He didn't tell me how or why he developed this phobia; it was probably a dream he'd had a long time ago.

Arguing or upsetting him emotionally at this point would only worsen his angina, so I dropped the subject for the time being and continued to check him carefully at even more frequent intervals, adjusted his therapy, and did whatever I could to improve his circulation. He was very cooperative; he'd do anything except undergo heart surgery.

Over the next few weeks his symptoms became more frequent and severe. I now feared for his life. Enough was enough; I could humor him no longer. I decided not to mince any words. "Martin, I've gone along with this *mishigas* (Yiddish for 'lunacy') as long as I could. I've done everything possible to protect you. Unless we get an angiogram *now*, find out what's wrong with your coronaries, and fix it, you're going to have another heart attack—or worse. I can't take that responsibility. If you won't accept my recommendation, then you'll have to find another doctor. I won't stand by and see you kill yourself."

He was clearly torn—and frightened. "OK," he said. "I can't fight you because my family won't back me on this. My wife is pressuring me to go ahead with the angiogram. No one believes me when I tell them that I will certainly die."

I seized this momentary weakness and scheduled him for an angiogram that week. I've never seen anyone so scared about this relatively safe procedure. Thankfully, it went smoothly, and he was relieved when the ordeal was over.

"See?" I said to him in the cath lab when the test was finished. "I told you there was nothing to it."

"It's not the angiogram I was afraid of. It's what it will show that worries me. If I need a bypass, it will kill me."

I went down to the viewing room after the film was developed. It showed critical narrowing of all three coronary arteries, as well as a significant blockage in the left main vessel, the artery from which two of the three coronaries come off. When that vessel closes, its two tributaries that supply most of the heart have no blood supply. The result is usually a massive heart attack. My patient urgently needed bypass surgery. I went back to his room to tell him that there was no alternative to an operation.

When he heard the "verdict," he seemed resigned to it and agreed to have the operation. In order not to prolong his anxiety and afraid that he might change his mind, I arranged for the operation to be done the very next morning.

He remained in the hospital and asked me to come to his hospital room that night. I got there at eight o'clock and found his entire family by his bedside—his wife, two children, their spouses, four grandchildren, and his lawyer—all there to say good-bye. I'll never forget that scene (it was more like a wake) and his farewell speech. After all the assertions of love for his family, he turned to me and said, "I know you're doing what you think is right. I am irrevocably convinced that this operation will kill me, but neither you nor my family believes me, and I'm prepared to go ahead with it. I wanted you here, doctor, so that you can hear me tell my family that I am not blaming you for my death. To prove it, I've asked my lawyer to come here tonight so that I can add a codicil to my will, in which I'm leaving you fifty thousand dollars after I die." (I noticed that he said "after," not "if.")

Frankly, this made me very uncomfortable. Doctors recommend what they believe to be best for their patients, but there's just so much responsibility one can take. I suggested a second opinion. He refused it because he wasn't questioning my diagnosis or recommendation. He knew he needed the surgery but was terrified and unable to control his fear. I was sorely tempted to tell him that I'd had enough and that he could do whatever he wanted. But having gone this far, I reassured him once more, watched him sign his will, said good night, and left.

I came by early the next morning to escort him to the operating room and remained there during the entire procedure. After the surgeon opened the chest and exposed the heart, I had rarely seen such diseased arteries. The surgery went without a hitch. Later that day, when Martin awoke from the anesthesia, he was genuinely surprised to find himself not in heaven or anywhere else but right here on earth.

Today, in 2009, he is eighty-nine years old, still active at his work, and totally symptom-free. His chest pain is only a memory, his ECG and stress test are normal, and he plays tennis every weekend (doubles). We often reminisce and laugh about his superstition, thankful that he was wrong. And it's the only time in my life I was happy to forego a fifty-thousand-dollar windfall.

There is no question in my mind that had Alfred dealt with his phobia as well as Martin had with his, he too would be alive today.

But There Are Times When a Doctor Is Helpless

1999: A woman in her early seventies, who had been my patient for many years, came to see me for a routine checkup. She'd always been cheerful and optimistic; today she was quiet and looked very sad. She was also a lot thinner than the last time I'd seen her several months earlier. When I commented about her weight loss, she admitted that she'd dropped about fifteen pounds in the past month. She said that her appetite was good, but she was too depressed to eat. Then she became silent, answering my questions in monosyllables— not responding to my attempts at humor, as she usually did. She clearly was not ready to tell me what was troubling her. So we just sat and made some small talk for a few minutes.

I subtly explored several potential reasons for her apparent profound sadness: Was it rooted in a failed friendship or financial problems? Apparently not. And then suddenly she opened up. She burst forth with a torrent of words and an outpouring of emotion and tears that caught me off guard.

"For thirty years my youngest daughter was happily married to a man who had always been in excellent health. However, in the past few months his appearance changed radically: his face lost its fullness, he tired very easily, and he could no longer do his usual thirty minutes on the treadmill every morning. He had no fever or pain, no lumps or bleeding to suggest cancer, nor any chest pressure or shortness of breath due to heart trouble, yet there was obviously something terribly wrong. After a few visits to his doctor, he was diagnosed with myotonic dystrophy, which he was told is a progressive muscle disease caused by a defective gene. The doctor said that other muscles in his body would probably soon be affected."

Myotonia is an abnormally slow relaxation of muscles after they have contracted. So when someone with this disorder shakes your hand, he or she may have trouble relaxing the grip and letting go; after chewing food vigorously, the jaw may lock painfully. The affected muscles also become weak. When the facial muscles are involved, these unfortunate individuals often lose their facial expression. They often have cataracts, too, especially adults, and the heart muscle may also become weak. Myotonic dystrophy is a terrible disease.

This poor man would eventually end up with at least some of the foregoing symptoms, as well as lung problems and difficulty swallowing. Tragically, there is no cure for myotonic dystrophy. My patient's son-in-law's sudden illness was enough to cause her emotional devastation.

But there's more to the story.

The defective gene that causes myotonic dystrophy is transmitted from generation to generation. To make matters worse, this gene is "dominant," which means that receiving it from just one parent can give you the disorder. If either your father or your mother has it, there is a 50 percent chance of your developing myotonic dystrophy, too.

My patient managed to continue with her sad tale:

"When my son-in-law heard his diagnosis and all that it implied, he had his children undergo genetic testing to see if any of them also had this gene. You won't believe this—eight of his nine children tested positive, including my youngest granddaughter, a beautiful young woman of nineteen who was engaged to be married in a few weeks. We were all so happy planning the event: bridal showers, stag parties, meetings with the pastor, and house hunting. This lovely young couple was filled with expectations of a wonderful, long life together—all shattered, for when told about the medical findings, the groom's parents convinced their son to call off the wedding."

My patient stopped and stared at the floor. She couldn't go on. She was living with the fact that eight of her nine grandchildren, along with her son-in-law, were all doomed! This was reason for her insomnia, weight loss, and sadness. There was no way I could help her. All I could do was hold her hand as we shed tears together.

I'm sure that with all the advances in gene therapy, there will one day be a cure for this terrible disease. But this was years ago, and it was already too late for that family.

30

WAS I WRONG?

1 986: A very prominent and wealthy European financier, influential in his country's political circles, had been my patient for several years. I liked him; he was humble, sincere, and totally unpretentious. One day I read in a front-page story in the *New York Times* that he was implicated in several major financial scandals, and that he was rumored to be a mafia front man and the kingpin in several vast schemes of criminal corruption. I found it hard to believe any of this, but I was wrong. He was tried in this country, found guilty, and sentenced to a federal penitentiary. This one-time friend and mogul was now washing dishes in a jail somewhere in the Midwest.

Because many of his crimes were committed in his native land, its government was unrelenting in its attempts to extradite him. He was brought under guard for a hearing in New York and imprisoned in a federal detention facility during these extradition hearings. One night he took a lethal dose of digitalis to end his life. I don't know who provided it to him or how it was smuggled into the jail.

Digitalis is widely used to help regulate certain cardiac arrhythmias and to strengthen a weakened heart muscle. However, amounts even only slightly more than those prescribed can be toxic. The huge quantities he took quickly caused his death by causing a fatal cardiac arrhythmia.

My patient was found unconscious in his prison cell and brought to a hospital in lower New York City. His family, living here during his judicial proceedings, called me at home near midnight to tell me that he was near death and asked for my help. I rushed to the hospital emergency room to find it filled with police and federal marshals. There I witnessed one of the saddest sights of my life. This elegant man I remembered with such affection was lying on a bare examining table wearing only a pair of soiled undershorts. He was semiconscious, foaming at the mouth, and thrashing about uncontrollably. I examined him briefly, looked at his ECG, and diagnosed digitalis intoxication, which was confirmed by a drug blood level measured in the hospital laboratory.

There was no cure for digitalis poisoning in 1986, which is why it was so often used by sophisticated people who wanted to do away with themselves (or others). As I stood looking at him in desperation, I remembered reading a recent report that researchers had come up with an antidote to digitalis overdosing. I couldn't remember who they were or where they had made their discovery—and this was before the days of Google. With this man closer to death as each minute went by, despite the late hour I began desperately calling some of my cardiologist colleagues who might be of help. I hit pay dirt on the fifth call! One of my doctor friends at New York Hospital remembered reading the study. He told me it had been done by an acquaintance of his at Harvard. He wasn't sure at which hospital the research had been carried out, but he thought it was the Massachusetts General. Armed with this skimpy information, I called Mass General, told the operator that this was an emergency, and asked to be connected to this doctor's home. Thankfully, she agreed, and a very surprised, sleepy physician answered the phone. I described the problem to him and asked if he could make available some of the drug he'd found that reverses digitalis toxicity. If so, the government would send a plane for it immediately. He was wonderful! He went right to his lab and sent us what we needed by private jet provided by the federal government. I received it four hours after my call and administered it immediately. It is an antibody to digitalis (Digibind) that removes the digitalis from the body.

I remained in the holding area of the emergency room with my patient, who was under guard. His cardiac rhythm gradually returned to normal, and he awakened in a couple of hours!

Normally, a patient is grateful when a doctor saves his life. Sometimes, even when someone tries to commit suicide, they have second thoughts and are happy that they failed. Not this man! I'll never forget his rage. He accused me of betraying him when he learned what I had done. "Why?" he asked. "Why did you interfere with what I wanted so badly to do? Why did you spoil my plan? What is my life worth? Why have you prolonged my suffering? I thought you were my friend."

I had no answer, and to this day I regret saving this man's life. A few weeks later, he was extradited by his country, jailed, and murdered in the prison to which he had been sent.

What would you have done in my place?

31

DANNY KAYE

A Third Opinion Might Have Saved His Life

Every case adds to a doctor's experience, knowledge, and judgment. Danny Kaye's case was no exception. For the last twenty-five years of his life, he and I were as close as brothers. This brilliant entertainer of stage and film was my hero on the screen long before he became my very special friend and patient.

In 1964, I was invited to Mary Lasker's annual Christmas party at her beautiful town house in New York. Mary was the Florence Nightingale of American medicine; Mary's charm and assets greatly furthered medical research in this country. She eventually received the highest civilian award our country can bestow, the Congressional Gold Medal. Her party invitation list almost always included America's political, medical, social, entertainment, and business elite, and sometimes even the president and first lady. Because she was my patient and friend, she invited me too.

That night, while I was mingling with an assortment of the rich and famous at her home, I spotted the actor and comedian who had been my idol for as long as I could remember! Even though I was not prone to hero worship, I asked Mary to introduce us. Danny and I chatted, mostly about medicine and exchanged a few jokes. I was convulsed with laughter at his brilliant imitations of some other guests present that night. That meeting was the beginning of one of the closest friendships of my life.

Danny was born and raised in Brooklyn; his parents, like mine, were Jews from Eastern Europe. He learned his craft as an entertainer while he was still a teenager—working in the Catskills, doing old-school vaudeville shtick on the Borscht Belt. His first big Broadway hit was *Lady in the Dark*, in which he sang the showstopper, "Tchaikovsky," a rapid-fire recitation of the names of a multitude of Russian composers. He went on to star in more than forty films, as well as scores of performances on stage and television. If you're too young to have known about Danny Kaye, do yourself a favor and rent *The Court Jester, The Inspector General, The Secret Life of Walter Mitty, Jakobovsky and the Colonel, White Christmas,* or any one of his films you can lay your hands on! You're in for a real treat.

Danny was the most multitalented person I had ever met. In addition to singing, dancing, acting, and performing hilarious comedy routines, he also conducted symphony orchestras throughout the world (although he could not read music). He was a superb chef, as well as a pilot with a commercial license (he piloted the first DC-10 tour around the world). Despite all these skills, I suspect that had Danny been able to live his life over again, he would have chosen to be a doctor. I really think we became such close friends largely because he loved to discuss medicine. He was interested in every new medical breakthrough and was always asking me for details of my recent experiences. He was so interested in medicine that chatting about show business with me was always taboo.

One day, while Danny was in New York, Dr. Michael DeBakey invited me to give grand rounds at the Methodist Hospital in Houston. I asked Danny to join me.

"Only if you'll come home with me to Los Angeles when you're through in Houston," he stipulated, and I accepted. Going to Danny's house was always a treat, not only because he was the best chef of Chinese food I knew but because his guests were always so interesting.

Danny and I flew to Houston together. On our flight, he posed as a steward on the plane and served cocktails. I think his nose was out of joint when some passengers didn't recognize him, and this caused him to go into one of his comedic routines. During my lecture the next morning, I scanned the audience looking for Danny and didn't see him. I thought that was strange, seeing as how he came to Houston with me ostensibly to hear me speak. What I didn't know was that Dr. DeBakey had invited him to attend a heart operation—and he took the better offer. He could hear me talk anytime, but how often would he be able to see the famous Dr. DeBakey operate on someone's heart?

DeBakey had not only invited him into the operating room but also had him scrub up and watch the operation close-up. Danny stood there enthralled, wearing a surgical cap, gown, mask, and gloves. This was the stuff his dreams were made of! DeBakey asked him to watch carefully while he placed a stitch around a small bleeding vessel in the chest. What happened next turned out to be an unforgettable experience for Danny.

This world-famous heart surgeon then turned to Danny, the actor, handed him the needle holder, pointed to another small bleeder, and said, "Here, you do this one." (He had previously obtained the patient's permission to have Danny put in just one stitch under his scrupulous supervision.)

Danny didn't hesitate for a moment. Leaning forward as if he'd been doing it all his life, he stitched the bleeding vessel absolutely perfectly. No jokes, no shenanigans—and no leaks after he was finished. This wasn't a movie take: This was the real thing. (Much as I liked Danny, this was the only time I disagreed with something Dr. DeBakey did. I would never have allowed a layman to put a stitch in a patient's heart, no matter how talented! Can you imagine the medico-legal consequences, or the cross-examination in court, if that patient had died, for whatever reason?)

DeBakey later told me that Danny was more skilled with his hands and fingers than were many of the numerous residents he had trained over the years. Danny didn't know it, but as he was placing that stitch, a photographer with a long telephoto lens was taking his picture, which DeBakey later presented to him. Danny treasured that photo, and it remained on his bedside table until the day he died.

I was only one of Danny's doctors, because he lived in Los Angeles most of the year. However, from time to time, when he was in New York, he'd ask me to give him a "going over." During one such checkup, I noticed some *minor* abnormalities in his postexercise electrocardiogram. Since he had no symptoms, I suggested he control all his risk factors and let me know if he ever experienced any shortness of breath, chest pain, or pressure on exertion. "These ECG changes are minor and not anything to be concerned about," I said.

"We often see them in normal people. Just watch your weight, be careful about your diet, let's try to lower your cholesterol, continue to exercise regularly, and check your blood pressure from time to time. (He was not a smoker or a diabetic.) I'll have another look at you when you get back to New York."

I was being honest with him about the significance of those changes after exercise in his electrocardiogram. My father-in-law and I had spent the last twenty years working together analyzing the post–stress test ECG, and together, we had published some forty papers in the medical literature on how to interpret the changes that occur after exercise. Most doctors still use our criteria. I was not worried about Danny's stress test. Had I been, I wouldn't have permitted him to leave for California.

A few weeks later, his wife, Sylvia, called me from Beverly Hills. "Danny's just had a coronary bypass operation—and something's gone wrong. Can you come right away?"

I was stunned! Why did he have a bypass, and why didn't he tell me about it? Was it an emergency procedure? Perhaps he'd had a sudden heart attack and there just wasn't time to call me. I couldn't imagine that he would undergo such a major operation unless it was absolutely necessary.

I later learned what happened. After I had told Danny that his stress test was not entirely normal, he consulted another cardiologist in Los Angeles. The test was repeated and the tracing revealed the same changes. The doctor suggested an angiogram to which Danny agreed. It revealed some arterial plaques that were not critical for a man in his late sixties and that could easily have been managed medically, especially since Danny was symptom free. But his doctor informed him that he was a candidate for surgery, and Danny jumped at the chance to be "perfect" again.

Danny was a perfectionist. He told me later that he simply couldn't live with the fact that one or more of his coronary arteries *might* have been narrowed.

Clearly, he was not comfortable with my interpretation of his stress test and was entitled to a second opinion. But in such cases, it's a good idea to discuss that with the first doctor so that the second one has the facts. Patients all too often hold back important information from a second doctor in order to influence the decision. If the two doctors do not agree, then a third opinion may help.

Anyway, that's water under the bridge. Danny had the operation. Unfortunately, in his case, the catheter that is routinely inserted into the urinary bladder before the operation had ruptured an artery and caused a massive hemorrhage into Danny's pelvis. He required an immediate transfusion and ended up needing some *eighty pints of blood* during the bypass procedure—an operation that the surgeon, for some reason, decided to continue despite the heavy bleeding. He may have felt that Danny, after awakening from the anesthesia, would be upset to learn that the operation had not been done.

In the recovery room, when Danny realized his condition was critical, he asked Sylvia to call me. I took the next plane to Los Angeles. When I arrived, Danny was in the recovery room. He looked up at me, smiled, and said amid the sounds of all the support systems to which he was hooked up, "I'm a real *putz*—an idiot. Look what I went and did. What the hell happened?" He didn't understand why he needed all the blood transfusions. "Do you think I'll make it, Is? Boy, I hope they gave me Jewish blood. I want to leave here as smart as when I came in." He was always the comedian.

I examined Danny, reviewed his chart, and concluded that the heart surgery itself had gone well, without complications, despite the urological fiasco. The arteries in question had been successfully bypassed. Barring any unforeseen development, I reassured Danny that he would recover.

What no one knew at the time was that one or more of the eighty units of blood he'd been given contained the hepatitis C virus. He was one of some four million unlucky Americans who were similarly infected from blood transfusions received before 1990. Since then, all blood is tested for the hepatitis C and other liver viruses.

A few weeks after he left the hospital, Danny developed symptoms of hepatitis. He tired easily, lost his appetite, and became jaundiced. He suffered for the next four years and died quietly in his sleep in 1987.

Just as there is a little poison in every medication, so does every surgical operation carry a risk. Despite the favorable statistics associated with any given procedure, none are totally risk free. Before you agree to have any intervention, make sure that (a) it is absolutely necessary, (b) there is no nonsurgical alternative, and (c) whoever is doing the operation is qualified. Even if the risk of death is one in a thousand, it's 100 percent for you if you are that one. Finally, when two doctors disagree about a major decision, a third opinion is a good idea.

32

WHY I (NOW) PAY (MORE) ATTENTION TO A PATIENT'S INTUITION

Zero Mostel was a great actor, both dramatic and comedic. He is probably best remembered for his roles in *Fiddler on the Roof*, *The Producers* (the original nonmusical), and *A Funny Thing Happened on the Way to the Forum*. He was a great, lovable hunk of a man with two major medical problems that cost him his life: he was massively obese, weighing more than three hundred pounds, and he had high blood pressure.

Unlike many comedians, who are introverted, often moody, and reflective when not performing, Zero was always "on," at least with me. Whether it was in my office or socially, he was forever involved in some shtick. Although it was fun being his doctor, I was always apprehensive when he came to my office. For him, nothing was sacred— not my waiting room, my consulting room, or my examining rooms.

For example, he always carried a small marker with him. Whenever he was left alone for a few minutes in my office, he'd busy himself doing a number on my various diplomas hanging on the wall. His main targets were those that attested to the fact that I had given satisfactory evidence of proficiency and was therefore entitled to be a fellow or member of some professional organization or other. Zero would print the word "NOT" or "HASN'T" with his marker on the glass covering the diploma. When he left, my staff had to restore the correct wording. If they missed one, I had a hell of a time explaining it to the next patient. He'd also turn toward the wall the photographs of other stars who were my patients; Danny Kaye and Walter Matthau were his favorite targets. He had another use for his marker. Once, after I asked him to get ready to be examined, I came back to the examining room to find him fully clothed. He had drawn the outline of a body on the examining table paper (actually a very good one since Zero was a fine artist). "Why don't you examine him?" he said. "Let's you and I just talk."

On the rare occasion when he was without his marker or it had run out of ink, he was up to some other mischief. Once, while waiting for me to come into the examining room, he again left his clothes on but this time inserted a flashlight into his trousers and turned it on, and when I came in, he grasped his illuminated crotch, moaning, "Oh, doctor, I have a terrible burning there!"

He was no better behaved in the waiting room. One rainy day, as he was about to leave the office, there was one woman in my waiting room. She was South American and had never seen or heard of Zero Mostel. Like many other celebrities, especially actors, who complain about being bothered by the paparazzi, he resented *not* being recognized. He stared at this poor woman for a moment, and when she still didn't recognize him, he went through some of the facial contortions for which he was famous. He stuck his tongue out, winked at her, wiggled his fingers over his ears, and performed other selections from his hilarious repertoire. These are very funny if you know that Zero is a famous comedian. But if you're a foreigner alone in a doctor's waiting room, being approached by an obvious lunatic can be terrifying. When all these shenanigans failed to generate the kind of response he expected, Zero opened the door to the anteroom, where he'd left his galoshes and umbrella on this rainy day. He returned to the waiting room with one overshoe on his head and the umbrella handle hanging around his neck. As the petrified lady watched, he took his overcoat from the rack, put it on so the buttons were at the back, bowed, and said, "Good-bye, madam. You are about to see a great doctor. He will do for you what he did for me!"—and left.

Over the years, I tried without success to get Zero to lose weight. His extra hundred pounds were his trademark as an actor, and despite them, he was lithe on his feet. However, they were a strain on his heart, lungs, and blood pressure (which was high). It's much more difficult to normalize hypertension in someone who is so heavy, but I was able to do it. His obesity made it difficult to assess his heart size, because the X-rays could not penetrate his very thick chest wall. (In 1977 echocardiograms were not available.)

After his blood pressure was normalized, Zero was really motivated to work on his weight. He reduced his caloric intake and began exercising regularly. To my delight, he began shedding pounds week after week, soon tipping the scales at a mere 235 pounds, down from over 300. He looked and felt great.

One Sunday morning in September, on a beautiful sunny day, he came for lunch to our home in Westchester. He wore a blue suit from Brooks Brothers. "This is the first time since my teens," he said, "that I've been able to buy a suit off the rack."

Later that week he left for Philadelphia to begin rehearsals for *Sweeney Todd*, a new play that was to open on Broadway later in the fall. He'd been there about two weeks when he phoned me. "Doctor, I've got this funny pain in the left side of my back and shoulder when I breathe. Do you think I should come back to New York?" he asked.

"I don't think so, Zero. It's not as if you're somewhere in the boondocks. Philadelphia is a major medical center with excellent doctors and hospitals. Get the name of a good internist, and have him or her examine you. If there's any question, ask him to call me. It sounds like maybe you've got pleurisy—or a viral infection, that's all."

The next day, a physician called me. "I'm Dr. (I can't remember his name), on the faculty of Temple University. I've examined Mr. Mostel and can't find much wrong with him. I think he probably has pleurisy. His temperature, blood work, ECG, and chest X-ray are all normal. I'll give him something for the pain. I'm sure he'll be all right."

Later that evening, Zero called me again. "I just don't feel right. I think I should come back to New York."

"Zero," I said, "I'm always happy to see you, but it seems like such a pity for you to leave the rehearsals for something as benign as what this doctor tells me you have. Let's see how you are tomorrow."

The next day, his doctor called me again. "Zero is really a worrywart. The pain is a little better; he's not coughing and has no fever. His physical exam and ECG are normal. But I'll admit him to the hospital for observation anyway because he's so worried."

Zero called me later that evening from the hospital and told me that he was still uncomfortable, but since the doctor had found nothing wrong with him, he expected to be discharged the following day. He promised to call me in the morning. When I hadn't heard from him by noon the next day, I called his room at the hospital. There was no answer. I asked to be connected to the nurses' desk. "I was calling Mr. Mostel's room, and there's no answer. Has he been discharged?"

"Who are you, sir?" she asked. When I told her, she replied that Mr. Mostel had gone into cardiac arrest. His old friend, the actor Sam Jaffe, was visiting him when he suddenly pitched forward, unconscious. The cardiac team had tried to resuscitate him—without success.

You can imagine how I felt. What could have killed him? Why hadn't I let him come to New York? He must have had some intuitive feeling that made him call me time and again. Full of remorse, I called his doctor and insisted that they do an autopsy. He was just as puzzled as I about the cause of Zero's death. After all, people just don't die from a pain in the chest that's made worse by breathing when all the tests are ostensibly normal.

I was shocked to hear the results of the postmortem exam. Zero had died because of a ruptured aneurysm of the thoracic aorta in the chest. The aorta is the large blood vessel leaving the heart into which the blood is pumped with each cardiac contraction. After it leaves the heart, the aorta courses up and around, giving off major branches to the brain, then descends into the abdomen, where it supplies blood to the kidney and other vital organs.

When the walls of the aorta are weakened (as happens in long-standing, untreated high blood pressure), they eventually balloon out to form an aneurysm. Aneurysms continue to expand until, at some point, they begin to leak and finally burst. An expanding aneurysm, either in the chest or in the belly, can be repaired surgically if diagnosed early enough. When it ruptures, however, death usually ensues very quickly. If it happens while you're in the hospital and it's correctly diagnosed, your life can be saved by an immediate operation. Unfortunately, no one thought about this diagnosis in Zero's case.

Hypertension is a *silent* killer: it does not usually cause symptoms. Although headaches and nosebleeds sometimes do accompany elevated pressures, they are relatively uncommon. There's no way of knowing you have it unless someone takes a reading. I treated Zero's hypertension, but it was too late. He'd apparently been too busy to see any other doctor on a regular basis, and his pressure must have been elevated long enough to damage his aorta, but he was not aware of it. He developed chest pain in Philadelphia because his aneurysm had started to leak and blood was oozing into the walls of the aorta, tearing them apart. His ECG remained normal because the heart itself was not involved. The ruptured aneurysm might have been detected if his doctor had taken the blood pressure in both arms. Normally, the difference in reading is no more than fifteen points. It's much lower in the left arm in the presence of an aneurysm. That is why I always take the blood pressure in both arms and teach my students to do so, too.

If the aneurysm had been diagnosed, it could have been repaired and Zero's life could have been saved. I should have allowed him to come back to New York! It's too bad I paid no attention to his intuition.

I Promise You, Zero, Never Again!

I have never forgotten what killed Zero. I always consider a ruptured aneurysm whenever a patient has "unexplained" chest pain. Recently, this paid off for one of my friends. Henry was about seventy-five years old and in excellent health other than a modestly elevated blood pressure that had responded to medication. One day he called me at the office asking me to prescribe an antibiotic for his cold. Such a request is, unfortunately, still very common even though everyone knows that antibiotics do not help colds and can only result in bacterial resistance to these drugs when you really need them. People seem to think that applies to everyone but them. I asked Henry whether he had a fever, and he said he didn't.

"Why don't you stop by the office at the end of the day and let me take a look at you?" I asked. He came by about 4:30 in the afternoon. He'd made the right diagnosis—he had a cold. His nose was stuffy and running, he had a slight cough but no fever, and his lungs were clear. As he put his shirt back on, he casually mentioned to me that he had a strange pain in his left chest just below the shoulder. It had started earlier that afternoon and didn't seem to be going away. He thought it might have been the result of his playing tennis that weekend. If I hadn't remembered Zero's story so vividly, I'd probably just have taken an ECG and reassured him. Instead, I asked him to tell me a little more about this pain.

"Aw, it's nothing. It'll probably go away."

"I'd better get an ECG anyway," I said.

"I'm sorry I even told you about this. Remember, you took it two weeks ago and it was normal? Do you need the money or something?" (a thought that often goes through patients' minds when we do some test they don't think is necessary).

I ignored his remark and took the tracing anyway. He was right. It was normal. I ignored his smirk.

I then checked the pressure in *both* arms. It was 160/80 in the right arm and 90/60 in the left! I reexamined his chest carefully; everything was normal.

It was now a few minutes after five. I called a nearby radiology office and told them that I had a man with a significant difference in blood pressure in both arms complaining of left-sided chest pain. Would they please do a CAT scan of the chest for me? They suggested he come by at nine o'clock the next morning. If I was right, and he in fact had a dissecting aneurysm, he'd be dead by then. I hung up and called another office and this time asked a special favor. Would they, at this late hour in the day, do a CAT scan on one of my patients in whom I suspected an aneurysm? They accommodated me, and Henry went over to see them. About an hour later, the radiologist called to tell me Henry had a dissecting aortic aneurysm!

I immediately phoned Henry at home. There was no answer. How could I reach this guy? I called his office and got his answering machine. Fortunately I remembered that somewhere in his chart I had written his cell phone number. I called it, and he answered.

"Henry, where are you?"

"I'm down here at a little Italian restaurant on Lexington Avenue having some dinner. Why don't you join us?"

"Henry, get your ass over to the emergency room at the New York–Presbyterian Hospital right away!"

"Doc, you nuts? I haven't even had my dessert yet."

"Forget about the damn dessert and get a cab to the hospital emergency room immediately."

To make a long story short, he was operated on one hour later, the dissecting aneurysm was repaired, and Henry is alive and well today, three years later.

The moral of the story? There is always a reason for chest pain, whether it's from your neck, your belly, your lungs, or your skin (shingles), or an aneurysm. *Every one of these potential causes should be considered* and a final diagnosis made before you leave the doctor's office.

33

THE MEDIA BECKONS

Although my first twenty years in practice were gratifying and exciting, I felt there was something missing in my professional career. I enjoyed teaching, but my only "students" were the ten or fifteen patients in my office every day and the handful of young men and women in my classes at Cornell. That was not enough for me. In my practice, I was often appalled at how little the average patient knows about health matters—even those that affect them personally. The fifty medical papers I had published in peer-reviewed journals and the textbook I coauthored some twenty-five years earlier, *The Electrocardiogram and Chest X-Ray in Diseases of the Heart,* didn't satisfy my urge to communicate. Doctors have many sources of information; it was the layman I wanted to reach. And then it suddenly happened! Here's how:

In 1978, I was examining a seventy-year-old man, a noted magazine editor. He had just sat down on my examining table, and I started his physical exam by probing the space above his left collarbone with my finger. As I continued to do so, he just sat there, looking straight ahead, without any comment or reaction—not the least bit interested or curious. I finally asked him, "Alex, don't you care to know what I'm doing?"

"Frankly," he answered, "I never gave it any thought. I mean, I'm only a patient; you're the doctor."

What he was in effect telling me was that he didn't think it was any of his business to know what I was doing to *his* body. It was precisely this attitude in my patients that had always puzzled me. I think it's important, and also very interesting, for them to understand their medical problems and how their doctor approaches them.

I explained to Alex that this particular area above the left clavicle contains glands that are normally so small that they can't be felt. Their function is to filter the body's lymph fluid that flows through them; in other words, they are sieves. When cancer cells or bacteria are present in this fluid, they are trapped by these glands, which then enlarge so that the doctor can feel them. Lymph fluid to these particular glands comes mainly from the chest and the abdomen, so that an enlarged gland there may indicate a malignancy or infection in the chest or intestines. Something as simple as probing that space can tip me off to the presence of a serious problem. He was fascinated!

I went on to tell him that there were so many other interesting aspects of the physical exam. "For example," I asked, "do you know what doctors are looking for when they ask you to stick out your tongue, or why they strike your knee with a hammer or have you say 'ninety-nine' when they listen to your chest? Why do I, though not an eye specialist, look into your eyes with my ophthalmoscope? What am I looking for?"

"You tell me. Why do you do those things? This is so interesting," he said. And ever the editor, he asked, "Why don't you put this in a book for patients? They'd love it!"

And so I did. In 1978, I wrote *The Complete Medical Exam*, published by Simon & Schuster, the first of my twelve books for the layman. I hoped it would not only satisfy the curiosity of my readers as to what their doctor was doing to and for them during their physical—and why—but, more important, give them the tools to know whether they were getting their "money's worth," whether their checkup was as thorough as it should be. (I'm sorry I didn't call the book *Checkup or Checkout!*) It sold well for a first book by an unknown author.

The Complete Medical Exam led to something much more important than sales. One of the TV programs on which I was interviewed during a nationwide book tour was the nationally syndicated Gary Collins show. Its producers liked my presentation and asked me to be the program's doctor. For the next eight years, I appeared weekly on *Hour Magazine*, dispensing medical advice and information.

For the next thirty years, whether it was the CBS Morning News with Diane Sawyer, or currently the Fox News Network, television has been an integral part of my life. I have not missed a single week on national TV. I suppose that's the reason some call me "America's Doctor" and others consider me primarily a "media doctor." The fact is, however, that TV and writing are my *hobbies*. I am first and foremost a practicing physician, and I continue to see patients full time in my office and the hospital virtually every day.

During those thirty years, I wrote eleven more books for the layman, each with a different and specific theme, based on my practice experience. My second book, in 1981, was *Second Opinion*. I wrote it because I had observed that patients who came to see me for a second opinion about a diagnosis or treatment someone else had given them were often uncomfortable doing so. They asked me not to tell their doctor they'd been to see me; they thought it would be an insult. They didn't want the other doctor to think that they had lost confidence in him or her. When I told some of my colleagues that I would be writing this book to encourage people to get second opinions, some were upset and angry with me because they feared it would cause patients to lose confidence in their physicians. That attitude has changed. Today, most doctors actually encourage their patients to get a second opinion if they have any qualms or doubts about what they've been advised to do. Part of that motivation is probably because they are happy to share responsibility after making a major decision—and avoid litigation should problems arise. Some insurance companies even insist patients obtain a second opinion before reimbursing them for a particular test or surgical procedure.

There's an even more important reason to get a second opinion. I hate to admit it, but present company included, doctors make mistakes. When you're given a hopeless outlook or a diagnosis that can change your life dramatically, or advised to have a major surgical procedure, you are entitled to and should ask for another opinion.

When a "Second Opinion" Paid Off

Shortly after I wrote *Second Opinion,* a man who had recently moved to New York called my office for a new-patient appointment. He was in his early fifties and told my receptionist that there was no rush about it. He was feeling well, but he did have a heart problem and wanted to establish a professional relationship with a cardiologist in the area. We mailed him the usual questionnaire to get some idea of his medical profile and vulnerability.

According to his answers, this man had never been hospitalized and had always felt perfectly well. He stated that he was lucky enough to have had a "sharp" doctor who had detected evidence of "silent" heart disease in the electrocardiogram. I looked forward to meeting him, hearing his story, and interpreting the ECG that had tipped his doctor off to the diagnosis of heart disease.

When he arrived for his appointment, I observed a healthy-looking, relaxed male who actually looked somewhat younger than his stated age of fifty-two. As we chatted, I learned that his family, both on his mother's and father's side, had been long lived. He had none of the usual risk factors for premature heart disease: he didn't smoke, he exercised regularly, he was only slightly overweight, and his blood pressure, cholesterol, and sugar were all normal. "Ironic, isn't it," he said. "Just as my business is beginning to take off, I get the news that I have a bad heart."

"What did you do when the doctor told you about it?" I asked him.

"What could I do? My wife has a little money, and I had saved some; our only child, a son of twenty-two, is almost through college. My life is worth more than my job so I sold my business and retired. My wife didn't want me to take any chances. She preferred a live, poor husband to a wealthier, dead one," he laughed.

"Do you have any symptoms at all that might indicate there is something wrong? Are you prone to indigestion?" I asked. (So often people attribute heart symptoms to "gas" or "acid.") "Nope," he replied. "Nothing at all."

"Do you smoke?"

"Never."

"Did you ask your doctor for a second opinion?"

"Why would I? An ECG is an ECG. Either it's normal or it's not. Right?" The answer, of course, is "Wrong."

Having elicited this sad and puzzling history, I couldn't wait to see what kind of terrible ECG he had without any symptoms that prompted his doctor to give so bleak an outlook.

I stood by the machine as my technician recorded the tracing. His doctor was right; it was "abnormal," *but only in the sense that it didn't have the conventional normal appearance.* However, there is a wide variation of "normal," and unless a doctor knows what that is, he or she can diagnose trouble when none exists. (Remember Mrs. Patiño's *professeur* in Paris?) This man had what we call WPW (Wolff-Parkinson-White) syndrome, a congenital variation in the way the cardiac electrical impulse travels through the heart. The ECG *looks* abnormal, but a well-trained internist or cardiologist can easily recognize the characteristic pattern, which this patient's doctor had failed to do. Although it can cause palpitations, they are easily treated, and WPW is not a threat to life.

I then proceeded to examine this unlucky fellow, and as expected, I found him to be healthy. He was maybe five pounds overweight, his color was good, there were no cholesterol tags on the outside of his eyes or that white ring in the eye itself (both of which may indicate abnormal blood fats), his blood pressure was an excellent 110/72, his heart sounds were strong without any murmurs, and he had a regular heart rhythm. His total cholesterol level was a normal 150, and he was not diabetic. In those days, we did not test for C-reactive protein, a marker of inflammation, which, when elevated, suggests vulnerability to vascular problems even when the cholesterol is normal. Had I been examining this man for a life insurance policy, I'd have cleared him for any amount he wanted (even with his WPW). As far as I was concerned, he was in perfect shape.

This is a dramatic example of how a wrong diagnosis ruined a man's life. Although the doctor made a mistake, it was the patient who made the graver one—by not double-checking his situation with another physician.

I wrote my next book, *Modern Prevention,* in 1986 because I had become aware that doctors and patients alike were becoming more interested in *preventing* disease than treating it. That was much different from the days when I was a medical student, when the emphasis was to teach us how to examine a patient and diagnose an illness; there were few diseases we could prevent. In this second book, I described how to prevent or delay such common killers as heart disease, stroke, certain cancers, adult-onset diabetes, and stomach ulcers. After America's number one "guru," Ann Landers, endorsed *Modern Prevention* in her column, it immediately became a number one *New York Times* best seller (as did every one of my later books that she has recommended).

In 1989, I wrote *Symptoms,* perhaps my most successful book— and one that is still selling today in paperback. Why *Symptoms?* Because of our broken health-care system, men and women were even then having trouble finding or paying for a doctor when they needed one. Many were unsure what a symptom they'd developed meant, and whether it was serious. Without access to a physician, their only option was to go to the nearest emergency room and sit around for eight to ten hours for an answer. So in this book, I interpreted the most common signals that our bodies send—fatigue, weight loss, pain, nausea, cramps, headache, dizziness, weakness of an arm or leg, indigestion—and many others. I tried to indicate which ones suggest an emergency. A few years later, at a black-tie dinner where I received an award from the American Heart Association, Diane Sawyer, the master of ceremonies, introduced me very generously. She told the audience that her favorite book of mine was *Symptoms*. She kept it on her night table and referred to it whenever she wasn't feeling well. What a coincidence, she said, that earlier that very day, she had awakened with some puzzling symptoms; she looked through my book to find out what they might mean. The answer? According to my book, she was having prostate symptoms!

My Book Saved Jack Paar's Life

Diane's reference to *Symptoms* was a joke, but Jack Paar's reading it was not.

Jack Paar was the father of the late-night talk show and a legend in his own time. None of his successors have ever been able to duplicate his inimitable style and effectiveness. It's clear from watching videos of his broadcasts that the secret of his success, in addition to his natural wit, was his ability to listen. Paar did not *compete* with his guests; he stimulated them. And what a range of guests he had— from Fidel Castro and Albert Schweitzer to Richard Nixon and the Kennedy brothers! They all enjoyed the uninterrupted opportunity to portray themselves spontaneously and in depth.

I met Jack in 1989 at a friend's home. I had just written *Symptoms*. Months later, Paar, who was in his early seventies at the time, was awakened one night by an uncomfortable pressure in his chest. He'd never had any problems with his heart and attributed these symptoms to indigestion. He took some liquid antacid and tried to go back to sleep. However, the uncomfortable feeling in his chest persisted, he began to perspire, and he was becoming short of breath. At this point he awakened his wife, Miriam.

"I don't want you to panic, and I think that these symptoms I'm having are only indigestion, but do you remember meeting a

Dr. Rosenfeld a few weeks ago? Well, I bought his book, *Symptoms*. I know it sounds crazy, because I've never had anything wrong with my heart, but what I'm feeling now sounds exactly like his description of a typical heart attack. I have this painful pressure in the center of my chest, I'm short of breath, and—feel my forehead—I'm sweating. Rosenfeld says in his book that if you're over fifty, and even only *suspect* that you may be having a heart attack, to get to the nearest emergency room as soon as possible. They now have drugs that can stop a heart attack in its tracks and prevent a lot of damage. It's almost three in the morning. What do you think, Miriam? Should we see what happens and wait until morning, or get over to the Greenwich Hospital now?"

They dressed immediately and made the only mistake of the evening: she drove him to the hospital instead of calling for an ambulance—as I advise in my book. He was lucky and made it to the hospital without incident. Minutes after he got there, the emergency room doctors determined that he'd had an acute heart attack. Since his symptoms had begun less than three hours earlier, they injected him with tPA, medication that can dissolve the clot obstructing the coronary artery.

That same morning, Miriam called me at home. "Your book just saved Jack's life," she said, and described what had happened during the night. She asked me to come to Greenwich Hospital and see her husband in consultation. When I arrived a few hours later, Jack was feeling much better; his pain was almost gone. However, I was concerned about the persistent abnormalities in his electrocardiogram. When tPA is successful, the chest pain clears completely (Jack still had a little discomfort), and the acute ECG abnormalities subside dramatically. His did not. His doctors and I agreed that the coronary artery that had closed up had been only partially reopened by the tPA, and that Jack needed an angiogram to confirm our clinical impression that he should have an angioplasty, that is, to balloon open the partially obstructed blood vessel.

At the time, angiography was not being done at Greenwich Hospital. The nearest facility was at the nearby White Plains Hospital, but since we had to move Jack anyway, I decided to bring him to my hospital in New York. Time was of the essence, and since it's a one-hour drive by ambulance from Greenwich to Manhattan, I decided to airlift him by helicopter to a landing pad very near New York Hospital.

The flight took about fifteen minutes, and we had Jack in the cath lab within the hour. An angiogram confirmed our suspicions.

The artery that had closed and caused his heart attack was still 80 percent obstructed. That's better than 100 percent, but not good enough. The cardiologist introduced a balloon catheter alongside the clot, inflated it, and pushed the clot aside toward the arterial wall, opening the artery completely.

Paar made an uneventful recovery and left the hospital three or four days later. He recounted his story several times on national TV, often joking that the main reason I had arranged for the helicopter was to get him frequent-flier miles. He remained well and active for several years and then had another arterial closure. This time he required a coronary bypass operation. He lived ten more productive years after that.

In 1991, I wrote *The Best Treatment.* Medicine had been making tremendous strides; many new drugs were becoming available for all kinds of diseases; new and more sophisticated tests were being developed, some of which were very expensive or even risky; there was a host of innovative surgical procedures available to treat a wide variety of conditions. A patient's options were virtually limitless. If you had a given condition, it was essential that you know *all* your options. Unless your own doctor was aware of them, which wasn't always the case, you wouldn't benefit from these advances. I described a wide array of common disorders and illnesses, listed the various ways in which they could be diagnosed or treated, and encouraged patients to discuss these options with their doctor.

In 1995, I reacted to the dieting craze by writing *Doctor, What Should I Eat?* My advice was based largely on the recommendations of the American Heart Association (which, incidentally, keep changing quite frequently. That's not a criticism; it's a good thing for the establishment to respond to new information.). The bottom line? I emphasized and described a balanced diet, advised how to avoid excessive cholesterol and fat, and stressed the importance of regular exercise. This was in contrast to many books on the market written by all kinds of "experts"—movie stars, TV commentators, physical trainers, and doctors (who'd previously specialized in disorders of the feet or sinuses!). Some of these other books were good, but many contained information that was wrong, conflicting, and ineffective. People bought one diet book after another, desperately looking for an answer to their weight problems (real or perceived), testing every different recommendation as it became available—from Dr. Atkins to the South Beach Diet. The American public has ended up (and remains) as confused as ever, undecided whether to consume high carbohydrates or low carbohydrates, and uncertain about what kind of fats are best for you. The most recent studies, completed in 2009, indicate that as far as weight is concerned, it makes no difference what you eat; it's how *much* you consume that's important. The answer to losing weight remains calories-in vs. calories-out.

In 1996, I wrote *Dr. Rosenfeld's Guide to Alternative Medicine* in response to the explosion of interest in "natural" medicine. Conventional medications were becoming prohibitively expensive and didn't always work; health food stores were springing up throughout the country, stocking their shelves with products they claimed could cure everything from baldness to impotence. The implication, especially on the Internet, was that "natural" is always safe and effective, while prescription drugs are artificial and usually cause side effects. I was eager to write this book because of an experience that had left me with an open mind on the subject.

Some twenty years earlier, I had witnessed an open-heart procedure in China *performed under acupuncture without any anesthesia!* This confirmed my belief that there are effective procedures and drugs that the medical establishment shuns largely because it doesn't understand them. For that book, I researched all the available scientific evidence I could find about most of the widely used herbs and alternative therapies, ranging from acupuncture to echinacea. The evidence for some was convincing; the efficacy of others was largely anecdotal. Shortly after this book was published, the U.S. government established, as part of the NIH, the commission on alternative medicine that is still actively and scientifically evaluating these alternative treatments. The main point of my book was that doctors must have an open mind when it comes to suggestions and ideas to help reduce human suffering. Departments of integrated or complementary medicine, as they are now called, have since sprung up in virtually every major medical school in the country. Conventional physicians no longer scoff at alternative medicine.

In 1999, I wrote my next book, *Live Now, Age Later,* for the rapidly increasing elderly population. In it, I emphasized that we are not only living longer but also living better. At the beginning of the twentieth century, the average life expectancy in this country was about forty-eight years. Today it is pushing eighty years. Older people are in better health; they have their teeth and they have Viagra, but they also have Alzheimer's. My point was that many of the manifestations of aging—cataracts, macular degeneration, prostate enlargement, osteoporosis, and so many others, even Alzheimer's, are preventable, are reversible, or can be delayed—if you know what their risk factors are and how to prevent them.

I wrote *Power to the Patient* in 2002 to help people cope with our inadequate health-care system. Doctors are no longer always free to prescribe what they think is best for their patients because the executives of managed care and other health insurance companies are looking over their shoulders trying to cut costs; the doctor-patient relationship is not nearly as strong as it used to be; many people are not free to choose a doctor they like but are apt to be sent to one selected by their health plan. You may see one physician one day and another the next. If you're sick, you may well have no access to anyone on weekends and end up in an emergency room, where you're treated by someone who doesn't know you or care about you personally, even though he or she is technically proficient and able to solve your immediate problem.

I tried to explain how best to deal with these realities in this book; how to improve your chances of getting the best medical care; and if nothing else works, how and where to challenge any adverse decision by your insurance carrier.

My Life on TV

As a result of having written these books, my frequent interviews eventually led to my own show, *Housecall,* on the Fox News Network. It is broadcast nationally and worldwide. I take this responsibility very seriously because the lay public depends on medical information from the media. It's more than curiosity or intellectual interest; people want and need to know what makes them tick and what makes them sick. In the old days, you could call your doctor for the answer. That's not so easy these days. Even if their doctors are accessible, most patients hesitate to call for an explanation of the endlessly new and contradictory reports that appear daily in the press and on television. This information is often superficial, conflicting, and inaccurate, especially on the Internet, where hype is often difficult to distinguish from fact.

I believe that it's up to professional medical communicators to clarify for the lay public the torrent of news to which they are subjected. That's what I try to do in my medical writing and broadcasting. It's very gratifying to deliver an important message not only to the ten or fifteen individuals I examine every day, but to millions everywhere. They send me hundreds of letters and e-mails every month from every corner of the world thanking me for sharing important health news with them. A few have told me I've saved their lives—whether it's because they heeded my warnings about the early detection of ovarian cancer, or my explanation that their "indigestion" might reflect angina or a heart attack, or my advice that lowering their cholesterol or measuring their C-reactive protein could reduce their risk of having a heart attack or stroke, or my opinion about why a routine total body CT scan may not be the best thing to have. On television, I try to impart this information as if I were talking to a patient across my desk or on my examining table. It is extremely important for a medical communicator not to base a report on a summary or headline reported by a news agency. I always read the original paper because the abstract or headline may not tell the whole story.

Here are some other rules I try to follow:

I never use "medicalese" that no one understands. Some doctors do so, in their offices and on the air. Listeners and patients may hold them in awe because what they're saying is incomprehensible. They're flattered to be made privy to something so complicated and sophisticated that they can't understand it! In my own practice, I end every patient session with, "Did you understand *everything* we talked about? Do you have any questions?" That's also my frame of mind in my TV broadcasts. There's no use delivering news that your readers or listeners don't understand.

I limit the information I impart to items that are of practical importance—things that matter to most people. A farmer in Iowa is not interested in an outbreak of tsutsugamushi fever in Africa!

It's frustrating when there's no breaking medical news to report, but rather than report trivia, I use the time to give important advice—about lifestyle, side effects of medications, vaccination schedules for children and adults, or the latest news about HIV-AIDS and other sexually transmitted diseases. I often discuss medical ethics, economics, and the health-care system.

I never call something a breakthrough unless it really is. An important breakthrough is exciting enough and does not need additional hype. If the results are at odds with previous studies, I point that out too.

I have also developed a thick skin over the years. No matter how carefully I research the information I'm providing, there is always someone who criticizes it. That's because for every fact accepted by the medical establishment, there are many passionate naysayers. For example, after I discussed the importance of statin drugs to lower cholesterol, I received a letter accusing me of being a tool of the pharmaceutical industry. That's because there are some who do not believe that cholesterol is important or that high blood pressure should be treated or that tobacco is bad for you or that anyone should have a bypass operation (they believe chelation is better) or that children should be vaccinated. Those who take these minority positions look for every opportunity to criticize anyone who disagrees with them—and they're often abusive. That does not deter me from telling what I know or believe to be the truth. Although I give equal time to legitimate conflicting opinions, I do not feel obliged to publicize a crackpot position that, if widely disseminated, could cause harm.

I always make it clear that I am *reporting* the news, not creating it. If I decide to comment about any study, I emphasize that it is *my* opinion, to which I feel entitled on the basis of my experience as a practicing physician. That's something with which no one can argue.

For me, bringing medical information to the lay public is another way of practicing medicine and carries with it the same responsibilities. I am always aware that doing so can have the same effect as actually writing a prescription.

So that's *my* modus operandi. But just as there is a crisis in the delivery of health care in this country, media coverage of medicine has become increasingly suspect. Readers and listeners worry that some medical communicators are promoting rather than just informing. They are aware that increasing commercialization of scientific research is interfering with fair and accurate dissemination of medical news, and that some communicators overstate the benefits of a particular "breakthrough" and minimize its potential harm. They worry about the ties between industry and science, and between reporters and the magazine or TV station for which they work. And there is some justification for their concern.

The fact is that the value of stock market shares in biotechnology and pharmaceutical companies rises and falls in response to media stories. Some researchers try to attract investors by promoting stories before they publish their work in scientific journals; "good news" medical stories can mean big business for everyone concerned—the manufacturer, the TV station, and sometimes the reporter. That's why ties between doctors and the pharmaceutical industry are the subject of ongoing review by the AMA.

So I believe that the cardinal rule for anyone engaged in reporting medical news is that one must scrupulously avoid any commercial influence in relationships. I have never received a penny for recommending any medical product. I feel that once I accept payment for endorsing anything, no matter how impressed I am with it, I will lose all credibility.

When TV Bleeps and Pauses Saved the Day

In my five-minute segments on Gary Collins' *Hour Magazine,* I reported and interpreted the latest medical news for my viewers, much as I currently do on my weekly Fox News Sunday *Housecall* show. There was one particular segment I will never forget.

There had recently been a spate of publicity about Tourette's syndrome, a condition in which the afflicted person cannot control his or her explosive utterances—often obscene. The Tourette's Society wanted very much to educate the public about this disorder so that anyone exposed to its victims would be understanding and tolerant. I thought it would be a public service to draw the attention of our millions of viewers to this problem. I asked the Tourette's Society for names of anyone so afflicted who might be willing to appear on national TV. They selected a man of about thirty who had overcome his problem with the aid of the newer drugs and counseling. He was now even working as a radio announcer—impressive proof that this was a treatable condition. I wanted him to tell our viewers what it was like to have Tourette's and how he had overcome it.

Bob lived in a small city in the Midwest. We arranged for him and his girlfriend to fly to Denver and then connect with a flight to our studio in Los Angeles. The first leg of the journey was a disaster and gave us enough reason to cancel the broadcast. But we didn't.

Here's what happened. About a half hour into the first part of the flight, the African American stewardess in first class asked our "star" if he'd like any refreshments. He smiled at her, and replied, "Yes, nigger, nigger, nigger, nigger." She was aghast, turned on her heel, and ran into the cockpit to tell the flight crew what had happened. The angry captain stalked back into the cabin. "What the hell do you think you're doing?" "I'm sorry," Bob replied. "I couldn't help it." That infuriated the captain even more, who obviously didn't know about Tourette's. "Listen, Buster, you'd *better* help it, because if you ever say anything like that again on this plane, off you go. I wish we could get rid of you right now." With that, he returned to the cockpit. The stewardess no longer offered our friend anything to eat and drink, but every time she passed his seat, he muttered audibly, "nigger, nigger, nigger." That was too much for the crew. The captain made an unscheduled stop at a small airport and evicted his "obscene" passenger.

The young man's girlfriend, who was accompanying him, phoned the studio in L.A. and told us what had happened. The only way for us to get them there in time for the show was to charter a private jet.

Later that day, Bob arrived. I greeted him in the green room and introduced myself. "I'm Dr. Rosenfeld, the doctor on this show, and both Gary Collins and I will be interviewing you in front of a live audience. Do you think you can handle it?" He seemed self-assured. "No problem," he said and then added, "kike, kike, kike." I should have told him my name was Featherstonhaugh.

I laughed. "Look, you're going to have to do better than that. I don't want you lynched. Between the niggers and the kikes, you'll make a lot of people mad." He apologized, as he had on the plane, and said that he would do all he could to control himself. However, the more nervous these patients are, and the harder they try, the less successful they are. I reassured him that I wasn't offended and that I knew he'd be fine on the show.

I then showed him into the makeup room, where an attractive young woman was to do his face. He smiled sweetly at her and said, "fuck, fuck, fuck." She was horrified, but fortunately I had accompanied him and explained the problem to her, and she continued to apply the makeup.

It was now time to go on camera for this live show being broadcast all over America. Gary told the studio audience of several hundred men, women, and children that we had a special guest who'd tell us all about Tourette's and how he had overcome it. After the first few guests, Gary and I welcomed Bob. I explained what Tourette's is, and its symptom, and said we had a guest who had conquered the disease, thanks to modern medical science. I introduced Bob, who took one look at me and again said, "kike, kike, kike." And as we continued, every four-letter word you can think of exploded compulsively from this man who had been recommended for national television to show what medical science could do for the victim of an unfortunate disease. Thank goodness for bleep technology.

I know of no other live TV show in which there were more bleeps than words in a broadcast—and I doubt that there ever will be one.

Doctor, Why Don't You Practice What You Preach?

After appearing on national TV for so many years, I presume I am a health model for some people, who expect me to practice what I preach. I forgot that one day when my wife and I were in L.A., window-shopping along Rodeo Drive. As we passed Nate and Al's deli, the aroma was irresistible; we went in and both ordered triple-decker pastrami sandwiches, sour pickles, and some french fries. The waitress who took our order glared at me and left without a word. "I wonder what's bugging her," I asked my wife. "How could she tell I'm a poor tipper?" A few minutes later, the waitress returned with our order and literally slammed the dishes in front of us. "Is that all?" she asked, barely able to contain her hostility. "Yes, thank-you. But is there anything wrong?" I asked. "Wrong?" she replied. "Wrong?" *You,* who tell us week after week what to eat and what not to eat, you come in here and order *this*?" With that, she angrily walked away, never to return, not even for her tip!

34

HOW I BECAME A WINE CONNOISSEUR

Some people spend a lifetime learning a hobby. I became an "expert" the easy way. I love good wine and have a very nice cellar because of one interesting experience. When I was growing up in Montreal, the only time we ever drank wine at home was at the Passover seder, when, even as children, we were allowed to sip kosher Manischewitz in small amounts. Shortly after I started practicing medicine, one of my patients brought me a bottle of red wine. I telephoned my wife, told her about it, and suggested we have some for dinner that night. "Good," she said, "We can finally use some of the wine glasses we were given for our wedding."

When I came home that evening, she had put the children to bed and set up a very romantic dinner for two, with candles and the bottle of red wine on the table. We sipped it throughout the delicious meal she'd prepared, and I must say, we both felt very good. More important, there was romance in the air. "We really ought to do this more often," I said, "It's fun."

"I agree," she replied, "but how do we know what wine to buy?"

"No problem. We love this one, so let's order more of the same." I looked at the label for the first time. The wine was a burgundy, a

Pommard, 1959, and the bottler was Henri Boillot. I called the neighborhood wine store and, feeling very sophisticated, I ordered a case of this Pommard.

"You're getting *a whole case* of twelve bottles? Will it keep?" my wife asked with concern. Remember, we had never previously had wine with a meal. "I'm sure it'll keep, and it's only $3.50 a bottle." (It's several hundred dollars today. I wish I had bought more and kept it.) Our wine arrived, and from then on, we had some with dinner two or three times a week. When that case ran out, we bought another—always the same—1959 Pommard, bottled by Henri Boillot. Why experiment with any other vintage when we liked that one so much? Whenever we dined out, we asked for this specific wine—nothing but Pommard '59, although we didn't insist on a specific bottler.

A year or so later, my wife and I went to Europe for a short vacation. We met her aunt and uncle in Paris. He was Herbert Lehman, the former governor of New York and later its senator. He was very well known internationally because he had been director general of UNRRA (United Nations Relief and Rehabilitation Agency). The Lehmans invited us to a very posh restaurant called Le Grand Véfour. After we ordered dinner, the sommelier handed the wine list to the governor. Lehman was not a connoisseur and asked him to select something he thought we might like.

A few minutes later, the wine steward returned with a bottle of wine wrapped in a white towel. He was about to pour some for the governor to taste, but Uncle Herbert suggested that I do it. Ham that I am, I swirled the wine around my glass as if I knew what I was doing. I had seen real wine experts carrying on in this way (mostly in the movies). "Nice burgundy, Pommard, eh what?" A bit English, but chic. The steward nodded appreciatively, probably surprised that an American would be this knowledgeable. As he poured the wine into the other glasses at the table, I took another sip and said, "1959." This wasn't a question; it was an assertion. This time the sommelier gave me an even more respectful look. He was impressed! "Very, very good indeed, monsieur." I never realized how easy it is to pose as an expert, even when you don't have a clue. I wasn't about to quit now. I was having too much fun, and it was beginning to go to my head. I decided to go for broke. "And if I'm not mistaken, this Pommard was bottled by Henri Boillot." Stunned silence, all mouths were agape—the senator's, his wife's, and the sommelier's—everyone's but my wife's. "*Je n'ai jamais rencontre un tel expert*," the sommelier exclaimed (I've never met such an expert). "To know the kind of wine, OK; the year too, impressive; but also to identify the bottler, that's incredible!"

Uncle Herbert was even more astounded and impressed than the wine steward. "Is, you never told us you're a wine expert. That was really impressive! How long have you been interested in wine?"

"Uncle Herbert, it's a joke," I confessed. "I know nothing at all about wine. This happens to be the only name I'm familiar with. It's a coincidence, that's all."

"Yeah, right. Some coincidence," he said, obviously taken not only with my expertise, but even more with my modesty.

From that time on, whenever and wherever we dined with the Lehmans, I was asked to select the wine. I had no choice but to learn something about it. And I did. I went to wine tastings, I joined wine clubs, I subscribed to wine magazines, and I began to discuss wine with my friends and patients. Soon people started sending me wine for my birthday and other occasions. Before long, I had acquired a very good selection. For one of my birthdays, Camilla even had a wine cellar built in our basement.

Wine became a passionate hobby. Because of all the publicity about it being good for the heart in modest amounts—raising the good HDL cholesterol and preventing abnormal clotting—I have been able to discuss it without appearing to be a wino. People just assume I wax enthusiastic about wine because I am a good cardiologist promoting effective therapy.

35

WALTER MATTHAU—
MY TWIN!

People used to tell me I looked like Walter Matthau—that I walked like him, talked like him, and had the same mannerisms. When he was alive, I was often greeted on the streets of London, in Montreal, the boardwalk in Atlantic City, New York, and even in faraway Turkey with, "Mr. Matthau, may I have your autograph?" I enjoyed being mistaken for this famous movie star and stopped by adoring strangers who asked *me* to sign *his* name. And I always did. I mean, why not? Every time someone approached me with pencil and pad in hand, I hoped it was *my* autograph they wanted. Alas, it was always Mr. Matthau's.

Walter Matthau was one of the nicest people I've ever met. I don't know of any film star who was so universally loved. Mention his name to any moviegoer, and you'll get the same response. "I really like him." The interesting thing about Matthau is that he was the same funny, relaxed, lovable guy in real life as he was on the screen. He wasn't acting!

The most dramatic effect of Matthau's fame on *me* occurred a few years ago. My wife and I had been invited on a friend's boat to cruise the Turkish coast. After a few idyllic days at sea, we docked in the tiny seaport village of Kas. We left the boat and walked toward the center of town, which was nothing more than a large open-air market with hundreds of rugs for sale. A few hundred feet from the boat, a swarthy Turk with a big, black handlebar mustache ran toward me. "Insh Allah!" he cried. "Insh Allah! I never dreamed that I would see you here in Kas. Oh, please, may I have your autograph? Wait till my brother in the U.S. hears about this!" I was thrilled. We were halfway around the world, none of my books had yet been translated into Turkish, and yet here was a fan asking for my autograph! As I was about to inscribe "Isadore Rosenfeld," my Turkish admirer said, "Mr. Matthau, what an honor this is for Kas. I must tell my cousin, the mayor. You must let us fête you tonight. A banquet. A parade, maybe." For a moment I thought I could pull it off and that it might be fun. But then I looked at that mustache and got cold feet. Imagine what would have happened to me if, during a gala parade through town, someone exposed me as just another American doctor, and not the venerated Walter Matthau.

"Ah, I truly wish that we could stay. But there is someone sick on our boat, and we must leave immediately," I said, as I penned "Walter Matthau" on his sheet of paper.

"Let's get out of here fast," I said to my wife. When this guy finds out that I'm not Matthau, he'll slit my throat." So we literally ran back to the boat, lifted anchor, and sailed away. I am happy to have given so much pleasure to that gentleman who now treasures my ersatz signature.

I wanted very much to meet Matthau, not only because I was so often mistaken for him, but also, because, like so many millions of moviegoers, I admired his work. My chance to do so came one day when Danny Kaye called to invite me to one of his special Chinese dinners on a Friday night that he knew I was going to be in L.A. Was there anyone special I wanted to meet? "Yes, yes. Walter Matthau."

"Why Matthau?"

"Well, I'm always being asked for his autograph, and it would be exciting finally to meet him after all these years."

"No. He's a hypochondriac, and when he finds out you're a cardiologist, he'll monopolize you."

I was disappointed, but it wasn't my house, my party, or my cooking, so I couldn't do much about it.

The next week I flew to L.A. When I arrived at the gate, a man holding a pencil and paper approached me. "Not again," I thought, determined not to pose as Matthau, especially here in his hometown.

Well, I wasn't Matthau . . . but he was—in the flesh! He came up
to me, smiled, and said, "Mr. Matthau, may I have your autograph?"
You can imagine how we both laughed. And there was Danny, who
had set it all up, convulsed with laughter in the wings.

Walter and I became close friends. We had chemistry. We saw
each other whenever he came to New York or I went to L.A. We
spoke regularly on the phone. He also helped me fulfill one of my
great ambitions by arranging for me to appear in a movie with him!
Here's how it happened.

In 1995 I was invited to lecture at a hospital in Minneapolis. Walter, Sophia Loren, and Jack Lemmon were shooting *Grumpier Old Men*
at that time in the lake country of Minnesota. When I told Walter I
was coming to Minneapolis, he asked me to stay at his hotel so that
we could have dinner together. If I was lucky, Sophia would join us.
I made the necessary room reservations. A few minutes later, he called
me again. "When is your talk?" he asked.

"Saturday morning."

"Why don't you get here Friday afternoon? I asked my director
to give you a part in the outtake (that's the scene at the end of the
film when all the actors fool around as themselves).

"Great!" I said, and early that Friday afternoon Walter met me at
the airport and drove me to the set.

"What role do you want to play? My twin brother or my doctor?"

"Whatever the script calls for," I replied.

"What script? There is no script. You and I will make something
up. The director doesn't care because it's in the outtake."

"OK, let me play your doctor. That's a little closer to the truth."

We then decided on the following script. I would wear a fisherman's outfit, complete with rod and pail, and wait in a small, win-
dowless, wooden fishing hut for the signal to come out. When I
did, I would say, "Hello, Max." Walter, standing by his station
wagon, would look up and say, "Hey, there's my doctor," to which I
would reply, "Max, did I ever tell you the one about the fisherman
who lost his pole?" Matthau would then say, "Doc, don't you remember, you told me that in the office last week?" Annoyed, I
would walk away muttering, "That's the last joke I'll ever tell him in
the office."

We arrived at the set and I found it all very exciting—the cast, the
hundreds of crew members milling around, the trailers, the cos-
tumes, and all the hubbub involved in shooting a Hollywood film.

Walter explained to the director what he and I would be doing. I signed my application for membership in the Screen Actors Guild to commemorate my Hollywood debut. We rehearsed the scene once, and I was ready to go. I was sent in to the little hut, where I waited for the director's instructions to come out. "Five, four, three, two, one. OK doc, come out." I opened the door, and there, standing in front of me, was *Sophia Loren*, not Walter Matthau! I had no script for this. For a moment I thought this was a dream. I was to greet one of the most beautiful women in the world—with the cameras rolling! She approached me, smiling, arms outstretched. "My doctor," and embraced me. I had to say something. My film career was at stake. In desperation, I blurted out, "You look very familiar. Have we met?" At this point, Matthau came in on cue, and we completed the rest of the scene.

That night, Sophia, Walter, and I had dinner. They didn't say so, but I know that they also felt that our scene was a momentous one. I was sure that because of it, *Grumpier Old Men* would certainly be in the running for an Oscar. It wasn't, largely because I would later learn that my scene ended up on the cutting-room floor! *Grumpier Old Men* arrived at the movie houses without me. The $578 check I received as base pay (scale) for a speaking part was a small consolation for my disappointment, and that of the thousands I had alerted in the weeks after the film was made to watch for my acting debut. But all was not lost. Even though I never made it to the silver screen at that time, news of my acting talent spread like wildfire. A few years later, Ron Howard asked me to play a small but obviously key role in *A Beautiful Mind* (Don't miss it!). And two years later, Milos Forman begged me to costar with Jim Carrey in *Man on the Moon.* It's amazing how word gets around! I had about six words in each film, but as I tell my film admirers, it's not what you say but how you *act* that's important. If you do see these two movies, try not to sneeze. If you do, you'll miss my performance.

A few years later, Sophia Loren consulted me in New York about a minor problem. Unfortunately, she's in good health, so I don't see her nearly as often as we'd both like.

The Matthau story came full circle when Walter called me one day. "You know how you're always being asked for my autograph? Well, I gave yours yesterday. I was in a deli in Santa Monica when a woman rushed over to me. 'Dr. Rosenfeld,' she said, 'I'm so glad to see you here. I need your advice. My husband has a serious liver problem, and his doctors want to do a portocaval shunt operation. What's your opinion?' I said to her, 'Madam, if your doctors say he needs it, he probably does. But if you're not sure, get a second opinion.' That's what you would have told her, isn't it? Anyway, she asked for your autograph, and I gave it to her."

36

HELP! I NEED AN EXTERMINATOR

The Duke and Duchess of Windsor used to spend a good deal of time in New York, although the world was their playground. They rarely if ever traveled by plane, arriving instead on ocean liners with more luggage than most planes would accept.

The Windsors were celebrities, but not because they were widely loved: the duchess was neither a Princess Diana nor a Princess Grace, and the duke was a far cry from that other famous royal personage of the time, Yul Brynner, the King of Siam. Nor were they especially talented, intellectual, or rich. They were social icons simply because of who they were: the former King Edward VIII of England, and the woman for whom he had given up his throne. Wherever the Windsors went, someone else picked up the tab because their presence enhanced their hosts' social standing.

Nathan Cummings, a prominent American industrialist and philanthropist, who was my friend and patient, developed a close relationship with the Windsors despite his modest Jewish Canadian background. Their friendship was one of give and take: he gave and they took. Nathan fed the Windsors, clothed them, and invited them to dinner parties at his royal apartment at the Waldorf Towers ("royal" because the Windsors had once briefly lived there, a fact commemorated by the hotel with a plaque outside the suite). Cummings displayed the duke and duchess much as he did some of his beautiful paintings. His parties were great fun, and New Yorkers vied to be invited to them. Despite his friendship with the royal couple, he was always "Nate," and she was always "duchess." (The duke, though unwelcome in his homeland, remained "Your Royal Highness" to the very end of his days.) Since I was Nate's doctor, he used to invite me to some of these royal soirées.

Frankly, perhaps because of my Canadian background, I was also impressed by royalty, and I was thrilled when the duke himself phoned my office one day for an appointment. When the voice at the other end said, "This is the Duke of Windsor," I thought one of my friends was putting me on. When His Royal Highness arrived at my office, I was ecstatic. Just to be in the same room with my former monarch, let alone shake his hand, talk with him, and, miracle of miracles, actually examine him, was breathtaking! (His cooperation and conspiracy with the Nazis before the war and his plan to return to the throne after Hitler had vanquished England were not yet known.)

Being the Windsors' doctor did not pay the rent. They would come to the office, be examined, thank me, and leave. I never billed them, and they never asked how much they owed. I would never have charged my former king or his wife, but why didn't they at least go through the motions? The duke did bring me some mint English stamps, made when he was briefly Edward VIII and inscribed them to me. I imagine they're quite valuable today. That kind of bartering was their currency, and I didn't mind it.

I can't remember a single substantive comment ever made to me by either the duke or duchess. It was essentially all small talk. The duchess was clearly the dominant partner, since he was a nebbish, but I never heard her demean him in any way. I remember when I once referred to him as "your husband," she retorted, "You mean 'His Royal Highness.'" However, she didn't expect any aggrandizement of her own title. When one of my nurses referred to her as "Your Royal Highness," she corrected her: "I'm a duchess, not a royal highness."

The Windsors were always impeccably dressed. It seemed a shame to ask them to remove their beautiful clothes and don one of my examining gowns! The duke usually wore gray hound's-tooth suits; she was attired in the latest fashions and always wore a hat. They always came together to see me. While she was being examined, he'd sit in my consulting room and read the *Wall Street Journal*.

During one such physical, I wanted to check the back of the duchess' eyes. Many patients don't realize that this funduscopic exam, as doctors call it, is a very important part of the physical. It's the only place in the body where a doctor can actually see your arteries. Everywhere else we feel them or listen to them, but when the doctor looks into the back of your eyes with the ophthalmoscope, he can diagnose many diseases, including diabetes, high blood pressure, TB, multiple sclerosis, embolism—and on and on. Often, when I am about to perform this exam, patients will tell me that they've already been to the eye doctor and that it's not necessary for me to do it again. The fact is, the eye doctor and the internist look for and see different things.

In order for the doctor to be able to study the interior of the eyes, the patient must not move them, so that the doctor doesn't have to play a game of tag with the structures he's examining. On this occasion, the duchess was sitting on the edge of my examining table facing a blank wall about eight feet away on which I had penciled a black X.

"Now, Duchess," I said, after she had moved her hat over to the side, "I want you to fix your gaze on that black mark on the wall while I examine your eyes. Don't move them. Just keep looking at the mark." As I began the exam, her eyes drifted to the right. I repeated my instructions. "Duchess, please focus on that spot on the wall." This time she shifted her gaze leftward. I couldn't understand why she didn't just look straight ahead. "Doctor, I'm doing exactly what you told me to. I am looking at the spot, but it's moving!" she said, obviously irritated. I took a closer look at my mark. She was right. It was moving! There were two marks there—one penciled by me, the second a "fly" crawling along the wall. As luck would have it, she was looking at the latter.

I have sanitized this story only in as much as it was not actually a fly. Flies don't crawl. We were in an older building in midtown New York, so you can guess what was really crawling on the wall. From then on, the duchess preferred that I examine her at her home in Paris.

37

WHEN MEDICINE
AND POLITICS MIX

D r. Theodore Cooper was, in my opinion and that of many other cardiologists, the best chief the National Heart, Lung, and Blood Institute ever had. He was modest and brilliant, he inspired confidence, he had vision, and he presided over the most impressive achievements in cardiovascular research conducted or funded by his institute. His administration was responsible for setting up most of the task forces that studied hypertension, cholesterol, and various aspects of coronary artery heart disease. He was also a most effective advocate for more research money from Congress.

After he had held this job for several years, the position of assistant secretary of health, a presidential appointment, became vacant. This is the number one health job in government and is always held by a doctor. (The secretary of health, now also "and human services," is a political appointment and only occasionally filled by a physician.)

Cooper was the natural choice for this prestigious position: the AMA wanted him, the American Heart Association and the American College of Cardiology were lobbying for him, and medical schools throughout the country were pressuring the government to have him appointed. Despite all this backing, the Ford administration allowed the post to remain vacant. No one understood why.

One evening in 1975 my friend, Ambassador Hushang Ansary, then the Shah of Iran's minister of finance, invited me to a formal dinner at the Iranian Embassy in Washington to celebrate an important trade agreement between his country and the U.S. I was impressed to find myself at his table along with then Secretary of State Henry Kissinger, coarchitect of the deal, one or two noted Washington columnists, and Donald Rumsfeld, then President Ford's White House chief of staff.

I was seated next to Rumsfeld. In the course of our conversation, he asked what my specialty was. This gave me the chance to discuss cardiology in general and my friend Ted Cooper in particular. "Mr. Rumsfeld," I said, "I don't know much about protocol, and forgive me if what I am about to ask you is impolite, impolitic, or out of order. I know how much you and President Ford care about the nation's health. Physicians don't understand why the key job of assistant secretary of health continues to remain vacant. You must know that Dr. Theodore Cooper is the choice of virtually every branch of organized medicine. May I respectfully ask why he hasn't been named?"

Rumsfeld was charming and quite willing to discuss the subject. "Well, we've certainly been considering him. I agree that Cooper is very good, and he's definitely on our list. But the problem is that he's a registered Democrat, and this is a Republican administration."

I couldn't believe it! "What difference does that make?" I rejoined. "There's nothing partisan about this job or Dr. Cooper. In my opinion, you're making a big mistake not selecting him for political reasons."

Rumsfeld smiled. "You're right. I'll tell you what. If we appoint Cooper, would you be willing to write a letter to the *New York Times* praising President Ford for his impartiality in naming a registered Democrat to such a high position in his Republican administration?"

"With pleasure," I replied.

"Well," he said, "consider it done."

I was elated. After the dinner, I rushed back to my hotel and phoned Ted at home to tell him the good news. "Ted, I think I got you the big job!" I then proceeded to give him a blow-by-blow account of my conversation.

"Gee, thanks," he said. "I guess you'll have to keep your promise and write that letter, even though they had already decided to appoint me several days ago. The FBI has been running checks on me all week. I guess Rumsfeld just wants to get a little more mileage out of it."

One week later, President Ford announced the appointment of Dr. Theodore Cooper as assistant secretary of health. But I had made a promise, and so I called the late Sydney Gruson, a close friend and senior executive editor at the *Times*. I told him about my conversation with Rumsfeld. "Sydney, you've got to help me. I promised to write that letter. Please do whatever you can to get it published." He said he'd try. I penned a letter, thanking President Ford on behalf of the medical community for his fairness and impartiality. The letter was published.

As we all expected, Cooper did an excellent job as assistant secretary, and vacated his position after the next election. Incoming President Reagan offered him the cabinet post of secretary of education, which Ted declined. He wanted to stay in medicine, his first love. So I helped persuade him to come to Cornell Medical School as dean of medicine and vice provost of the university. He accepted, did a great job there too, and later left to become the president of the Upjohn Company.

Although I had not, in fact, gotten Ted that job in Washington, my temporary delusion that I had done so was exhilarating. But whenever he was asked about it, Cooper told everyone that it was I who had persuaded the president of the United States to appoint him.

The lesson that I learned from this little drama was that medicine and politics don't mix.

38

I Make a House Call with the First Lady!

In the late 1970s, I was invited to a big publicity bash in Acapulco by my friend and patient Harding Lawrence, then the president of (now long-gone) Braniff Airways. Lawrence and his airline had transformed Acapulco from a sleepy Mexican town into a busy, prosperous tourist resort, and the company was celebrating the inauguration of a new route from Houston to Acapulco.

Guests of the gala were flown to Acapulco, mostly on Braniff planes, and lodged at the Las Brisas Hilton, one of that area's most attractive hotels. It consists of many separate cottages spread out over a hillside, each with its own little swimming pool and deck. The main building is for administration only and has no residential suites.

The guest list was star-studded with such luminaries as Ladybird Johnson, Mary Lasker, the Robert Strausses (chairman of the National Democratic Party at the time), the noted columnist William Safire, and the CEOs of several major international corporations.

On the day we arrived, our hosts threw an elegant cocktail party on the terrace of the Lawrence villa at the hotel. Being the only doctor in attendance, I was very grateful to them for not serving raw vegetables, fruits, nonbottled water, ice, or any of the other myriad causes of Montezuma's revenge. I sipped the wine, ate the certified-pure canapés, and chatted with Helen Straus about the hazards of smoking because earlier in the evening I had seen her light a cigarette. I was obviously making a great impression on her, because as I was citing the statistics linking tobacco with lung cancer and heart disease, she took another cigarette out of her pack. Although there was no clap of thunder, divine providence must have also been offended by her terrible no-no, because as she struck the match, the entire book of matches she was holding went up in flames. She suffered an extensive, painful, superficial burn on her wrist. She turned to me for help. Well, how does one treat a burn at an Acapulco hotel on a weekend? Simple. Lots of cool compresses. The smoker's symptoms improved, we all had dinner, and then we retired to our respective cottages.

About two o'clock in the morning, my phone rang. "Doctor, this is Helen Straus's husband. My wife's burn is excruciatingly painful. We don't know what to do. I'd appreciate it very much if you dropped over and took a look at her hand. I want to make sure she doesn't need to be treated in a hospital." I told him I'd be happy to come by (an overstatement, to say the least), but I didn't know where their villa was located. The front desk was closed, I had no car, and it was pitch dark outside. Then I had an idea. "The Secret Service agents with your friend, Ladybird Johnson, have a car. If they pick me up, I can get to you. Just turn on the lights in your cottage, and we'll cruise around until we find it. I'll call Mrs. Johnson. I'm sure she'll let me have the car." Helen's husband thought that was a good idea.

I had the switchboard connect me with Mrs. Johnson. That took a lot of nerve at two a.m. I told her how sorry I was to wake her, but her friend Helen had a painful burn and had asked me to come see her. Would it be possible to borrow her car, with or without her agents, to take me there? I was surprised and disappointed by her answer. "I'm sorry, doctor. My Secret Service detail is not permitted, by law, to leave me at any time, or to allow their vehicle to be used. You can be sure that if it were up to me, I'd certainly oblige, but I'm afraid that even if I asked them to, the agents would not comply." I told her that I understood fully, and was about to hang up, when she added, "But there's another way. Why don't I get dressed and pick you up? Then we can both go to Helen's cabin."

Which is what she did. To the best of my knowledge, I am the first and only American doctor ever to make a house call in the middle of the night, in a foreign country, accompanied by the first lady of the United States. I wasn't surprised when Mrs. Johnson later confessed to close friends that she'd always wanted to be a doctor.

Another First Lady

1992: Secretary-General of the United Nations Boutros Boutros-Ghali invited Camilla and me to dinner at his official residence, a town house on New York's fashionable Sutton Place. We were greeted in the foyer and shown the seating arrangements. There were three tables of ten; I would be sitting with the secretary-general, and on my right was Ambassador Janet Jagan, wife of Dr. Cheddi Jagan, president of Guyana.

All I knew about Guyana was that it had been a British colony, that it was somewhere near South America, and that some nine hundred members of the Jim Jones cult had recently committed suicide there under Jones' direction. Mrs. Jagan was her husband's personal envoy to the UN. She was a fascinating dinner companion—pleasant, educated, warm, and unassuming. I was riveted by her passion for her country and its struggle for independence and democracy. Mrs. Jagan told me that Guyana had became an independent republic in 1966 and is the only nation in South America where English is the official language. Almost 50 percent of the population is of Indian (from India) descent, a third are black, and the remainder is a mixture of East Indians, Chinese, and other Asians.

I was puzzled because Mrs. Jagan was Caucasian. How come Guyana had a white first lady? My interest was further heightened by the fact that she did not have an Indian or South American accent. As a matter of fact, the more she spoke, the more she sounded to me like someone from this country, and Jewish to boot. An American Jewish woman, the first lady of Guyana? Impossible!

As the evening wore on, I became increasingly convinced that I was right. But how does one ask such a dignitary in this august diplomatic setting whether she is Jewish? I decided to do it deviously, by introducing a Yiddish word into my conversation and assessing her reaction to it. We were talking about some unpopular world figure (maybe someone like Saddam Hussein), and I said, "You know, I think he's a *meshugener*" (the Yiddish word for "crazy"). Entirely unfazed, she replied, "Of course, everyone knows he's a meshugener."

"Mrs. Jagan, you're Jewish!" I said in astonishment. "Yes, of course," she answered, as if every first lady is. And then she told me her story. She was born in Chicago, where she went to nursing school, but ended up a social worker. While at college, she met Cheddi Jagan, a native of Guyana who was studying dentistry. They married while he was still in school, but after he received his dental degree, they decided to return to Guyana because he was passionately interested in the welfare and politics of his country, which was then still under English rule. They formed a political party called the PPP that captured the imagination and support of the Guyanese, and Dr. Jagan was elected president.

After Dr. Jagan died in 1997, his seventy-seven-year-old feisty wife was named to head the political party that she and her husband had founded. She was nominated in the election to fill the presidency and she won it by a comfortable margin. My former dinner companion was now President Janet Jagan!

She retired from the presidency, and lived in Guyana until her death.

39

ON A HELICOPTER WITH
A PILOT WHO NEEDS
NITROGLYCERIN!

few years ago I was asked to see a patient in Italy. My flight
from New York landed in Milan, and my patient, who lived
in Turin, sent his helicopter to pick me up. I love flying in
helicopters, and this was a particularly comfortable one. We buckled
our seat belts, took off, and flew several hundred feet over northern
Italy's rice fields. What a beautiful sight! Ah, this was the life! I was
so sorry for all those people driving their cars and struggling with the
traffic as they drove from Milan to Turin.

A few minutes into the flight, the one pilot on the chopper (most
that I'd been on had two) took a little bottle out of his pocket and
showed it to me with a queried expression on his face. He didn't
speak a word of English, but he obviously wanted to know what I
thought about these pills he was taking. Maybe he had read the Italian translation of *Second Opinion* and wanted to pick the brains of
the physician that his rich boss had flown in all the way from New
York. I looked at the pill bottle and my heart sank. It contained nitroglycerin, the medication people slip under the tongue to treat their
angina pectoris. This pill can cause a drop of blood pressure, cause
light-headedness, and even result in fainting. That's all I needed on

this flight—a pilot who develops chest pain and then passes out. I told him this was a very good medication, and for the next few minutes until we landed, I watched with keen interest every move he made flying the aircraft in the unlucky event that I had to take over.

We landed safely! I now had a dilemma. Should I tell my patient that his pilot has heart trouble? At first it seemed obvious that I should, but then I had second thoughts. When that man asked me a medical question, he established a doctor-patient relationship with me that I would be violating if I revealed anything to his employer. "On the other hand," as Tevya would have said in *Fiddler on the Roof,* my patient's life might be in jeopardy because of this man. I agonized about what to do and finally decided that I owed it to both the pilot and my patient to disclose the truth. This guy shouldn't be flying a helicopter with nitroglycerin in his pocket, for his own sake as well as his passenger's. (I was about to make arrangements for the return trip to Milan by car. I now looked forward to seeing those beautiful rice fields at eye level.)

The next morning, I said to my patient, "I have something very important to tell you." He looked worried, for I had just taken an ECG on him. "Your pilot is a sick man. He shouldn't be flying helicopters."

"What's wrong with him? He always looked fine to me. And how did he tell you what his symptoms are? He doesn't speak English." "He showed me his bottle of nitroglycerin." My patient burst into laughter. "That's not *his* nitroglycerin. It's mine. I sent him to a drugstore in Milan to pick it up for me, and he was just checking to see if he'd gotten the right medication!" And then he showed me the bottle that had worried me so much!

I was more relaxed on my return helicopter flight back to Milan the next day. I much preferred it to a car, and everyone knows that rice fields are much more beautiful from five hundred feet than they are at eye level.

40

WHY I LOVE COPS

One hears a great deal about police brutality these days—cops everywhere, from Los Angeles to New York, viciously beating defenseless suspects. But for every one of these "atrocities," there are infinitely more acts of bravery by cops. Unfortunately, they are not reported often enough because they are "part of the job." I witnessed one such scene.

In 1976, during our nation's bicentennial celebration, there was a spectacular event in New York City harbor. Ships from virtually every country in the world came here and were viewed by millions of people. The president of the United States arrived in a destroyer to take the salute from these vessels, large and small. The site of the flotilla of ships, with their different flags, was breathtaking. The banks of the Hudson River were packed with throngs, some camping on shore, others sitting in grandstands. The celebrations started early in the morning and ran well into the evening.

The New York City Police Department has several small craft that patrol the East River and the Hudson River. These boats perform a vital function; they rescue people who jump off bridges, fall into the water, or leave helicopters and planes that make unscheduled landings in the rivers.

Several senior police officers were invited that day to board one of these patrol boats and get a good look at the festivities. Since I am a New York City police surgeon, I was included in that group. It was a thrilling experience. Our police boat was permitted to sail to every nook and cranny of the waters, alongside President Ford's destroyer and wherever our curiosity took us. We had a close-up, firsthand look at all the ships from faraway places.

The festivities ended at about 10 p.m., and we were heading back to our dock in Brooklyn when suddenly we received an emergency message on our radio. A grandstand along the Hudson River had collapsed, and there were scores of people in the water! We were to proceed at full speed to take part in the rescue operations, along with other units. We changed course and sped toward the accident scene, sirens wailing and lights flashing.

There were only three regular cops on duty on that boat; the rest were senior officers in their fifties and early sixties. They were no longer patrolmen; all of them held desk jobs. Some were overweight; one was wheezing with chronic bronchitis; another was convalescing from a heart attack and about to be discharged from the force. And then there was me, unable to swim. Some rescue team! Yet every single cop on that boat, young and old, sick and well, removed his uniform and donned a life jacket, ready to jump into the cold, dark waters of the Hudson River to try to save whomever they could find.

I was embarrassed because I'm a floater, not a swimmer, and floaters can't save drowning people. Had I jumped in with them, they'd have had one more person to rescue. When I apologized to my colleagues, they assuaged my guilt by reassuring me that I would be more useful treating the survivors they would be bringing on board.

I now understand why this police department is called New York's Finest. There they all stood, as the boat sped up the river— captains, inspectors, and other high-ranking officers—shoes, socks, and clothes removed, in their underwear, wearing life jackets, and ready to plunge into the dark waters. As we approached the scene, a second report came over the radio. "Disregard the alert. It was a hoax."

The fact that these men did not, in the end, have to rescue anyone from drowning did not diminish by one iota my admiration for their courage. I was so moved, I described the scene in a letter to the editor of the *New York Times.*

It's important to remember that despite some bad apples, the police are really there to protect us, and when the chips (or grandstands) are down, they do so, even at risk to themselves.

41

WHY I BELIEVE IN
FORTUNE-TELLERS

My parents came from Eastern Europe. Mischa Rosenfeld,
my father, was born in 1896 in the area of Russia that is
now part of the Ukraine. His home, the village of Volochisk, is situated on the *eastern* banks of a narrow river bearing
the same name. My mother was born on the *western* bank of that
same river, directly opposite my father's town, in the Polish village
of Podwoloczyska. Though only a stone's throw apart, these two
communities had little in common; they were in different countries,
with languages, politics, cultures, and lifestyles as dissimilar as Berlin is from Beijing or Tokyo from Toronto. Even their Jewish communities did not communicate with each other, because, despite
their common religion, the differences between them were too
great. Hate may be too strong a term, so let's say these two communities disliked each other. The Poles viewed their Russian neighbors as uncouth peasants and tradesmen; the Russians considered
those across the river to be snobs and dilettantes. They rarely visited each other, either for social reasons or even to trade. So it was
astonishing that my Podwoloczyska mother eventually became the
bride of my Volochisk father—especially since she had been very

much in love with a boy in her hometown whom she'd known most of her life.

My mother was two years younger than my father. Until she was sixteen years old, Galicia, the area of Poland where she was born, was part of the Austro-Hungarian Empire, and her family always considered themselves Austrian, not Polish. They were poor; there was no tradition of commerce in the family, and most of their ancestors had for generations been impecunious scholars. My mother and her sister—identical twins—studied history, philosophy, and art. They had kept steady company with two brothers in this village from the time they were thirteen years old. The four of them, "near-betrothed," would spend hours planning their marriages and the children they would someday bring into the world.

One Sunday, a traveling road show passed through Podwoloczyska, complete with clowns, Polish-style cotton candy, jugglers, and a Gypsy fortune-teller. Such visits from the outside world were rare, and so the couples joined the fun. After playing games at the various booths, they ended up at the fortune-teller's "to see if she could predict when we would marry." With the earnest demeanor of true believers, they watched the old lady as she peered into her crystal ball. After a few minutes, she looked up at my mother's sister and said, "You will marry this nice young man and have three children together—two sons and a daughter." When she turned to my mother, and her face darkened. "I see a Russian in your future," she said with some reluctance. "Yes, there's no question. He's wearing a uniform. He's a soldier. You will marry him and move far away from here."

They thanked the old lady and couldn't wait to get out of her earshot so that they could explode with laughter. Marry a Russian, a boor, and a soldier to boot! Move away with him, from her twin sister and the parents she loved so much! Preposterous! No more plausible than going to the moon.

On the Russian side of the river, my grandfather was a grain dealer, from whom my father learned his trade. Dad was very different from the boy my mother was planning to marry, physically and intellectually. He was shorter than he, and a horseman, an athlete—a man's man; the other guy was a bookworm. The Russian Rosenfelds didn't read much; my father would not have enjoyed the discussions of philosophy and literature at my mother's home. He had no formal schooling (Jewish children were not educated in Czarist Russia), but he learned to read and write Yiddish and Russian from local teachers.

When he turned nineteen, Moishe was drafted into the Russian Army. He wasn't happy about it. The Russian government encouraged anti-Semitic attacks on Jews and their property. The Jews viewed these "pogroms" as facts of life and bore them with resignation, much as Americans endure hurricanes.

Mischa and his family were relieved when his platoon was assigned to patrol the enemy territory in Podwoloczyska across the river, and not sent to the front lines. There was no resistance to their entry into the town. Some of the Russian troops were making sport with the unlucky inhabitants; they had no hesitation robbing, raping, and pillaging, especially after a few drinks. One day, my father and other members of his platoon were ordered to conduct a house-to-house search for hidden weapons in the village. The real reason was probably to keep the troops busy and free of ennui, since there were no hostilities in the area. My mother's home was one of those on the list to be "inspected." The Russian soldiers, my dad among them, pounded on the door of the small cottage where my mother's family, the Friedmans, lived. Standing behind the cowering middle-aged couple were two beautiful teenage girls. The intruders rubbed their eyes in disbelief, as if suffering from double vision, for the maidens were absolutely identical in appearance—from their hairdos to their clothes. Before the "fun" could begin, my father stepped in. With an "I saw them first" wink, he cajoled his friends into leaving, and he stayed behind. He assured the terrified family that they had nothing to fear and that he would see to it they were not molested by anyone. This Russian soldier had fallen in love with my mother at first sight. Was it possible that the Gypsy's prophecy was destined to be fulfilled?

Totally smitten, my father was now delighted to be in the Russian Army as long as he was stationed in Podwoloczyska. He spent as much time as he could with the Friedmans—and their beautiful daughters. Although her sister remained enamored of her boyfriend, my mother now became more interested in the handsome Russian suitor who not only protected them but also brought them food and fuel to heat their home. He began to spend evenings with them and even feigned an interest in their discussions of philosophy, little of which he understood.

The possibility of a future together seemed to vanish in 1917 when the czar was overthrown and the new Soviet government dropped out of the war. Demobilized, my father returned to Volochisk. The border with Podwoloczyska was now closed, and there was again no traffic between the two river towns. However, not to be deterred, my dad, athlete that he was, plunged into the river and swam across to the other side at every opportunity. I don't know how long he could have continued this feat, but the Communist authorities solved the problem for him. They decided that he and my grandfather would no longer be allowed to conduct their commerce and that they would have to seek gainful employment in jobs selected for them by the state or leave the country.

My grandfather reacted by contacting his relatives who had left years earlier for the U.S. They sent immigration papers for him, his wife, and their son, Mischa, all of whom were now free to move to Terre Haute, Indiana. Dad's parents left Volochisk for the U.S., but he remained behind and took his last swim, a one-way trip from Volochisk to Podwoloczyska. He would not leave my mother, even though there was yet no formal understanding between them.

He became a virtual boarder in the Friedman home, until 1921, when he and my mother decided to marry. Exactly nine months later—and not a day sooner—my brother Shachna Beryl was born.

Life was less than idyllic for them in Poland. Many of the Friedman's neighbors and friends had moved to Austria, which they considered their mother country, and were replaced by strongly anti-Semitic Polish peasants. My mother's brothers came home on weekends from Lemberg (now called Lwow), where they taught school, and told of signs such as "Jews and dogs not permitted" throughout that city. Anti-Semitic discrimination and vandalism were as commonplace in Poland as they had been in Russia across the river during my father's childhood.

My dad came to believe, as did my mother (with some trepidation) that they would be better off moving to the U.S. He contacted my grandfather, who was now living with the rest of the family in Terre Haute (one of whom was the Republican district attorney), and a visa arrived in short order for his young family. But when the chips were down, my mother could simply not bring herself to leave her family. My father would do whatever she wished (he continued to worship her until the day he died), and so they didn't take advantage of their American visa.

A few months later my father's permit to remain in Poland was about to expire. He asked to remain in Poland as the husband of a Polish citizen and the father of a child born in that country. The Polish government didn't see it that way; the official who had secured the temporary permit for my father was no longer there. Russians were not greatly loved in Poland (then or now), especially if they were Jewish, and so his application was rejected. After several futile appeals, it was clear, even to my mother, that they no longer had any choice. They'd have to leave Poland. By the time they reapplied for an American visa, the immigration laws had changed, and the doors of the United States were no longer open to them. Now my father was truly a refugee with nowhere to go. Desperate, he applied to Canada for permission to immigrate there. They were accepted, and a few weeks later, my parents and my brother sailed to Montreal from Holland on the *Volendam*. I was born in Canada a few months later.

As it turned out, I owe my life to the Jew-hating Poles who wouldn't allow my father to live in Poland. If they had, I would have perished with all the Friedmans in the Nazi gas chambers.

42

MY FATHER IS WANTED BY THE ROYAL CANADIAN MOUNTED POLICE!

My parents remained in Montreal for the rest of their lives. They were distraught when my wife and I moved to New York, but their sadness was in part compensated for by their frequent visits to us. My father, in particular, loved to come to the Big Apple, not only to see Camilla, the grandchildren, and me, but also to shop. There were so many things he could buy here that were not available in Canada, at least at a price that he was prepared to pay. Like his younger son, he loved gadgets—radios, little TVs, anything electronic.

During one of his visits, I received a call from my brother in Montreal. "Is, we're in trouble!"

"What's wrong, John?"

"It's Dad. He's wanted by the Royal Canadian Mounted Police."

"You've got to be kidding. What the hell are you talking about? Dad doesn't even know what RCMP stands for. And the only possible crime of which he may conceivably be guilty is jaywalking. What's it all about?"

"I don't know. The RCMP came by yesterday looking for him. I asked them why they wanted him, and all they would tell me was that it was for a federal offense."

"OK, John. Let me see what I can find out."

I hung up the phone and joined Dad in the living room, where he was playing gin rummy with my mother. I didn't want to upset him. I couldn't burst into the room and ask, "Why does the RCMP want you?" out of a clear blue sky. That kind of question would worry anyone, and I had to be particularly careful in Dad's case to avoid causing him chest pain and the need to take nitroglycerine. How could I break this terrible news to him without giving him a heart attack?

"Dad, so how's everything at home, in Montreal?" I asked casually. He looked at me as if I had a screw loose. He'd been in my house for several days, and we had talked about all the little things in our lives.

"What do you mean? Everything is fine."

"Business OK? Pay your taxes on time?"

"What are you getting at, Issie? I can tell there's something wrong. What is it?"

I had no choice at this point. "Dad, it's obviously a mistake of some kind, but John just called and said the Mounties are looking for you back home. Can you think what they might want? Have you had any legal problems? Is anyone suing you?"

He thought for a moment. "No, I have no idea what they want." And then he blanched, held his chest, and slipped a nitroglycerine tablet under his tongue.

My father knew why the police wanted him! "Dad, you'd better tell me so that we can take care of it. If you did break the law in some way, I'm sure we can explain it. Please don't worry."

"No, there's nothing you or anybody can do. I've known for years that this moment would come and that I'd have to face up to it." He took a deep, painful breath. "I'm a murderer."

Murderer? My father, who wouldn't hurt a fly, killed someone? "Dad, what the hell are you talking about? You never killed anyone!"

"Issie, come sit down. I should have told you this a long time ago."

It's a good thing I don't have angina; this was enough to give anyone a heart attack.

Dad continued. "Issie, listen. When I was seventeen years old, living in the Ukraine, there were marauding anti-Semitic bands that used to attack our shtetls, rob and pillage our homes, and rape our women. There was no rule of law. They could come and go whenever they wanted. I decided to organize some of the older boys and young men in our village. We trained; we learned how to shoot. We wanted only to protect our families. There were no police you could call, no justice for Jews. We wanted to stop these bastards from attacking us. One day we learned from a neighboring village that these gangsters were on the way to us. My men and I waited on the outskirts of our town. In about half an hour, they came on their horses, rifles slung over their shoulders. They were drunk, laughing, and singing. I knew what was in store for us. We began to throw rocks at them to divert them. One of the Cossacks took his rifle and started shooting at us. I had a gun and returned the fire. I killed him! The rest of their gang ran away. I've known all along that some day I would have to pay for what I did."

I was incredulous. He had never told me this story before. I started to laugh out of sheer relief. "You think the Mounties are after you, a Canadian citizen, because sixty years ago you thwarted a pogrom in Russia?" It took some doing to convince him that he would not be charged with murder. But we still had to find out why the RCMP was looking for him. I called a friend named Alan Macnaughton, who was then a member of Parliament with ties to the Mounties. I begged him to find out how my father had broken the law and promised I would return with my father to Canada to face the music.

Alan called me back a couple of days later. "Your dad apparently passed a counterfeit U.S. twenty dollar bill in New York at his last visit there. He bought a car radio, paid in cash, and when the dealer took his daily receipts to the bank, they spotted the phony bill. He remembered your father very clearly. He got the name from the bill of sale. Your father was the only one who paid in cash that day. The FBI contacted us, and they want to extradite him."

"Thanks, Alan. I'll take care of it. Dad no more knowingly passed a bad bill than you or I would. I'll find out where he got it."

Dad was waiting in the other room. "What did I do?" he asked plaintively. I told him about the bill. He explained that he had received it from the Royal Bank of Canada, where he had gone to exchange some Canadian money for U.S. currency. It was a bank teller who had given him the bad bill!

Guilt can remain in one's conscience forever. My dad was a hero who had saved his town from killers; he deserved a medal. Instead, he carried with him to the grave the guilt of having killed someone, even though it was in self-defense.

43

THE POWER
OF A (SIGNED)
PRESCRIPTION

Richard Avedon, the noted photographer, was a good friend and patient. One day, when my kids were still at college, he telephoned my wife. "I'd like to surprise Isadore with a family portrait for Christmas. When will all your children be home for the holidays?" My wife checked the schedules and gave him the dates, on one of which they all secretly went to Avedon's studio to be photographed.

A few days later, Avedon called my office and asked if he could see me for a few minutes at the end of the day to discuss a personal matter. He showed up with a bundle of photographic proofs of my wife and children that he laid on the desk. "These are for you—for Christmas. Pick as many as you'd like, in whatever sizes you want and I'll have them for you in time for the holidays."

I was overcome, not only by his generosity and thoughtfulness but also by the beauty of the photographs he had taken. (They still adorn several walls in my office and home.) I must have selected at least twenty-five. "No problem," he said, although I suspect he was somewhat taken aback by the number of pictures I had chosen.

A few days later, he returned with a package of finished photos and proudly announced, "These are for you. Merry Christmas!" I opened the bundle and there were all the photographs I had selected—absolutely stunning! I had never seen better portraits of my wife and four children. I was thrilled and grateful. Here, after all, was one of the foremost photographers of our time, personally delivering a slew of pictures he had taken of the dearest people in my life.

At the bottom left of the top photograph was the unmistakable signature—AVEDON. I went on to admire the next photo—equally striking and beautiful, but unsigned. I figured he skipped one by mistake. But the third photograph had no signature either and neither did any of the others. "Dick," I said, "you only signed the first picture. Did you forget about the others?"

"No, Is, I didn't forget. You see, when we do a batch of photographs, we only sign one."

"Why? Are you afraid I'm going to flood the Avedon market?" I countered. And then I was embarrassed at seeming ungrateful and apologized.

The next day, before I'd had a chance to distribute the photographs to my wife, children, and parents, I received a call from Avedon's secretary. "Mr. Avedon needs the following six prescriptions. Would you please write them, and I will send somebody to pick them up?" Avedon's wish was my command, especially after that wonderful gift. So I promptly wrote the prescriptions he asked for, put them in an envelope, and a messenger collected them. A couple of hours later, a puzzled Richard Avedon telephoned. "Doc, you only signed the top prescription! You forgot all the others."

"Aha," I replied.

Later that afternoon, Richard Avedon returned to my office, muttering under his breath as he signed all twenty-five of my photographs. In return, I signed his remaining five prescriptions. Quid pro quo!

44

WHEN A DOCTOR IS ARROGANT

Doctors don't usually like to testify against each other in court, or to criticize one another publicly. But you can be sure that if you have a legitimate malpractice complaint, your lawyer won't have any trouble finding a medical expert to appear on your behalf. It's also highly unlikely that any doctor you're seeing for a second opinion will agree with a diagnosis or recommendation he knows to be wrong. Although from time to time, charges or complaints against doctors are launched out of spite or to make a buck in a lawsuit, I can assure you, as a former chairman of the New York County Medical Society's board of censors, that unethical and unqualified doctors *are* being censured and losing their licenses all the time. We haven't yet reached zero tolerance against the misfits among us, but that's often as much the fault of the legal system as it is of the medical profession.

I personally witnessed how the ego and arrogance of one medical practitioner threatened the life of a patient: the doctor's name is not important; I'll refer to him as Dr. Talbot.

One rainy evening in the dead of winter several years ago, a close friend called me at home in New York City. "Issie, a pal of mine whom you don't know has been admitted to White Plains Hospital with a stroke. His family is very worried. I hate to ask you this, but would you run up there to see if he's getting the best treatment?"

"Gee, Lester, it's eight o'clock, the weather is lousy, White Plains is forty miles away, and he's in a good hospital. Do you think I really need to go now? Who's his doctor?"

"Talbot. He's been looking after George for many years. It's not that the family doesn't have confidence in Dr. Talbot. It's just that this is such a serious thing, and they'd feel better getting another opinion."

It was hard for me to argue with anyone who wanted a second opinion for a major illness, especially since I had just written a much-publicized book on the subject. What's more, Lester was a good friend. So I agreed to drive forty miles on a nasty winter night.

"Ask the family to let Dr. Talbot know I'm coming." This was the ethical thing to do. "I'll be there at about nine tonight, so please have him arrange permission for me to examine his patient and review the chart." Medical ethics again. You just can't pick up a chart or examine someone without permission in a hospital where you are not on staff. "Call me back after he clears it."

A few minutes later, Lester phoned again. "Talbot says you're wasting your time and the patient's money. It's a clear-cut stroke, he's treating it properly, and there's no reason for you to come. But if the family insists, he'll arrange for you to have access to the chart and patient. However, he's not coming to meet you there; he says there's no need for him to do so." Most doctors normally extend that courtesy to a consulting colleague, especially one who has made a long trip in lousy weather.

When I arrived at the hospital, the patient's family was waiting anxiously for me. Dr. Talbot, who had previously told everyone he wasn't coming, was true to his word. He wasn't there. The nurse gave me the chart, and I studied it. It was evident from the record that this patient did have a neurological problem. He was a fifty-five-year-old man who had been admitted to the hospital the previous day because of a severe headache, visual problems, and weakness of his right leg. Pretty straightforward so far. But he had none of the predisposing risk factors for stroke such as high blood pressure, elevated cholesterol, a cardiac arrhythmia such as atrial fibrillation that might have caused a clot to dislodge and travel to the brain, or a history of some bleeding disorder that might cause a brain hemorrhage. Why, I wondered, had he been stricken?

After talking to the patient's wife and daughter, I went in to his room to examine him. The only abnormal neurological findings were slightly slurred speech and some weakness of his right leg. What concerned me in the history were the recurring severe headaches that had started a few weeks earlier. He'd never had them before, and Dr. Talbot had told him that they were probably due to stress. (What would we doctors do without stress and viruses to blame for the multitude of symptoms whose causes we don't understand?) He told me that the pressure in his eyes was normal and that his vision and glasses were fine too. The headaches always started late in the day, continued into the night, and were worse in the morning. It was only a couple of days ago that he became aware of some weakness in his right leg.

So these symptoms had not started abruptly, as is usually the case with a stroke. This entire story sounded to me more like the symptoms of a brain tumor. By the time I had finished taking the history and examining him, I felt even more strongly that this was a real possibility.

I wasn't sure, but if this was, in fact, a tumor and not a stroke, then the blood thinner he was getting—the correct treatment for stroke—could cause bleeding into the tumor. I didn't tell the family that I suspected a tumor; I wanted to discuss it first with Dr. Talbot. The nurse gave me his home number. By this time, it was almost ten o'clock. He answered the phone himself. "Dr. Talbot, this is Dr. Isadore Rosenfeld. We haven't met, but I know of your reputation. I'm sorry to disturb you at home. As you were told, the patient's family asked me to see him in consultation. I have just reviewed his chart and examined him. I wonder whether you considered the possibility of a brain tumor?" I proceeded to tell him why this seemed like a reasonable diagnosis. "I'm concerned about the anticoagulants, Dr. Talbot, and their potential for causing a hemorrhage into the tumor."

Dr. Talbot was silent a few moments, then replied. "Dr. Rosenfeld, are you a neurologist?"

"No," I answered, "I'm not."

"Neither am I. I'm a cardiologist, like you. I called a very good neurologist to see this patient this afternoon. He agreed with the diagnosis of stroke, and I'm satisfied that he and I are right. Thank-you for your input, and good night." With that he hung up, leaving me holding the phone, speechless. He wanted no dialogue. His mind was closed, and he clearly resented my interfering with *his* patient.

Had I felt less strongly about the possibility of a tumor, I'd probably have left it at that. However, I was furious that my opinion should have been given such short shrift when there was so much at stake. I didn't know what to do. How could I leave this patient in jeopardy? What recourse did I have? And then I had an inspired thought. I called my good friend, Dr. Fred Plum, at home in New York. Dr. Plum is one of the most famous neurologists in America and was, at the time, chairman of neurology at Cornell Medical School. It was now pushing ten thirty. "Fred, I feel terrible asking you to do this. It's late, and the weather is lousy, but would you do me a great favor? Would you come out to White Plains?"

"When? You don't mean tonight, do you?"

"Yes, Fred. I do. And here's why." I then recounted the details of my consultation. "I'm not sure I'm right, Fred. You're the best one to make the final diagnosis. But if this man has a tumor, continuing the present therapy may hurt him. And that bastard doctor of his didn't even give me the courtesy of discussing or considering that possibility."

To his everlasting credit, the president of the American Neurological Association drove forty miles in the middle of a rainstorm and arrived at White Plains Hospital near midnight. We reviewed the chart together; he examined the patient, and then said to me, "You know, for a cardiologist, you made a pretty good neurological call. This man almost certainly has a brain tumor."

"Fred," I asked. "Do me another favor. Call Talbot and tell him the news." Now, you've got to know Fred Plum to understand why I relished this moment. Fred tends to be imperious, especially given his credentials. I suspect he was also looking forward to making the call. He dialed Dr. Talbot's home. "Good evening. Dr. Talbot? This is Dr. Fred Plum, the Anne Parrish Titzell Professor of Neurology at the New York Hospital–Cornell Medical Center, and chairman of the department. I have just examined your patient here at White Plains Hospital. Dr. Talbot, I believe this man very probably has a brain tumor. I have told him and his family that it is in his best interest to be transferred immediately to New York Hospital by ambulance. They've agreed and asked Dr. Rosenfeld and me to take over the case. We plan to stop the anticoagulants immediately and do the necessary tests to confirm the presence of a tumor first thing in the morning. If we find one and re able to remove it, the patient will return to your care, if he so chooses. Do you have any questions, Dr. Talbot?"

Talbot was as speechless as I had been a little earlier when he'd hung up on me. We called the ambulance and transferred the patient to our medical center within the hour. The next day, we found that he did indeed have a brain tumor. Happily, it was benign, it was completely removed surgically, and the patient was cured!

You'd think that Dr. Talbot would have been mortified by his behavior and its consequences. But about a month later, at a meeting of the New York County Medical Society's board of censors, of which I happened to be the chairman at the time, there was a letter from Dr. Talbot complaining that Dr. Fred Plum had behaved unethically by "stealing" a patient from him! I recused myself from the deliberations after giving the other side of the story. You can imagine what the board did with that letter and how much I enjoyed reading its reply to Dr. Talbot.

The moral of this story is simple: second opinions can save lives, and doctors must keep an open mind.

45

WHEN I VOTED RIGHT— AND WHEN I VOTED WRONG

It's not easy to challenge the establishment and win. The laws, customs, and decisions established by those in power are almost always binding. You either conform and obey or end up a social outcast, or worse. Some years ago, I was offended by one such fiat handed down from above. But this time, I was in a position to do something about it.

In 1985, I was elected president of the New York County Medical Society, the largest local doctors' organization in the nation and a member of the American Medical Association. Its physicians represent all the specialties in Manhattan. Over the years, it has come to be viewed as the bellwether of medical opinion in the country.

Midway through my one-year term as president, we received a notice from the World Medical Association (WMA) that its next meeting would be held in Johannesburg, South Africa. The WMA is composed of all the medical associations of the Western world, including our AMA. In 1985, South Africa was still in the throes of apartheid. I was shocked! Why would the AMA (and my society to which it belonged) participate in a meeting in a country where blacks were so badly treated? I could not justify going along with this edict, not only because of my own conscience but also out of respect for our African American members.

I learned that, anticipating resistance to having the meeting held in its country, the South African government and that nation's medical society (which, incidentally, was all white) were prepared to waive all restrictions on visiting black physicians for the duration of the meeting. How decent of them! For me, the decision of the AMA to go there was very much like going to Berlin during the Nazi era because the Germans promised they would not enforce any of their racial policies on visiting Jews for the duration.

I felt strongly that even if the AMA persisted in its folly, the New York County Medical Society should boycott the meeting—and do so in a very public way. I called an emergency meeting of my board of directors to enlist its support. I was surprised that my view was not unanimously shared. Some directors rationalized that since the AMA, our parent organization, had decided that we should all go to South Africa, we in New York were morally obliged to do so. You can't have splinter groups in medicine, they argued. Others felt that it was too late to back out, since every other country, including the U.S., had already agreed to participate. It must have taken a tremendous amount of work to organize such a large international meeting, and it would be a formidable task to start all over again in some other locale.

I was appalled by this position and told my board that I couldn't care less what commitments had been made on our behalf: this was a matter of principle. We had an obligation to black doctors *and* to our own code of ethics not to meet in a country that discriminates so blatantly. We, the largest affiliate in the AMA, had not been consulted, had not agreed to anything, and I did not feel bound by its decision. In fact, I said that I'd resign as president unless there was unanimous consensus on this matter from my board. I would not continue to serve if they did not share these very basic sentiments.

After some further discussion, the entire board of directors of the New York County chapter of the AMA voted unanimously against attending the meeting in South Africa. We further drafted a letter of "no confidence" in the AMA leadership that had perpetrated such an outrage and insisted that it withdraw from participation unless the WMA changed the site of its meeting.

A few days after we sent this letter, I received an irate phone call from AMA headquarters in Chicago. "Who do you think you are? We've committed ourselves and all our members to attending this meeting. We received assurances that any blacks attending would be well treated."

"Would you go to South Africa if you were black, even with such assurances?" I asked.

"I certainly would," he answered disingenuously.

"Then you're even less sensitive than I thought," I replied, and added, "Here's the bottom line: we are not going to Johannesburg, and I hope to persuade enough American doctors not to go either."

The next day, I met with several medical student leaders at Cornell, both black and white. I informed them of what had transpired and asked for their support. They offered it unanimously. The students organized a march on the South African Mission to the UN, complete with placards, three days hence. I telephoned AMA headquarters to advise them of our plans. "Hold off the march," they pleaded. "We're reconsidering our participation. We'll call you in a day or two."

A few days later we were notified that the forthcoming meeting of the WMA would be held in Brussels, not Johannesburg.

And When I Voted the Wrong Way

There is an ironic twist to this next story. I had for many years served on the Albert and Mary Lasker Foundation Medical Research Award jury. It was chaired by Dr. Michael DeBakey and made up of leading scientists and researchers in various fields of medicine. Our jury reviewed the most important contributions made in every area of medicine during the past year and awarded the prize to the one considered to be the most significant. In 1974, Dr. John Charnley, a British orthopedist, was nominated for the Lasker award in recognition of his invention of the artificial hip. In the discussion that followed, I voted against his receiving this award. Yes, I knew that many people were disabled by hip disease, but in my opinion it was much more important to recognize someone who'd made a major contribution in the field of cancer or vascular disease, from which millions of people worldwide die every year. I emphasized that I felt sorry for anyone with hip problems, but I did not consider this to be a major area of concern. I argued in vain. The jury voted to give Dr. Charnley the Lasker prize.

We all make mistakes in judgment—and this was one of the more ironic ones in my life. Without Charnley's invention, as you will discover in a later chapter, I would have spent the rest of my life in pain and in a wheelchair.

46

TO RUSSIA—WITH LOVE?

In the early 1970s, at the height of the cold war, the Nixon administration decided to change its Soviet policy from one of confrontation to détente in order to relax international tensions and reduce the threat of nuclear war. Détente was to consist primarily of scientific and artistic exchanges between our two countries. Among the scientific programs proposed by the administration, and welcomed by the Soviets, was a cooperative study of sudden cardiac death. The National Heart, Lung and Blood Institute appointed a team to meet with Russian heart specialists and share experience and technology in identifying those most vulnerable to sudden cardiac death and to find ways to prevent it. In this country, of the roughly half-million people who die from heart attacks each year, about 350,000 do so suddenly, often before they can receive any medical help. The same is true in Russia.

Having been a member of several government task forces in such areas as arteriosclerosis, hypertension, and special cardiac devices (the artificial heart among them), I was chosen as one of five members of this new joint Soviet-American team. The group was headed by Dr. Bernard Lown, a pioneer in electrical defibrillation of the heart, and also included Dr. William Roberts, chief of pathology at the National Heart, Lung, and Blood Institute, and Leonard Cobb, who had recently trained rescue teams in Seattle to provide the public with emergency cardiac care. His program was responsible for saving many lives in that city.

Despite the administration's attempts to relax international tensions, relations between Russia and the U.S. remained tense. We were scheduled to leave for Russia in October 1973. A few days before our departure, war broke out in the Middle East. Henry Kissinger, Nixon's secretary of state, was shuttling back and forth between Washington and Moscow. The Soviet bloc supported the Arab nations, and the Americans backed Israel. Our access to Middle East oil supplies was at stake. It was in this difficult climate that our sudden cardiac death team was to leave for Moscow.

Shortly before our departure, we were summoned to Washington for a briefing. The Jewish members of the team were told that if they had any reservations about going to Russia at this time, in view of that nation's support of the Arab cause, our resignation would be understood and accepted. None of us did so. We were warned about conditions in the Soviet Union; we would be watched, our conversations would be monitored in every closed area that lent itself to "bugging"—hotel rooms, homes, and even some public places. We were advised to be very careful about what we said; never to discuss sensitive political matters among ourselves or with a Soviet citizen except in a park or on the street; not to make disparaging or critical remarks about our hosts, their government, its political system, or its policies.

Most important, we were cautioned to scrupulously avoid any illegal financial transactions. Dollars were worth ten times more on the black market than they were at a bank—and we were warned that if we were caught in any such shenanigans, our government would not bail us out. Also, we were instructed never to take any letters back to the U.S. The Soviet Union was full of people who wanted to leave, and they were constantly seeking help to do so. Someone might plead with us to please take a letter to a relative in the United States. "Don't ever do it. The 'letter' may be a plant and contain some pseudo-secret information that Russian agents will find on your person and accuse you of espionage. You may then become 'trading fodder' for a future spy exchange." This bugging mania and suspicion were translated into the strictest security precautions inside our Moscow embassy. (On one of my visits to our ambassador there, we chatted in a clear plastic room hanging from the ceiling, in which there was no electricity and no plugs! It was a "container" that could not in any way be monitored.) Strangely enough, one warning we were *not* given was to avoid being seduced by a member of the opposite sex.

This stark briefing certainly didn't whet my appetite to go to the Soviet Union at this time, given the uncertain international political situation. But one week later we were issued our official U.S. passports and departed on our mission.

We flew to London where we rested for a day, and then left on the Soviet airline, Aeroflot. A dour Russian stewardess greeted us at the door of the plane. She waved my four colleagues into the economy section of the aircraft. However, she directed me into the first-class cabin! Why me? Was this the start of some intrigue against which we had been warned? Was the enemy with whom we were "détenting" trying to bribe me? Ridiculous! I had no secret information!

Anyone who's ever visited a police state knows that there is no arguing with authority, even that of an airline stewardess. I looked quizzically at the hostess before I entered the luxury cabin, and she said tersely, "Economy class is full." I decided to enjoy my lucky break; at the curtain separating the peasants from the elite, I waved at my four friends squeezed into their little economy-class seats and returned to my wide, comfortable one.

Four hours later, we landed safely in Moscow—in those days, that wasn't something you took for granted on Aeroflot. The weather matched the climate of our Washington briefing: gray, cold, and rainy. The Moscow terminal was drab; soldiers patrolled the airfield and the airport with submachine guns. However, inside, our Russian hosts were waiting, all smiles and very cordial. We were warmly welcomed; they were really happy to see us. They facilitated the entry formalities, and we were soon on our way in to Moscow. For me this was a homecoming of sorts; it had been some fifty years since my father had left Russia.

The road from the airport was a straight boulevard dotted with huge signs showing happy workers and their families, often with fists clenched in determination—a testimonial to their "happiness" under communism. We passed the memorial marking the closest point the Nazi troops had reached on their drive to Moscow in World War II some thirty years earlier.

We checked into our hotel, a drab, overheated, boxlike structure in downtown Moscow. Just outside the elevator on each floor sat a grim-faced lady whose job, as far as we could tell, was to monitor our comings and goings. Our rooms were small but adequate. Fortunately, I had brought my own toilet paper. I was also glad I took along some soap: the fifty-cent-size piece I found in the bathroom produced neither suds nor scent.

Our Russian colleagues hosted a dinner for us in the private dining room of the hotel that night. It was a banquet to end all banquets. Mounds of black and red caviar, each egg the size of a pearl, a huge variety of smoked fish, fresh vegetables—an extraordinary feast. There were eleven of us—five Soviet physicians, five Americans, and an interpreter, Olga, who was seated beside me. She was a beautiful, dark-haired woman in her twenties, who spoke excellent English and easily translated back and forth. About an hour after we sat down at the table, in the middle of the meal, I became aware of her hand gently squeezing my thigh. I looked at Olga with surprise. She smiled sweetly and said innocently, "I love you."

Frankly, women have always been attracted to me, but the speed of Olga's response to my charms was suspiciously rapid. My mind hearkened back to my briefing in Washington. But what could the Russians hope to achieve by subverting me with this beauty? Despite my natural inclination to assume that Olga's overtures were the result of my overwhelming sex appeal, I concluded that I was being set up. The quickest, most appropriate response I could make to her overtures was to remove her hand gently but firmly and say, "Not here. Not now."

I did not tell either my colleagues or my hosts about Olga. After all, love is a very private matter. She remained on the job throughout our entire stay and took every opportunity to tell me how much she loved me. One day she said, "I know you think I am spy. We can go to Finland for weekend." I got out of that one by telling her I didn't have a Finnish visa. In any event, she cried when the Russian team came to the airport to see us off.

When we returned for a second visit to the Soviet Union six months later, Olga was nowhere to be found. I asked our same Russian hosts where Olga was. They looked puzzled. "Olga? Who's Olga? We don't remember any Olga?" So much for the KGB.

When we left on our first mission, the fighting in the Middle East had just begun strong. Once we arrived in the Soviet Union, we had no way of knowing whether America's or Russia's allies would win. Because the situation was so tense, when we left the U.S., my patient Averell Harriman insisted that I take with me a letter of introduction to a very important Soviet official, Georgi Arbatov, head of the U.S. Canada Institute, a think tank that provided the Russian government with information about the West.

A couple of days after I arrived in Moscow, I went to see Comrade Arbatov at the institute. His office was large and sparsely decorated, with a big desk at one end. I gave him Harriman's letter, and we made some small talk. I was anxious to know how things were going in the Middle East, even if it meant getting only his side of the story. He started a tirade against America's pro-Israel policy. And then he gave it away. "Even if the Israelis win this battle, they cannot win the war against the entire Arab world." I immediately knew that the Israelis had won the war. He continued with, "The Arabs control the world's oil supply. Even if they lose this fight, they will strangle the West by withholding their oil. When that happens, and Americans can no longer drive their cars and have to queue up at the gas stations for hours, there will be a terrible outbreak of anti-Semitism in your country. Americans tolerate Jews as long as things are going well. Mark my words. There will be trouble." He obviously emphasized the Jewish angle because he knew I was Jewish. I pointed out to Arbatov that the West was the Arabs biggest *customer*—they weren't *giving* us their oil. I figured that some of the sultans and sheiks might think twice about their policies if their sales dropped too much for too long.

When our deliberations on sudden cardiac death started in Moscow, I was dismayed by the lack of equipment and facilities in that country. We brought with us technology that was commonplace in the U.S., such as the Holter monitor, which allows us to record a continuous ECG for twenty-four hours while the patient is up and about. A Holter monitor is one way to spot disturbances of heart rhythm that may be precursors of sudden death—yet there was not a single such unit in all of the Soviet Union. But what the Russian doctors lacked in equipment they more than made up for in scientific thinking. It was a pleasure to work with them.

During this and subsequent visits to the Soviet Union, I became aware of the depth of discontent in that country and that for many people, the government was indeed unpopular and ruled by virtue of fear and terror. One day, a senior Russian scientist asked me to go for a walk with him in the park. He was an important member of the Communist Party and was obviously trusted by the government that had appointed him to this joint task force. When we were out of earshot, he said to me, "Why is your country doing this? Why are you sending us all this equipment? You're perpetuating an evil system."

This was long before Ronald Reagan's "evil empire" speech. "We have the resources to make the best medical equipment, but everything is going to the military. If you leave us alone, the people will rise up against this tyranny. Any help you give us now only delays the inevitable and perpetuates our suffering." I thought, at the time, that his was a voice in the wilderness. When the Reagan administration decided to follow my friend's advice and play hardball instead of footsie with the Soviets, their system did indeed collapse.

One of the upshots of Dr. Lown's chairmanship of this Soviet-American committee was the friendship he developed with his Russian counterpart, Yevgeny Chazov. Chazov, like Lown, was a fine scientist and was the first to demonstrate that enzymes given intravenously to someone with an acute heart attack could dissolve the fresh clot responsible for the problem. This became standard treatment all over the world. Chazov and Lown also shared a commitment to peace and a terrible fear of nuclear war. Together, they formed an international medical society called the Physicians for Social Responsibility and began a worldwide campaign for nuclear disarmament. Chazov, who was the doctor to every Soviet leader, later became the Minister of Health, and ultimately introduced Lown to Mikhail Gorbachev. Lown and Chazov were credited with the input that led to the international nuclear arms agreement, as a result of which their organization was awarded the Nobel Peace Prize. Here's an ironic twist. At the presentation of that prize, one of the journalists in the audience had a sudden cardiac arrest. What a stroke of luck for him that two doctors on the Soviet-American task force on sudden cardiac death were there receiving the prize. They resuscitated him!

The sudden cardiac death task force was a great success. I remained part of the team for ten years, during which time we went to the Soviet Union once or twice year, and they came to the U.S. just a often. Our cooperation in this area resulted in some very important joint research findings and the development in both countries of important new drugs to prevent and treat sudden cardiac death. In addition, it led to deep friendships with our Russian counterparts that persist to this day.

47

To Russia—
with Averell Harriman

I first met Averell Harriman in 1972, shortly after he married Pamela Churchill Hayward. They were a very happy couple; he was in his early eighties and she was some thirty years younger. They had first met in London during the Second World War, when she was married to Randolph Churchill and Averell was President Roosevelt's personal envoy in charge of Lend-Lease and other aid to embattled Britain. I'm not privy to the nature of their relationship at that time, but I assume that it was amiable, at the very least. After the war, they went their separate ways, but obviously retained a soft spot for each other. When, in the course of their convoluted lives, it was possible for them to do so, they finally married—and remained happily together until he died at the age of ninety-four.

Harriman was one of those personalities who inspired genuine awe: a handsome, imposing, and intelligent man of patrician bearing. He didn't have a great sense of humor, at least by my standards; when someone told him a funny story that he usually didn't quite understand, he'd titter politely, being the gentleman he was. On rare occasions, however, when he did get the joke, he'd enthusiastically pound and slap his knees.

Born to great wealth, Harriman devoted his life to public service after his success in the business world. The scope of his career was breathtaking—U.S. envoy to Churchill and Stalin, then U.S. ambassador to Moscow during World War II, peace negotiator in our attempts to end the Vietnam conflict, governor of New York, and presidential troubleshooter during the cold war. It was during this latter time that I was his personal physician. In the years that followed, while I may have improved the quality of his life, and perhaps on occasion even saved it, he certainly enriched mine.

Shortly after Harriman became my patient, I detected a small cancer in his prostate gland during a routine physical exam. This was before the era of PSA tests and ultrasound exams of the prostate. The diagnosis was confirmed with a biopsy. The malignancy had not spread outside the prostate gland, and its cells were not aggressive. He was over eighty and had a new wife. The available therapy in those days—surgery, radiation, and hormones—or a combination thereof—would almost certainly give him unpleasant side effects; the "nerve-sparing" operation that reduces the likelihood of impotence and incontinence had not yet been devised. There was no acceptable way to treat prostate cancer successfully or humanely in those days for a man in his eighties, especially one recently married and still able to enjoy sexual relations. So since the tumor was not causing any symptoms and it had not spread, I decided on a course of "watchful waiting"—an option that is still widely practiced today. I monitored the governor at regular and frequent intervals until the time of his death at age ninety-four. In all those years, his prostate cancer remained dormant.

There is an important lesson to be learned from Harriman's experience. Urologists these days are often too quick to implement aggressive therapies for this malignancy in the elderly. These tumors often grow very slowly in older men; a conservative approach such as I took with Harriman should always be considered. Indeed, in Sweden, small, nonaggressive prostate tumors are routinely left alone in seniors. And recently, in this country, it has been suggested that we not even bother performing a PSA test in the blood to make the diagnosis after the age of seventy-five. Surgery, especially the new sophisticated procedures, can cure, but it can also kill, especially elderly men who have some heart, lung, or other disorders. Even though radiation is now much better tolerated, it can cause unpleasant side effects.

Harriman became virtually blind and deaf before he died. He had severe macular degeneration, which caused him to lose his frontal vision, although he did retain some peripheral sight. His deafness was too severe for the hearing aids then available; one had to speak clearly and in a loud voice in order for him to hear. Despite these infirmities, which would have daunted lesser men, Harriman remained active and productive to the day he died, both in his personal life and as the envoy to the Soviet Union of a succession of American presidents.

Harriman was especially effective in his dealings with the Russians. He had started trading with them back in the 1920s, and since then, in the various government posts that he'd held, had come to understand the motivation and psychology of the communist leadership better than most. And so, whenever the need arose during the cold war, he was often asked by the White House to "straighten things out" in Moscow.

Harriman invited me to accompany him on these missions, probably at the insistence of his wife, who was worried about his health. However, he did not want to convey an image of frailty and was concerned that if I always came with him on these travels, it would be assumed that he was a sick man. He resented anyone holding his arm while he climbed stairs or walked in unfamiliar surroundings. Since I'd been going to the Soviet Union as a member of the sudden-death task force, he always introduced me as a close friend, an old hand in Soviet-American relations, and only incidentally as his physician.

Over the years, I learned how to be unobtrusive in his life of high-level diplomacy, while at the same time offering him protection should he need it. Our personal friendship soon overshadowed the doctor-patient relationship, and our trips together to Moscow were fun and fascinating. I learned something about diplomatic parlance, nuances, innuendo, and even the body movements that few laymen appreciate. Remember, his missions took place during the height of the cold war, when tensions between the United States and the Soviet Union were very high; when the Soviet government was both anti-Israel and anti-Semitic; when it persecuted Jews but did not allow them to emigrate. Soviet-American relations were further strained by the Soviets' political and military support of the Arab states. The result was years of crisis after crisis, throughout which Harriman figured prominently as a mediator.

The Soviets liked and respected Harriman. They remembered how supportive he was as our ambassador to Moscow during the darkest days of World War II; they knew he had been instrumental in arranging the vast amount of military material that the Allied powers, especially the United States, had sent to them. At the same time, they knew that in this cold war era, Harriman was a very tough negotiator. The Russians called him "the alligator," and with very good reason. I remember one session when President Carter sent him to Moscow. Our government had learned that the Soviets were building bomb shelters in Moscow, a move that suggested a lack of confidence in the future of world peace. He asked Harriman to find out why the Russians were acting so provocatively and to persuade them to desist.

In one of his meetings with senior Soviet officials at the Kremlin, as Harriman pored over the files provided by our State Department, he couldn't find a particular document he wanted to discuss. After searching his papers, he turned to Mr. Gromyko, the Soviet foreign minister, and said with a perfectly straight face, "I don't seem to have what I'm looking for here. I probably left it in my hotel room. Oh, well, in that case, your people have probably already copied it. So take a look at it when you get home tonight, and we can discuss it in the morning." The Russians were astonished at his brazen candor, but smiled. Only Harriman could get away with such an undiplomatic comment. I doubt that he was serious, but with his poker face, there was no telling.

On one of our trips together, after the Harrimans and I arrived late one afternoon in Moscow after flying from London, someone from the Soviet foreign office called to ask confidentially whether the ambassador, as the Russians called him, would be too tired to have dinner that evening. (Of course, the Russians understood why I was there with him.) I told them I thought that Harriman was up to it. We all met at 8:00 p.m. in a private dining room of the hotel. There were ten of us at the dinner: the Americans were the Harrimans; Peter Swiers, a longtime confidant of Harriman's; an interpreter from our State Department (Harriman never trusted the Soviet interpreters and always traveled with one of his own, although to the best of my knowledge, none of them ever laid a hand on his thigh); and me. On the Russian side were Giorgi Arbatov and four other officials from their foreign office.

The dinner was spectacular. It began with endless amounts of caviar and other delicacies. The atmosphere was cordial and the conversation candid and interesting, despite the strained relations between our two countries at the time. Seated next to me was a young Russian diplomat with whom I made the usual small talk.

The entree was a small hen, grilled to perfection, accompanied by a container of liquid garlic with which it could be sprinkled. I love garlic and used it liberally years before I was even aware of its many health benefits. So I proceeded to douse my bird with it. The young Russian sitting next to me watched with interest, then leaned over to me and said in a quiet voice, "I see that Jews like garlic."

I couldn't believe his gall! (Had I not been in the Soviet Union, I would have used the word "chutzpah"!) I saw red! (No pun intended.) How dare this nasty, little communist anti-Semite make such a snide remark about Jews in such an august diplomatic setting? Such blatant racism evoked my worst childhood experiences of prejudice from French Quebecois.

I could not let it pass. I struck my wineglass with a spoon and called for everyone's attention. "Please," I said, "we have an expert on Jews here tonight. He has made some very astute observations on Jewish eating habits on which he appears to be quite an authority. He's obviously done important research on Jews. I'd like him to tell us what other pearls of wisdom his studies have yielded." There was a stunned silence in the room; this was a most undiplomatic thing for me to have said. The chap beside me reddened. He'd obviously not expected that I would embarrass him in this way in front of his superiors. "Professor, don't get excited," he said. "It's not what you think. You see, you have chicken, and you pour garlic over it. I have chicken; I pour garlic over it, too. You are Jew, I am Jew! Jews like garlic!"

It's a wonder Harriman ever invited me to Russia again.

When our dinner was over, this same young man asked me to join him for a walk in the park (that's what Russians did in those days when they wanted to talk privately without being monitored), to tell me the full extent of Soviet anti-Semitism. He'd only been invited there that night out of courtesy to me—a Jew!

In 1976, Harriman wrote a book about his wartime experiences, entitled *Special Envoy to Churchill and Stalin*. It was well received in the West and in the Soviet Union. Shortly afterward, President Jimmy Carter sent Harriman to Moscow to confer with Leonid Brezhnev, the general-secretary of the Communist Party. This was not long after the Harrimans had come to my fiftieth birthday party in New York and presented me with a pair of beautiful and unusual gold cuff links by Bulgari. They were semicircular, the kind that pinces the holes in the sleeve instead of going directly through it.

In Moscow, the night before Harriman's meeting with the general secretary, he was preparing to inscribe a copy of his book for Brezhnev. He wanted to be sure that what he wrote was politically correct, so we considered several different greetings, such as "To the General-Secretary, and your devotion to peace" (which we rejected because it might be misconstrued by the hawks back home). We finally settled on the rather innocuous "To the General-Secretary, in friendship."

At about ten that evening, the telephone rang. In those days, hotel phones in the Soviet Union rang at all hours of the day and night; often as not, there was just a dial tone when you picked it up. We never knew whether these false alarms were due to an antiquated faulty phone system or the KGB making sure that we were in our rooms and not causing mischief somewhere in Moscow.

Harriman took the call himself; it was a deputy foreign minister. "I'm calling to remind you, Mr. Ambassador, that we will have a car at your hotel at 10:45 in the morning to take you to the Kremlin for your meeting. And by the way, Mr. Ambassador, you do have a present for the general-secretary, don't you?"

Now, there's something that you should know about Averell Harriman. Much as I admired and respected the man, generosity was not one of his strong suits. Don't get me wrong. He was a philanthropist; he donated vast sums of money, millions of dollars, to support worthy causes throughout the world—including The Harriman Institute of Russian Studies at Columbia University, launched with a ten-million-dollar gift. But that only required phoning a bank and issuing instructions; it did not involve taking out his wallet and physically extracting actual money to *pay for* something—and that's what Harriman didn't enjoy.

His face, never full of color, blanched three more shades. "A present?" he mumbled weakly, and then with relief, added, "Yes, of course I have a present. I have just finished inscribing my new book for Mr. Brezhnev."

"No, Mr. Ambassador, not a book, a present." And then he added memorably, "The general-secretary is only human."

That threw Harriman for a loop. He hung up the phone, turned to his wife, and asked, "Pam, do you have something we can give

Brezhnev? I think this guy called to send me a signal that Brezhnev has a gift for me, and he doesn't want me to be embarrassed."

"You must be joking," Pamela replied. "What kind of gift could I have for him? I might have a piece of my jewelry for his wife, but what could I possibly give him?"

This was a diplomatic crisis. In any other city, in any other country, at any other time, one could go to a shop early the next morning and buy something suitable. But this was Moscow in the 1970s, where every store had long queues, and what they sold was not something you'd give the general-secretary of the Communist Party anyway. The foreign currency shops (*Beryoshkas*) for tourists had nothing fine or appropriate either and, in any case, didn't open early enough for us to go shopping. So we were stumped. Harriman was beside himself. "Maybe our ambassador has something I can give Brezhnev." But he was out of the embassy for the evening, and no one knew when he'd be back.

Then I remembered Harriman's birthday gift to me—the gold cuff links. I had brought them with me, intending to wear them some evening. "Gov," I said, "I've got Brezhnev's gift; your gold cuff links from Bulgari. They're still in their original chamois bag! I'll be sad to part with them, but—"

I'd never seen Harriman so overjoyed. "That's perfect, absolutely perfect. Thanks so much! I'll replace them as soon as we get home."

The next morning, after their meeting, as Harriman correctly predicted, Brezhnev presented him with a beautiful Russian winter scene set in inlaid semiprecious stones. In return, Harriman gave the general-secretary my gold cuff links. Brezhnev opened the chamois bag and took them out. He had obviously never seen the pincer variety and thought they were earrings! Puzzled, he put one up to his ear and exclaimed, "*Shto!*"—the Russian equivalent of "What the hell is this!"

When we returned to New York, Harriman replaced my cuff links, but he was so shaken by Brezhnev's reaction that the new pair was of the conventional design.

The highlight of all my trips to Russia with Harriman came at the conclusion of one particularly successful and cordial visit, when the politburo honored him at a farewell dinner. It was a gala affair held in the main banquet room of their foreign ministry, and all the brass were there. Official dinners in most countries, including ours, are usually boring—the food is so-so and the speeches are long. Not so in Russia.

Food for the bigwigs is fabulous, and instead of a few lengthy dis-courses by a handful of tiresome politicians, there are countless short toasts by everyone. They designate a witty toastmaster, called a *tamada*, who calls on everyone to say a few words. There is a pecking order; the most senior officials speak first and the list proceeds down the line of importance. Every toast is followed by an obligatory swig of vodka; otherwise, it wouldn't be binding, would it?

The subject matter also follows a descending order of impor-tance. So the first toast would be by Harriman on the U.S. side toast-ing Brezhnev and the Soviet Union; his Russian counterpart would reply with a toast to the president of the United States and our coun-try. After almost two hours of toasting and swigging, we mercifully reached the low end of the toasting totem pole. A minor Soviet offi-cial, who'd obviously had twelve drinks too many, staggered to his feet, held up his glass, and said, "I propose toast to Mrs. Garriman (as pronounced in Russian) and to women's lib, because without Mrs. Garriman is no women's lib." Everyone dutifully stood up, ready to validate those wishes with a little more vodka. But it was not to be, because a slightly more senior official interrupted with, "Moment. Moment. To Mrs. Garriman, OK; to women's lib, *nyet*, because wom-en's lib can also produce a Golda Meir." Unbelievable, right? Well, there he was, standing, glass held high, and the last words he'd ut-tered were "Golda Meir." Without a moment's hesitation and acting much more quickly than I usually do, I jumped up and said, "Here, here, to Golda Meir!" There was mass confusion; this was a totally unexpected turn of events. But the perception was that a Russian of-ficial had toasted Golda Meir, and so had an American. There must have been a sudden change in Soviet policy toward Israel of which they were unaware! Clearly they had no choice, so everyone stood up, lifted their glasses, toasted Golda Meir, and cemented it with a hearty gulp of vodka.

About a year later, I received a call from Dr. DeBakey in Houston. "Isadore," he said, "the Soviet minister of health is visiting me here and will be leaving for New York tomorrow. When I asked him to look you up, he said he knows all about you. He tells me that when relations between Israel and Russia were at their lowest point, you got the entire Soviet politburo to toast the prime minister of Israel!"

A year or two later, it gave me great pleasure to recount this story to Mrs. Meir on one of her visits to New York. Then we both toasted Averell Harriman.

48

THE TSUNAMI

The tsunami disaster that struck Indonesia on December 26, 2004, was so great that nations throughout the world were asked for whatever medical assistance they could provide. Many countries sent supplies and hospital ships. The United States decided to activate the U.S. naval hospital ship USNS *Mercy* and ordered it to sail immediately to the Indian Ocean. The *Mercy* had heretofore been sent to war zones to provide medical care for injured American troops. In peacetime it is kept in San Diego harbor, and its medical staff works in the San Diego Veterans Administration Hospital because there is nothing for them to do aboard the ship. After it had received orders to sail to Indonesia, given the magnitude of the disaster, it was clear that many more doctors, nurses, and medical technicians would be needed in addition to the *Mercy*'s normal medical staff. The navy asked Project Hope for help, and within days, scores of volunteers were selected to join the staff of the *Mercy*. Every one of them committed themselves to a thirty-day tour away from their jobs, homes, and families—with *no* pay.

During the next forty days, the personnel on the *Mercy* treated more than ten thousand patients ashore and afloat, performed nearly twenty thousand medical procedures, provided sanitation teams, immunized thousands, supplied oxygen to hospitals that needed it and engineering teams to repair engines and pumps, and carried out other public health measures. After most of these acute medical problems in the disaster area had been dealt with, *Mercy* set sail for home.

The navy suspected that on its way home via the rest of Indonesia, East Timor, New Guinea, and the Marshall Islands—*Mercy* might well find communities that also needed medical care.

I was invited to join the ship and to report to the nation—and the world—the extent of *Mercy*'s humanitarian impact. Why me? Because I was then the health editor of *Parade* magazine as well as host of Fox's *Housecall* show and could report to the American people in the world what our navy had done for these disadvantaged areas. So my wife and I (she refused to let me go alone) flew to East Timor and boarded this wonderful hospital ship.

My first view of *Mercy* was from a Blackhawk helicopter off the coast of Alor, Indonesia, as we were about to land on its deck. This vessel is nearly three football fields long and can accommodate one thousand patients. It has twelve well-equipped operating rooms, an intensive-care unit, and the latest medical equipment necessary to perform the most complicated surgical operations.

During our one week on board, I had never in my entire life seen so much rampant, unrecognized, undiagnosed, and untreated disease. Remember, this was not in the tsunami-stricken areas. This was "normal" countryside in this nation. Entire communities were riddled by malaria; tuberculosis, pneumonia, and other chronic lung diseases; malnutrition; blindness; cancers; abscesses that were spreading bacteria throughout their victims' bodies. Village after village had no access to any medical care whatsoever: their kids had never been vaccinated and had never used, or even seen, a toothbrush.

Spending only one or two days in each village, the *Mercy* staff set fractures, extracted abscessed teeth, repaired hernias, removed cataracts, handed out reading glasses, treated life-threatening infections, and instituted public health measures to prevent epidemics of everything from malaria to dengue fever to cholera. They repaired broken waterlines and sprayed hospital walls with mosquito repellent. One Project Hope doctor who refused to stop examining the hundreds of children lined up waiting for him in 100 degree heat collapsed from dehydration. Members of the naval staff carried child after child onto the ship for emergency treatment. I wish I could share with you the emotions of the scores of blind men and women who never expected to be able to see again whose vision Project Hope's volunteer eye surgeons restored by removing their cataracts. They were shouting, "I can see! I can see!" as they left the ship. I wish you could have seen the seven-year-old child who, several years earlier, had suffered burns on his knees and, because of all the scar tissue that it had formed, was unable to walk. After *Mercy's* surgeons removed the scar tissue, the boy was actually able to run off the ship! I wish you could have seen the kids brought on board with high fever and serious infections such as meningitis cured by high doses of intravenous antibiotics that had not previously been available to them.

Whenever our ship left a port, there were hundreds of men, women, and children standing at the dock, waving good-bye, many crying, and shouting: "Thank-you America!" All this led me to wonder why a ship like *Mercy* had remained anchored for fourteen years in San Diego harbor when she could have and should have been sailing to these and other parts of the world, not only to save lives but also to demonstrate the compassion and expertise that makes this country so great. These visits would not only be acts of humanitarianism, but also an antidote to terrorism against our country.

I learned an important lesson from my trip: that we can reverse the hostility that much of the world feels against America by performing such humanitarian acts. According to a BBC poll, almost 70 percent of all Indonesians, the most populous Muslim nation, formerly viewed our country with hostility before the tsunami. Another poll found that almost 70 percent of them now think favorably of us after our humanitarian help during their terrible crisis.

As the *Mercy* departed Banda Aceh, an Indonesian interpreter named Tamalia Alisjahban addressed and thanked the ship's staff: "You were first greeted with suspicion, then puzzlement, and then great fondness. And now nearly all the patients are saying how grateful they are and that we really can't thank you enough. There's nothing we could give to you to repay your kindness and care, it will have to be God who repays you. In Indonesia we say, *terima kasih,* which means 'please accept our love.' "

Exhausted and seasick, I disembarked from *Mercy* the evening before my flight home from Dili, East Timor. At 6 p.m., I received a call from the mission commander, Capt. Timothy McCully, who had planned to come ashore for a farewell dinner with me that evening.

"*Mercy* has just been ordered back to Sumatra," he said. "They've had an 8.7 magnitude earthquake that has already taken hundreds of lives. They need us. I expect a large-scale onboard medical-treatment operation, with multiple operating rooms working simultaneously."

Fifteen minutes later, from my hotel window, I saw the ship set sail with most of Project Hope's doctors and nurses, who had been scheduled to leave in the next few days, still on board. They'd volunteered for an extended tour of duty to help with this new tragedy. I had never met such a dedicated and hardworking group of men and women. I have never felt more proud to be a physician and an American.

I cannot imagine any of the children or parents I met on the *Mercy* embracing Osama bin Laden's anti-American vitriol or wishing harm to a single American or supporting the cause of any of our terrorist enemies.

Can we earn the respect—and accept the love—of millions of others around the world? The answer is a resounding yes. We most definitely can . . . and we must! I expressed my strong feeling about this in an editorial in *Parade* magazine. Shortly thereafter, I received a note from the director of Project Hope, John Howe. "Dr. Rosenfeld, your prescription for a healthier U.S. foreign policy works! The steps you outlined have in fact improved foreign attitudes toward the U.S., and we have the hard numbers to support it. At a time when people are questioning the U.S. approach to foreign policy, here is one solution that produced positive results!"

The U.S. has now decided to keep ships like *Mercy* constantly cruising areas where medical help is always needed, not only during acute crises.

49

SHOULD (AND CAN)
A DOCTOR TREAT
HIMSELF?

I'm convinced that it's a good thing for doctors themselves to get sick once in a while; it makes them better doctors. For example, a physician who was once a heavy smoker or drinker and quit, or who was overweight and endured the pangs of dieting, or who himself suffered a heart attack is better able to help others similarly stricken. I've found I empathize more with a patient who presents with an illness that I've had—especially if I was anxious about it.

When I was forty years old, something happened to me that had a great impact on my psyche and my outlook on life. I had always been in good health, worked hard, and enjoyed every minute of it. I had few of the usual commonplace disease risk factors in my health profile: I smoked only occasionally to be sociable and I drank wine in moderation (when this was not known to be good for you). But I also exercised regularly, watched my cholesterol level, kept my blood pressure normal, was happily married, and was considerably thinner than I am today.

Then one night, "disaster" struck. My wife and I had gone out for a Chinese meal with some friends. The food was delicious, and I probably ate a little more than my share. In those days, we knew nothing about monosodium glutamate and Chinese restaurant syndrome (which causes indigestion and a variety of other symptoms). We got home about ten in the evening, I read for a while, and then went to sleep. At about 2 a.m., I was awakened by a burning sensation behind my breastbone. I had seen enough of these cases to suspect that this might very well be a heart attack.

It's strange how one doesn't always practice what one preaches or accept what one knows to be true. I have warned countless patients to call the doctor immediately when they experience this particular symptom, and get to the nearest emergency room fast because their lives might depend on it. But when it happened to me, I rationalized it all away. First, I didn't want to waken and alarm my wife, sleeping so peacefully beside me. Then I thought that this was probably indigestion, a mistake so many people make, often with fatal results. I sat up to see if the burning would go away as often happens when the symptoms are due to gastric reflux—and it did! Reassured, I went back to sleep.

The following morning I awakened with trepidation and anxiety. Daylight brought me to my senses. Without telling my wife, I called one of my doctor friends and told him my story. He was appalled that I had waited so long. He had me come right over to see him. He examined me, took some blood for cardiac enzymes (in a heart attack certain chemicals are released from the injured heart muscle and enter the bloodstream, where they can be measured), and recorded an electrocardiogram. To his surprise and my relief, the tracing was normal, as was the physical exam. "You're lucky," he told me with relief. "Next time, practice what you preach."

I went home and felt I was now able to recount to my wife the details of the drama. She was understandably furious with me at my stupidity, and then we drank a toast to health—hers, mine, and everyone else's.

This was a spring Friday, and we were going to our place in the country. I spent the rest of that weekend hauling out the lawn furniture from the basement and doing other heavy chores. I felt perfectly well and gave no further thought to my close shave with a heart attack the night before. We returned to the city Sunday night, and early Monday morning I went to the hospital, where I was reading all the ECGs taken there. Sitting with me were three students I was teaching how to interpret the tracings. Suddenly, my doctor burst into the ECG lab pushing a wheelchair and accompanied by a staff nurse. "Isadore, I'm afraid I have bad news. Your cardiac enzymes just came back and they're abnormal. I couldn't get the blood results over the weekend. It looks like you've had a heart attack! You'll have to be admitted right away. I'll call your wife and tell her."

"Don't," I said, "let me phone her."

I was filled with fear and apprehension. I had conveyed this kind of bad news to hundreds of people over the years and always reassured them as best I could. But until this very moment, I never really understood the full emotional impact of such a diagnosis. This was before the days of all the wonderful things we can do for people with heart attacks—no angioplasties, no stents, no bypass operations, no lasers, no genes, and no stem cells. There were precious few drugs that made a real difference to one's outlook. The in-hospital death rate for acute heart attacks was about 20 percent, a statistic of which I was well aware as I was wheeled to my room.

On my way to the cardiac floor, I felt very self-conscious sitting in a wheelchair in my white coat with my stethoscope in the pocket. I tried to avoid the stares of other doctors and patients. My mind was in a whirl. How would I now be able to support my wife and four children? Who would take care of my patients while I was away? Would I be able to resume practice when this was over, or would I be an invalid—assuming, of course, that I survived? I berated myself for not having bought more life insurance. These were just some of the thoughts that ran through my mind. I was not a happy camper!

When I got to my room, I phoned my wife and told her as gently as I could what had happened. Her response? "They're crazy. There's nothing wrong with you." Well, better to have this unrealistic reaction than to fall apart.

My hospital room was ready for me. The oxygen prongs were placed in my nostrils, an intravenous was started, and I was hooked up to an ECG monitor. "Strange," my doctor said, "your tracing is still completely normal. Oh, well, as you know, it sometimes takes a while for it to show the heart attack." I didn't want to be my own doctor but I peeked at the monitor anyway. I loved what I saw, was encouraged, and yet it puzzled me. There wasn't even the slightest abnormality.

"Listen, David," I said to my doctor, "you and I have seen lab errors before. Do me a favor. Take another blood test on me and have them analyze it right away. I don't want to run my own case, but I honestly don't feel like I've had a heart attack. I worked like hell all weekend, and I never had any pain or shortness of breath. Maybe this was a lab error." He smiled patronizingly. He'd heard it all before, as had I. "OK, I'll check; I'll be right back," he said—to humor me.

"David," I begged, "before you go, will you tell them that it's all right for me to go to the toilet. I hate a bedpan."

"Sorry, doctor, I can't do that, much as I'd like to."

After he left, my wife arrived. "Please don't tell the kids anything," I begged. "I'll be all right. I promise you that."

With tears in her eyes, she said, "Of course you will. No one with a heart attack could have done what you did this weekend. Someone's made a mistake. I can't believe there's anything wrong with you."

Maybe she was right. After all, she was not only a doctor's wife; her father was the great cardiologist Dr. Master. Some of his clinical intuition may have rubbed off on her! As I vented some of my anxieties, she was adamant. "You'll see. It's all a mistake."

Two hours later, my doctor came into the room, all smiles. He yanked out the IV from my arm, removed the oxygen prongs, and disconnected the monitor. "You're a phony. There's nothing wrong with you. The lab had a problem with some of the reagents they use to measure enzymes. All the bloods that were analyzed over the weekend were abnormal, just like yours. When they ran the specimen again, it was completely normal. And so was the one we drew today. Get back to work."

Which I did and did not have a "recurrence" until some forty years later. That experience scared the hell out of me, but I'm a better doctor, and certainly a better cardiologist, for having been through it. I never base a diagnosis on one abnormal laboratory result, especially if it doesn't jibe with my clinical judgment. Contrary to what the younger generation of physicians tends to think these days, technology is there to back up the most important part of diagnosis—the doctor's insight, knowledge, and intuition. And, by the way, I rarely force anyone to use a bedpan.

50

AND NOW THE REAL MCCOY

I continued delivering medical care rather than receiving it for the next thirty-five years after my coronary false alarm. Then, suddenly, all hell broke loose. I was stricken in three different ways, once a year for the next three years—and I learned a lot from each of these illnesses.

In 2001, my wife and I were walking at a leisurely pace one morning on Worth Avenue in Palm Beach, Florida, when I suddenly developed the worst pain I'd ever experienced. My right hip felt as if it had been smashed into pieces; I could barely make it into a cab to return to my hotel only one block away. Once I got to the hotel and out of the cab, I needed a wheelchair to get to my room. My wife called an ambulance, and I was taken to the emergency room of a local hospital, where an X-ray revealed that my right hip had virtually crumbled. I was flown back to New York the next day and underwent immediate surgery to replace it.

Why had my hip disintegrated? Several months earlier, while in the Caribbean, I was infected with ciguatera, a poison present in some fish found in tropical and subtropical waters. This toxin had spread throughout my body, affecting my heart, muscles, and nervous system. I was in agony until the doctors made the diagnosis and began treating me with large doses of steroids. After a few days, my symptoms disappeared and I was back to my old "healthy" self. However, I had to continue taking cortisone for several weeks. Unfortunately, in a very small percentage of cases (perhaps 1 or 2 percent), such prolonged steroid therapy results in bone destruction, usually in the hip. Luckily, my left one was not involved. Two weeks after my hip replacement, I was completely pain free. Today, seven years later, I can't even tell which hip was replaced—though airport screeners can, every time I fly. That's why I regret having voted against Dr. Charnley receiving the Lasker award for his invention of the artificial hip (see chapter 45).

Diagnosing Myself in London—All Alone

My second major illness occurred a year later. I had been called to London to consult about a patient with a heart problem. I spent the afternoon evaluating the data, gave my opinion, and planned to return to New York the following morning. That evening, the patient and members of his family invited me to a sumptuous Chinese banquet in one of London's best Asian restaurants. I threw caution to the wind and ate whatever my heart desired, without regard to calories or content. Satiated, I returned to my hotel room at about 10:30 p.m. A few minutes after getting into bed, I developed a serious pain in my right upper abdomen. It came in waves, traveling up to my right shoulder, and around to my back. I didn't have to be a gastroenterologist to realize that I was having an acute gallbladder attack—the first one ever in my entire life! What bad luck for it to happen when I was all alone in a hotel room in a strange city. What to do? I knew that, even as uncomfortable as I was, this was not apt to be life threatening. I remembered my mother's many attacks over the years and my brother's as well. They'd both gotten over every one of them until one day they decided they'd had enough and had their gallbladders removed.

I did not know any English surgeons or to which hospital to go. I didn't want to sit for hours in a London emergency room. So I decided to take my chances, to endure the pain throughout the night, and leave for New York first thing the next morning. It was a calculated risk, one that I'm not sure I should have taken or would recommend to anyone else. I telephoned my office nurse at home, where it was late afternoon. I told her I'd be boarding a Concorde flight first thing in the morning and would be home by 11 a.m. New York time. I asked her to arrange for me to be seen by one of my surgical colleagues. I always travel with basic medications, so I took two broad-spectrum antibiotics as well as some extra strength Tylenol and went to bed. I tossed and turned for the next few hours, then got dressed and took a cab to the airport.

My flight home was uneventful; I ate and drank nothing—in anticipation of an operation. My belly hurt, but the pain was bearable. What bothered me most was having to say no to the champagne and caviar, which were staples on this luxury three-and-a-half-hour flight across the Atlantic. The stewardess and passengers had never before seen such willpower or dietary asceticism.

As soon as we landed in New York, I made a beeline to the hospital. I was immediately evaluated by an excellent surgeon who, after looking at the sonogram of my belly, decided I needed to have my gallbladder taken out ASAP. He made three small holes in my abdominal wall through which he inserted the appropriate instruments and removed a gallbladder inflamed and full of stones.

I found all of this incredible, since I had never previously had any gallbladder symptoms. Most patients with gallstones have recurrent attacks, especially if they do not rigorously follow the appropriate low-fat gallbladder diet. In any event, amazingly, I was discharged home the very next afternoon! I say amazingly because I remembered my mother's and brother's experiences. They'd both had their gallbladders removed through large abdominal incisions, remained in the hospital for almost two weeks, and were plagued by recurrent incisional infections. I also compared my experience with Aristotle Onassis' surgery in Paris twenty-five years earlier. (There is no doubt in my mind that he would not have had the postsurgical complications that took his life if his operation could have been done with the same minimally invasive laparoscopic technique that had been performed on me.)

There are very few operations today that cannot be done this way, even robotically. Virtually every major organ—from the prostate to the heart—can be removed or repaired laparoscopically. Instead of incisions, tiny holes are made in the belly wall through which the surgeon inserts the instruments. This results in shorter hospital stays, much less discomfort to the patient, and fewer postoperative complications. I was lucky that my gallbladder disease had remained silent until I could benefit from this major advance.

Just as was true for my artificial hip, living without a gallbladder has made absolutely no difference in my life. I eat what I like, or what I think is healthy, without fear of developing the severe pain I felt that night in London. And, of course, gallbladders never grow back.

This Time My Heart Problem Was for Real!

The third and most important medical event in my life occurred just one year later. I expected to develop some heart trouble as I grew older because of my family history (not only had my father suffered angina from the age of forty-seven, but my brother had required bypass surgery in his fifties and my mother had coronary artery disease later in life); I had an elevated cholesterol for many years (but was able to normalize it by diet and medication); my blood pressure was high (but I lowered that, too); and although I was aware of the importance of regular physical exercise, in recent years my schedule did not always permit me to do as much as I should. Finally, although not very overweight, I could afford to lose some twenty pounds. Still, my medical checkups had always been satisfactory, my physical exam was normal, my ECG was unremarkable, and a stress test taken a few years earlier was also normal.

So I was surprised when, one afternoon in 2003, while walking to a store a few blocks from my office, I suddenly felt an uncomfortable pressure in my chest. It wasn't pain; it was more like heaviness, as if someone was sitting on my breastbone. When I slowed down, the discomfort subsided; when I started walking briskly again, it came back. As a cardiologist and also having watched my father's attacks for so many years, I knew exactly what this symptom meant. It was clearly angina—not indigestion, not muscle spasm, not pressure on a nerve from my neck. There is only one disorder in which effort or emotion induces chest pressure that's relieved by rest—angina pectoris. The symptom is due to one or more narrowed blood vessels in the heart unable to deliver enough blood to the heart muscle. This time, unlike when I was a "kid" of forty, I did not fool around with denial. I cut short my shopping trip, took a cab back to my office, and called the cardiac catheterization laboratory at my hospital. I had enough clout there to ask one of the "invasive" cardiologists to schedule me for an angiogram first thing the following morning. I remained at home that night, ate lightly, and did not exert myself. I was prepared to call 911 if the pain recurred at rest because that would suggest a heart attack. Happily, I was without any symptoms throughout the night and next morning, took a cab to the hospital.

The doctors examined me, drew blood to make sure I hadn't actually had a heart attack, and recorded an ECG. It was normal. (Some 80 percent of patients with angina have normal electrocardiograms taken at rest, which is why stress tests are so important when angina is suspected.) I was taken on a gurney from my hospital room to the cardiac catheterization lab (to which I had always previously walked, accompanying patients who were to undergo the procedure that I now faced). I wasn't fearful. I knew that a coronary angiogram is neither painful nor dangerous: a catheter is inserted into an artery in the groin and threaded up to the heart. It is then injected with a dye that fills the coronary arteries. X-rays indicate whether there are any blockages in these arteries, their location, and their severity. When an obstruction is identified, a balloon is slipped up through the catheter into the artery alongside the obstructing plaque and is inflated, compressing the plaque toward the wall of the artery so that more blood can flow through it. This procedure is called angioplasty.

A coronary angiogram normally takes less than an hour. For some reason, mine was lasting longer than usual. The animated conversation the doctors were having at the onset of the procedure suddenly stopped. There was silence. I began to experience angina again. "What's happening, fellas?" I asked. Another uncomfortable silence. Finally one of the doctors told me that the largest coronary artery in my heart, the left anterior descending, was almost completely blocked. So what? That's what I was there for. Why didn't they go ahead and balloon it open? A 95 percent blockage is as easily removed as a 70 percent closure, so what was the problem? It turned out to be the composition of plaque itself, not its size. Instead of being soft and easily compressible by the balloon, as they usually are, mine was filled with calcium and rock hard. The balloon could not push it aside toward the wall and relieve the obstruction it was causing. I was going to need emergency open-heart surgery to bypass that diseased blood vessel. They didn't tell me, but my doctors had already alerted a heart surgeon who was on his way. While

they were waiting for him, they decided to try to break up the calcified artery with a "Roto-Rooter" (an instrument that vibrates against
the calcified plaque).

After they inserted the device, I could hear it whirring in my chest
as it attacked the calcified artery. I continued to experience angina
throughout this procedure because my artery was now narrowed not
only by the plaque but also by the instrument that had been introduced to remove it. At one point, the instrument got stuck in the
plaque and stopped whirring for several seconds, and my chest pain
worsened. I was sure I was going to die. But then, the whirring resumed, the pain subsided, and the doctors literally whooped with joy
as the calcium-laden plaque disintegrated and the artery was opened.
They then inserted a bare metal stent to keep it open—and it's been
there ever since, delivering all the blood my heart muscle needs. The
doctors assured me that I would be fine since the other arteries in my
heart were virtually free of disease. They were right. I haven't had any
angina since.

But that's not the end of the story. Remember Danny Kaye's experience with his heart surgery, when someone ruptured an artery in
his bladder while trying to catheterize him? Patients who undergo
angiography (as opposed to cardiac surgery) do not normally have a
urinary catheter because the procedure is usually over in less than
an hour. However, in my case, when it became clear that I might be
on the table longer than that, the doctors decided to have me cathe-
terized so that I would not have to retain a great deal of urine in my
bladder. When the nurse introduced this catheter, it hurt like hell; it's
not supposed to. After my coronary artery was opened, I was transferred to a private room in the hospital, with the catheter still in my
bladder. Patients are usually kept at complete bed rest for a few hours
after a cardiac catheterization and pressure is maintained on the
punctured artery in the groin to prevent it from bleeding. I was lying
there with the weight on my groin and the catheter in my bladder,
when I happened to look at the bottle beside my bed into which my
urine was emptying through that tube. I was shocked to see that
there was a considerable amount of blood in the bottle, not urine! I
asked the nurse to call the resident on duty. He was very reassuring.
Such bleeding was very common, he said, and told me not to worry.

There's an advantage to being a doctor in such situations and
knowing something about these things: I knew that what he told me
was nonsense. I phoned a urologist friend, told him what was happening, and asked him to come over as soon as he could. He arrived

a few minutes later, removed the catheter, and the bleeding stopped. That catheter that hurt so much when it was introduced into my urethra had burst a small artery. Fortunately, it was much smaller than the one that was torn in Danny Kaye. Still, had I not asked for help, I might also have required transfusions, and who knows where that might have led?

No matter what your occupation happens to be, doctor or dancer, if you suspect that there is something wrong during or after any procedure, let your voice be heard.

51

OUR BROKEN MEDICAL CARE SYSTEM

While I was a medical student, and also after I graduated and was working in hospitals during my residency and postgraduate training, it never occurred to me that anyone who was sick would be denied medical care because he or she couldn't afford it. We doctors were on call twenty-four hours a day treating anyone who needed it. But after I went into private practice, I was exposed to the harsh reality that the medical care system in this country is broken, and things have only gotten worse over the years. Patients are unhappy with their doctors (if they are lucky enough to have one); doctors are angry with insurance carriers and HMOs because of poor reimbursement; insurance companies are angry at the drug industry because of the high cost of medication; and everyone is angry at the government for failing to do something about it. The bottom line? Many millions of Americans either have no medical care whatsoever or have inadequate care.

As I see it, there are two options: (a) a government-run and government-financed system, such as is practiced in the United Kingdom, Canada, and most European countries, or (b) health care delivered by the private sector through private insurance plans and HMOs.

Early in my career, I was not impressed by or enthusiastic about universal health care run by the government. This may have been a holdover from my experiences in Russia during the cold war, and socialized medicine was something our communist enemy practiced. This bugaboo continues to dominate the thinking of many Americans to this day. In addition to its political stigma my family's experience in Canada had a great influence on my thinking about government-managed medical care.

I left Canada for the U.S. before the introduction of socialized medicine in my home country. The rest of my family—parents, brother, nieces, and nephews—remained in Montreal, and in 1966, they were thrilled when the Canadian government introduced a system of health care that seemed perfect. They were able to choose their own physician, and everything was free: doctor's visits, vaccinations, hospitalizations, and even most prescribed medications. "Free" meant that they never had to pay for anything up front. But when they got their next tax bill, they learned that nothing in this world is free. But that was acceptable to them and to most of their fellow citizens. The important thing was that this health-care system protected them against financial ruin in the event of catastrophic illness. It also meant that they could visit the doctor of their choice whenever they needed to. It's true that they often had to wait a long time for some procedure or operation, but that didn't bother them because most emergencies were treated promptly (and if the wait was too long, they could always cross the border to our country).

The Canadian health-care system saved my brother's family. After he developed leukemia in his sixties, he was cared for diligently at no cost for several years until he died in 1993 at the age of seventy-one. Had he lived in America, he'd have gone through all his assets and left his wife, children, and grandchildren destitute.

But then there was the other side of the coin. My mother, also living in Canada, took sick. What happened to her with access to all this "free care" raised some serious questions in my mind about socialized medicine, at least as it was practiced in Canada at the time.

One day in 1974 I received a call from my mother's doctor in Montreal. "Your mother passed some blood from her bowel yesterday," he told me. "She has no other complaints; no fever, no pain in the belly, no diarrhea or constipation. I examined her briefly and didn't find any hemorrhoids to account for the bleeding, so I guess she'll have to be evaluated."

"What do you mean, 'guess'?" I asked.

"Well," he said, "she's seventy-six, and, as you know, she has had some heart problems in the past. So it's not as if she is young and all that. I tried to schedule her for a barium enema [colonoscopies were not being done at that time], but there's a wait of several weeks. They have to take care of the younger patients first. You understand that, I'm sure."

"So do you plan to stand by and let her bleed to death or allow any cancer she may have to spread?"

"Look," he replied. "I know it's hard for you to be objective because she's your mother. The fact is there are two possibilities here. The first is that whatever is causing the bleeding will stop on its own and your mother will be fine. On the other hand, she may have cancer of the bowel. If she has cancer, it's probably too late to do anything about it anyway. We never think of our parents as old, but remember, Issie, she's seventy-six."

There was no point in arguing with this fellow. He'd been practicing under the "free medical care" system, with its priorities, for too long. Society there had accepted the fact that the elderly must take a back seat when it comes to survival. I was not prepared to accept this route for my mother. The next day, I arranged for her to fly to New York. Twenty-four hours later she was in our X-ray department for a barium enema. My worst fears were realized: she had a cancer the size of an orange in the large bowel, just where it courses by the liver (the transverse colon). Judging by its size, I was worried that it might have already spread, and it was too late to be cured. But even so, she needed surgery because, if left alone, the cancer would continue to grow and ultimately obstruct her bowel. That would be agony for her. I consulted an experienced bowel surgeon, and he agreed that we had no choice but to debulk the cancer, that is, remove as much of it as possible.

A few days later, my mother underwent surgery: The tumor was indeed malignant, but, miracle of miracles, it had not yet spread. The liver was clean and the tumor had not invaded any of the nearby glands. The surgeon was able to remove it completely, after which he reattached the two ends of the bowel, leaving my mother cancer free!

She recovered without a hitch. I never told her she'd had cancer. She might not have believed me that she was cured. I said we'd removed a polyp, and that she'd be fine. She died some fifteen years later, at the age of ninety-one! In the intervening years, she had the pleasure of seeing her grandchildren grow up and marry, she became a great-grandmother, and she enjoyed life to the fullest until the very end. Had she remained in Montreal and been "managed" as her doctor had planned, she would simply have been another old lady who died of cancer. What's so terrible about that?

I believe this form of triage can play havoc with the well-being and survival of old people. We'll never know how many elderly folk in Canada died in those years sooner than they should have for want of a diagnostic test.

But that was many years ago. Things are now better in Canada than they used to be because health care has been given greater priority and more resources. And that's the key to its success. Shortly after socialized medicine was established there, too many people who had previously thought twice about calling the doctor because they had to pay for it were suddenly wallowing in this free care. They did not hesitate to report minor problems that they used to ignore or treat themselves. And they also demanded all kinds of medical tests that they never before could afford. As a result, there simply weren't enough medical resources or money to satisfy that sudden demand. I am told that things are quite different now.

Every civilized country is struggling to find a way to provide adequate yet affordable medical care for all its citizens. Any nation motivated to do so, ours included, should be able to take care of its sick. In this country, almost fifty million citizens are currently without any health insurance because they can't afford to pay the premiums; another twenty-five million have nominal health insurance—but it does not provide even basic care. Ironically, in this era of prevention, when controlling risk factors can prevent or delay the onset of most major diseases ranging from cancer to heart disease, from diabetes to stroke, millions of Americans do not have access to a doctor. They must wait until they are critically ill, at which point they go or are taken to an emergency room to be treated. In most cases, these crises, some of which are life-threatening and even fatal, can be averted if you are able to discuss your symptoms with your doctor before they progress.

For those who can afford a private doctor, his or her reimbursement is so inadequate that you'll have only a few minutes together. In order to compensate for the low fees, doctors are seeing far too many patients to ensure optimal care or for any meaningful doctor-patient relationship to exist.

I have come to believe that only a government-run universal health-care system can provide medical care for all Americans, regardless of their economic status. I do not believe this can be achieved by the profit-motivated private sector. In order to make a profit, which is why the company exists, your insurer *must* spend less for your medical care than the amount of your premiums. Managed care and similar programs make no bones about the fact that they're in business to make money. Taking care of you is secondary. So their objective is to cut costs and care in order to end up ahead of the game.

We *can* have socialized medicine in a capitalistic society. Medicare is an excellent example. The government runs it, and though it has its problems, it does provide basic medical care for all our senior citizens. And that's the most important goal, as far as I'm concerned! We do not necessarily need to look to the U.K. or Canada as models for what we should establish here; other countries such as France and the Scandinavian nations provide their citizens with good, affordable care. Surely the United States can do so, too. But as long as there is no commitment to the nation's health as a top priority, we'll be stuck with what we have today.

In addition to the delivery of medical care per se, there are other serious problems that must be addressed. These relate basically to physician availability.

When I was in medical school, my fellow students and I couldn't wait to graduate so that we could start caring for the sick. That's not very often the case these days. Students early on begin to explore the specialties that generate the highest income and the best hours. The most popular choices are dermatology; orthopedics; ear, nose, and throat surgery; and radiology—all of which lend themselves to an 8 a.m. to 5 p.m. schedule five days a week. There is much less interest in family medicine and internal medicine residencies. This trend is the result of inadequate reimbursement for doctors who do not perform lots of special tests for which they are handsomely reimbursed. Neither the government nor insurance carriers pay a physician to talk to a patient or to educate him or her in the important guidelines of prevention and lifestyle. Because of the high cost of tuition, many students are deeply in debt when they graduate and are looking for a high income as soon as possible. Primary care physicians work long hours, have relatively little reimbursement, often can't cover their expenses, and are paying huge amounts for malpractice insurance. I predict that as a result of this shortage of primary care physicians, we will find more and more practices run by physician assistants—more trained than nurses, but not as well trained as doctors. They will function as "screeners," performing a basic physical exam and referring to the appropriate specialist anyone with a particular problem. They'll also be able to educate patients about a healthy lifestyle. However, I continue to believe that no health plan devised by the government will work unless there are enough primary physicians to provide the care.

52

POSTSCRIPT

Camilla and I have four wonderful children, all married with wonderful spouses, and nine children among them. My one daughter was a schoolteacher, but now devotes her time to raising her three children; two of my three sons are authors, and my middle son, Stephen, is a physician.

Stephen made me very happy when, at the age of fifteen, he told me he wanted to be a doctor. He went on to graduate from Cornell Medical School in 1985 and was responsible for one of the proudest moments of my life when, at his graduation, his dean invited me to lead Stephen's graduating class in taking the Hippocratic oath.

Later that day, Stephen asked me if I had any special advice for him at the beginning of his career. I gave him the following "tips." Always keep an open mind. I confessed to him, as he stood there with the M.D. diploma in his hand, full of everything he'd been taught in the last four years of his life, that most of what I had learned in medical school either is now out-of-date or was wrong in the first place—and that he could expect the same. New knowledge is a continuum; ideas change as the cutting edge of medicine move forward. Nothing is written in stone. Doctors must remain receptive to new ideas no matter where they come from or how much they vary from conventional "wisdom." I also told my son, the doctor, that nothing is impossible. Diseases and conditions that I thought were unconquerable when I graduated almost sixty years earlier—polio, smallpox, blocked coronary arteries, osteoporosis, deafness, even impotence—can now be either prevented or cured. He could expect the same for the challenges that face him—AIDS, cancer, Alzheimer's, and others. The key to success is being receptive to new ideas, no matter who proposes them.

But the single most important piece of advice I could give him was to lead his life as a physician by adhering to the Hippocratic oath he had just repeated after me. In the event that you, my readers, are not familiar with that oath, here is what Stephen and his classmates pledged when he became a doctor almost twenty-five years ago. It's something with which every patient should be familiar.

I do solemnly vow, to that which I value and hold most dear:

that I will honor the Profession of Medicine, be just and generous to its members, and help sustain them in their service to humanity;

that just as I have learned from those who preceded me, so will I instruct those who follow me in the science and the art of medicine;

that I will recognize the limits of my knowledge and pursue lifelong learning to better care for the sick and to prevent illness;

that I will seek the counsel of others when they are more expert so as to fulfill my obligation to those who are entrusted to my care;

that I will not withdraw from my patients in their time of need;

that I will lead my life and practice my art with integrity and honor, using my power wisely;

that whatsoever I shall see or hear of the lives of my patients that is not fitting to be spoken, I will keep in confidence;

that into whatever house I shall enter, it shall be for the good of the sick;

that I will maintain this sacred trust, holding myself far aloof from wrong, from corrupting, from the tempting of others to vice;

that above all else I will serve the highest interests of my patients through the practice of my science and my art;

that I will be an advocate for patients in need and strive for justice in the care of the sick.

I now turn to my calling, promising to preserve its finest traditions, with the reward of a long experience in the joy of healing.

I made this vow freely and upon my honor.

That says it all, doesn't it? No wonder it has endured so long. To Cornell's credit, I believe it is the only medical school that now introduces the Hippocratic oath to students, not only when they graduate, *but on their first day of medical school*!

INDEX